BATS
Learning to Fly

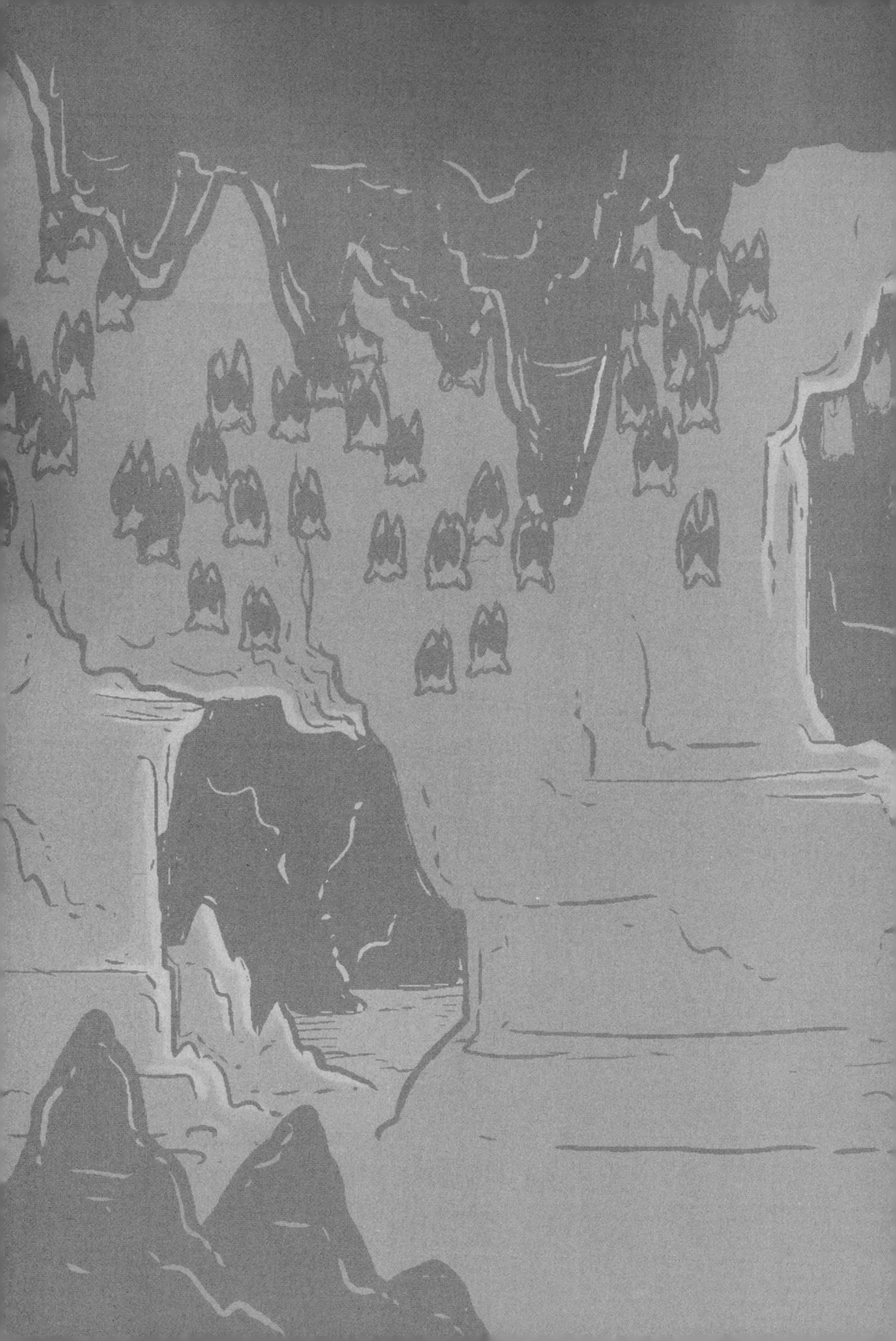

BATS
Learning to Fly

FALYNN KOCH

SCHOLASTIC INC.

For Tucker Waugh and Neal Koch

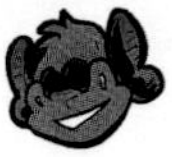

ISBN 978-1-338-24551-6

12 11 10 9 8 7 6 5 4 3 20 21 22

Printed in the U.S.A. 40

First Scholastic printing, September 2017

Penciled with a light blue Staedtler Triplus Fineliner and Manga Studio
Inked with a Maru-style digital nib and colored digitally in Photoshop

Book design by John Green

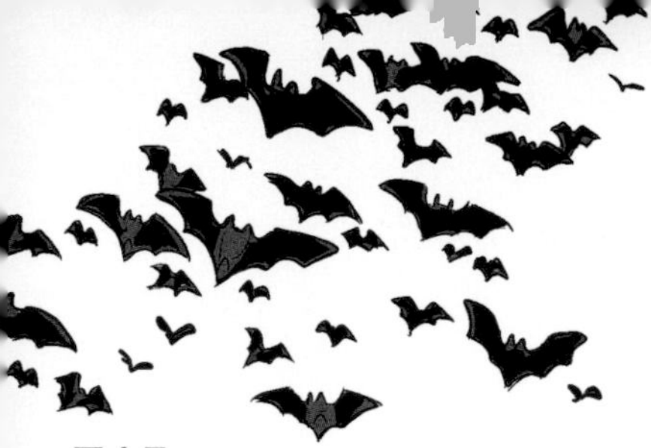

Were you afraid of the dark when you were little? Maybe you thought a monster was in your closet or maybe you were afraid of what was under your bed. You're probably not scared of the dark anymore, but even as we get older, things we can't see can still scare us. Bats, for example.

Bats are nocturnal, which means that they only come out at night. At dusk, they fly from their day roost to look for food. If you are in North America, the bats that live near you only eat insects or nectar—not humans! Even those bats that do feed on blood, the infamous vampire bats, much prefer cattle. And they only live in Central and South America.

Bats around the world eat other things—fruit primarily. This means that bats help humans a lot. All that bug, nectar, and fruit eating means that bats do us a big service in the pest-control, pollination, and seed-spreading departments. Without them, we would have to use more pesticides on our farms. And we wouldn't have nearly as many bananas, mangoes, avocados, dates, and figs to eat!

So we should all love bats, right? But not everyone realizes how important they are. People do things all the time that hurt bats either on purpose or by accident. Sometimes people kill bats if they find them in their house instead of just removing them. They cut down trees where bats live. And they use pesticides in their backyards. All of this means that bats are having a harder time finding healthy food to eat and safe places to live. So what does that mean for bats? They disappear. And when bats disappear, we have fewer choices of what to eat.

Now that you know that bats are important to have around, what can you do to help them? First, check out the Save the Bats Campaign by visiting savethebats.org. You can join millions of people across the continent working together to teach Americans about the importance of bats, the threats of extinction, and how we can work together to save bats.

You can also make your backyard or school a safe place for bats to live and eat. Putting up a bat house gives bat moms a warm, sheltered spot to raise their babies. Special bat gardens with plants that bloom at night attract the bugs that bats need to eat to be strong. And if you avoid using pesticides in gardens, you can make sure that bats aren't exposed to chemicals that can make them sick.

Tell everyone you know—your family, friends, and teachers—that we all need to do what we can to keep bats healthy. And next time it's dark out, don't be afraid—think about all the bats busy at work, keeping us—and our food—healthy.

—Rob Mies, Bat Expert and Founder of
the Organization for Bat Conservation

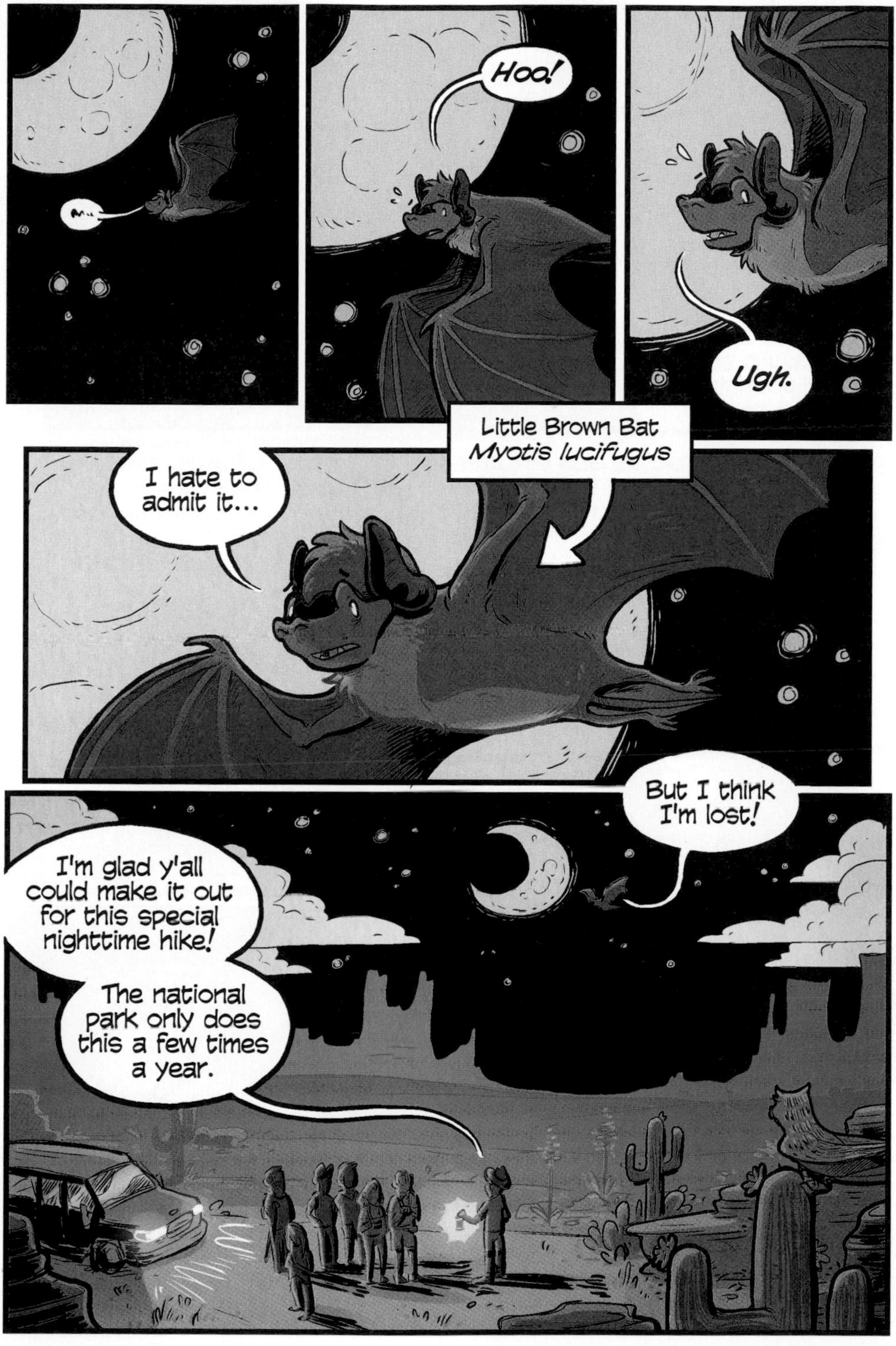
Hoo!
Ugh.
Little Brown Bat
Myotis lucifugus
I hate to admit it...
But I think I'm lost!
I'm glad y'all could make it out for this special nighttime hike!
The national park only does this a few times a year.

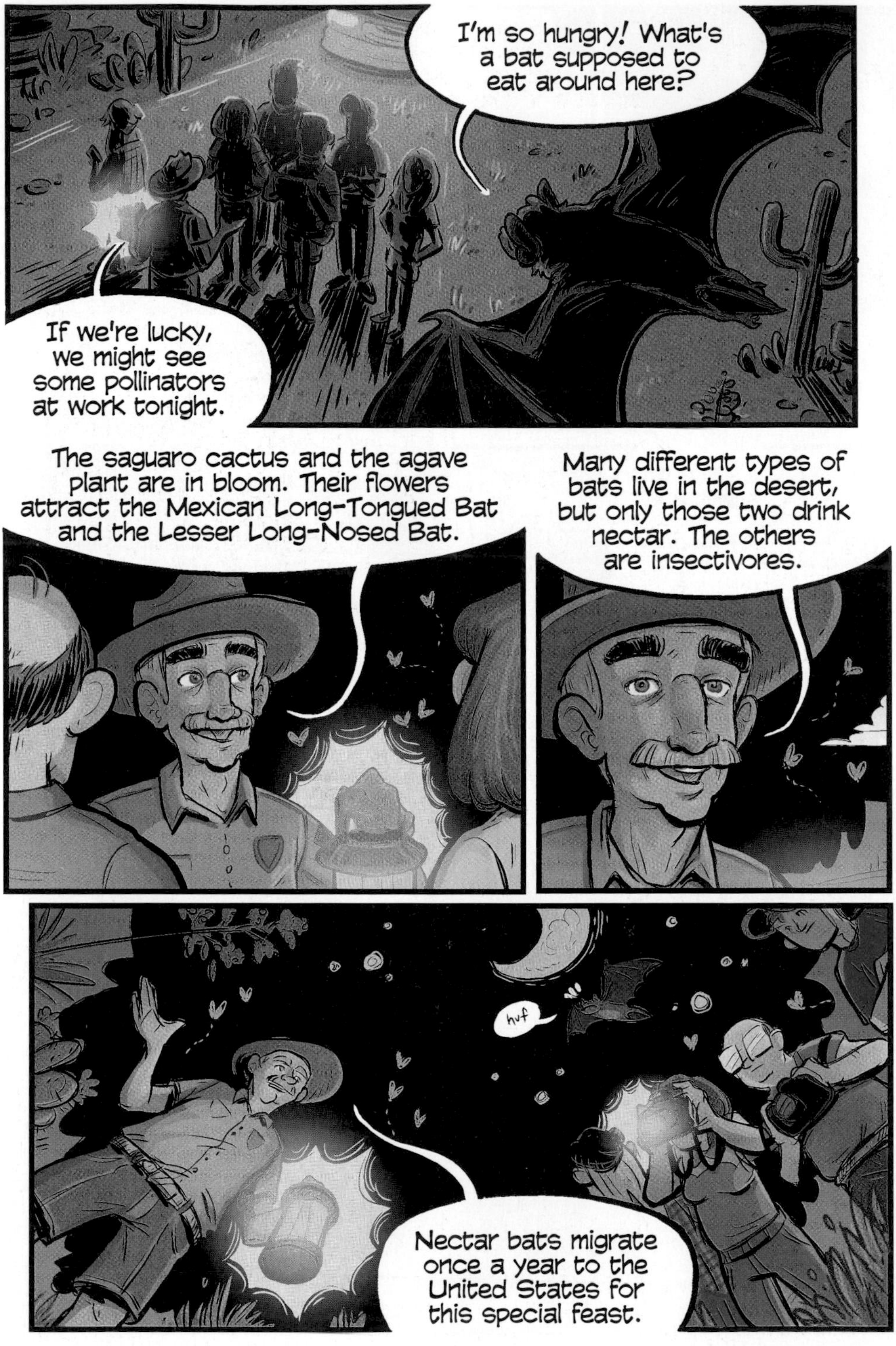

I'm so hungry! What's a bat supposed to eat around here?
If we're lucky, we might see some pollinators at work tonight.
The saguaro cactus and the agave plant are in bloom. Their flowers attract the Mexican Long-Tongued Bat and the Lesser Long-Nosed Bat.
Many different types of bats live in the desert, but only those two drink nectar. The others are insectivores.
huf
Nectar bats migrate once a year to the United States for this special feast.

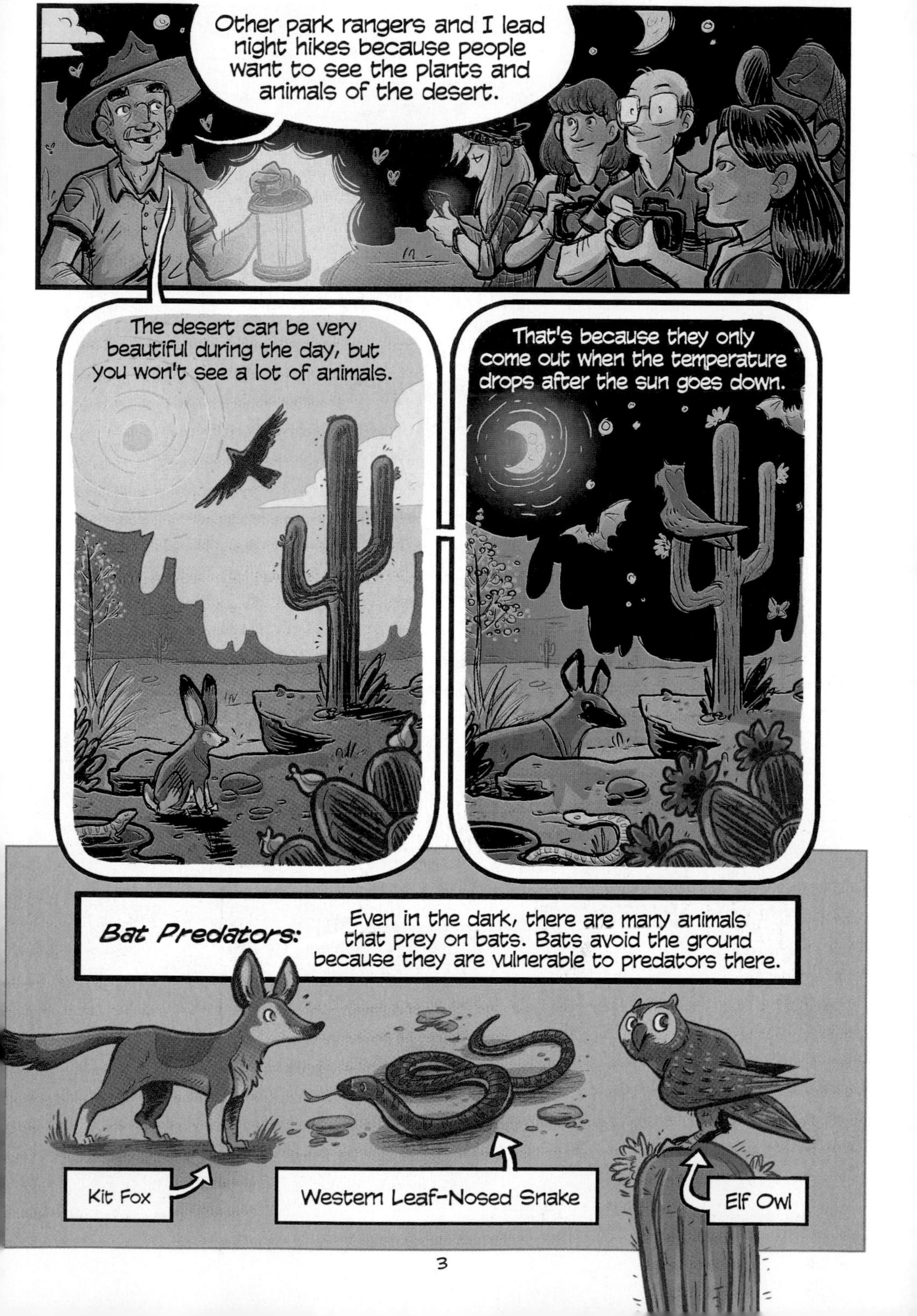
Other park rangers and I lead night hikes because people want to see the plants and animals of the desert.
The desert can be very beautiful during the day, but you won't see a lot of animals.
That's because they only come out when the temperature drops after the sun goes down.
Bat Predators:
Even in the dark, there are many animals that prey on bats. Bats avoid the ground because they are vulnerable to predators there.
Kit Fox
Western Leaf-Nosed Snake
Elf Owl

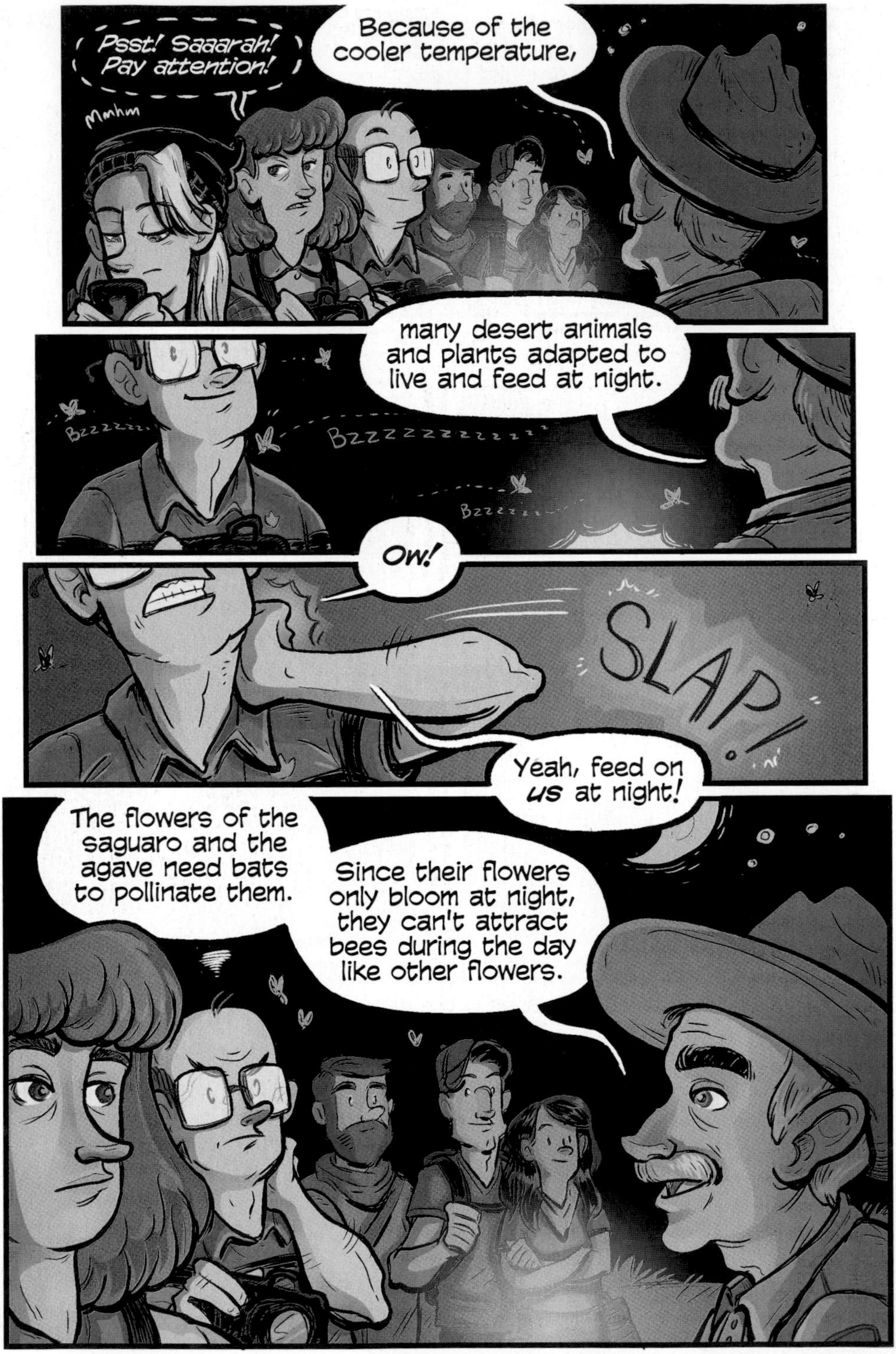

Psst! Saaarah! Pay attention!
Because of the cooler temperature,
Mmhm
many desert animals and plants adapted to live and feed at night.
Bzzzzzz
Bzzzzzzzzzzzz
Bzzzzz
Ow!
SLAP!
Yeah, feed on *us* at night!
The flowers of the saguaro and the agave need bats to pollinate them.
Since their flowers only bloom at night, they can't attract bees during the day like other flowers.

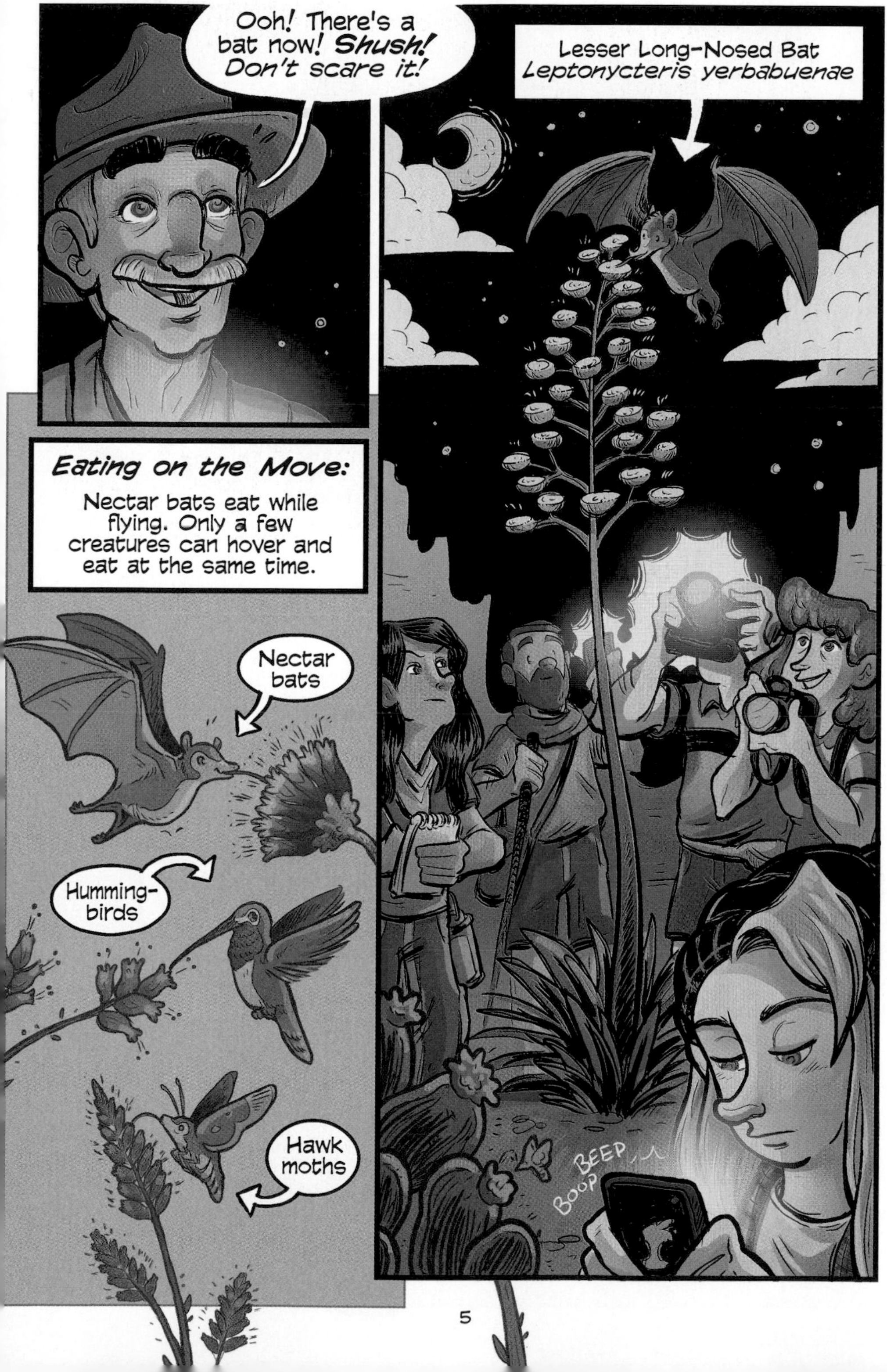
Ooh! There's a bat now! *Shush!* *Don't scare it!*
Lesser Long-Nosed Bat *Leptonycteris yerbabuenae*
Eating on the Move:
Nectar bats eat while flying. Only a few creatures can hover and eat at the same time.
Nectar bats
Humming-birds
Hawk moths
BEEP
BOOP

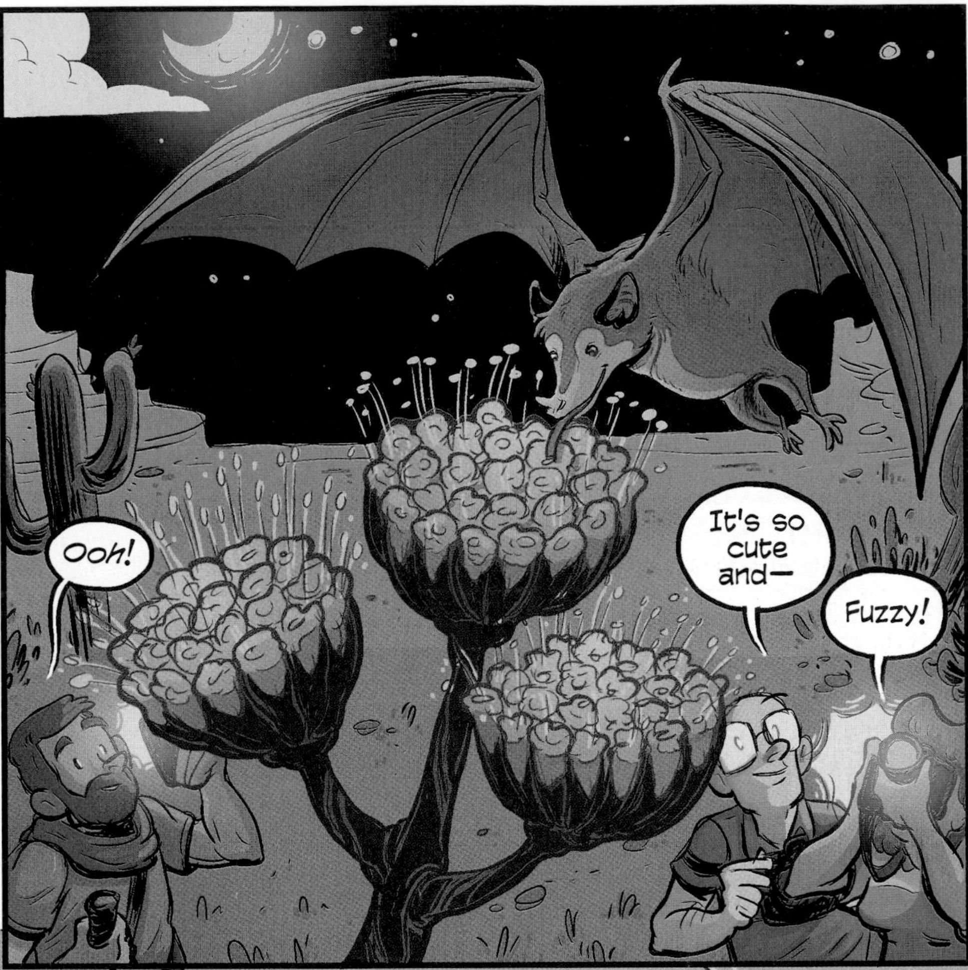
Ooh!
It's so cute and—
Fuzzy!

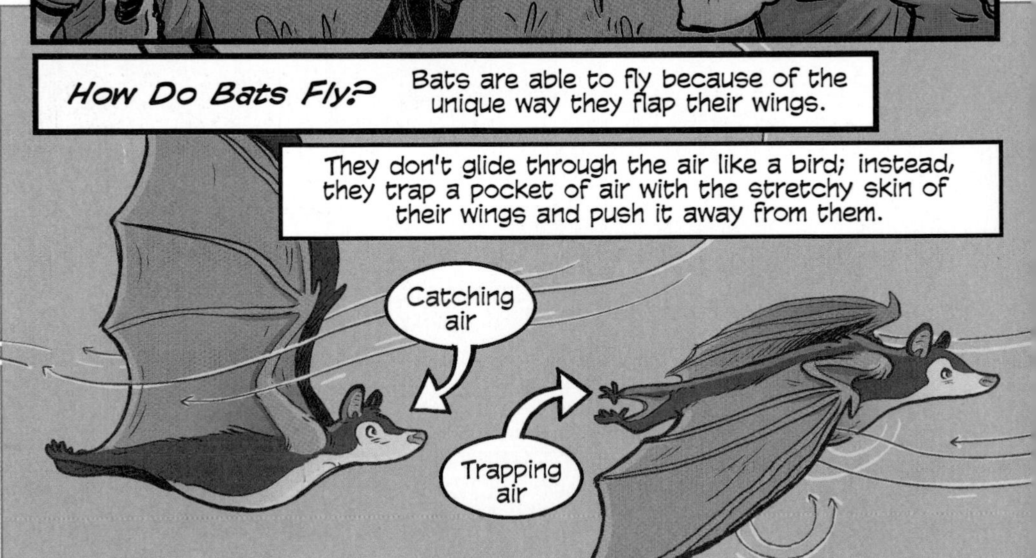
How Do Bats Fly?
Bats are able to fly because of the unique way they flap their wings.
They don't glide through the air like a bird; instead, they trap a pocket of air with the stretchy skin of their wings and push it away from them.
Catching air
Trapping air

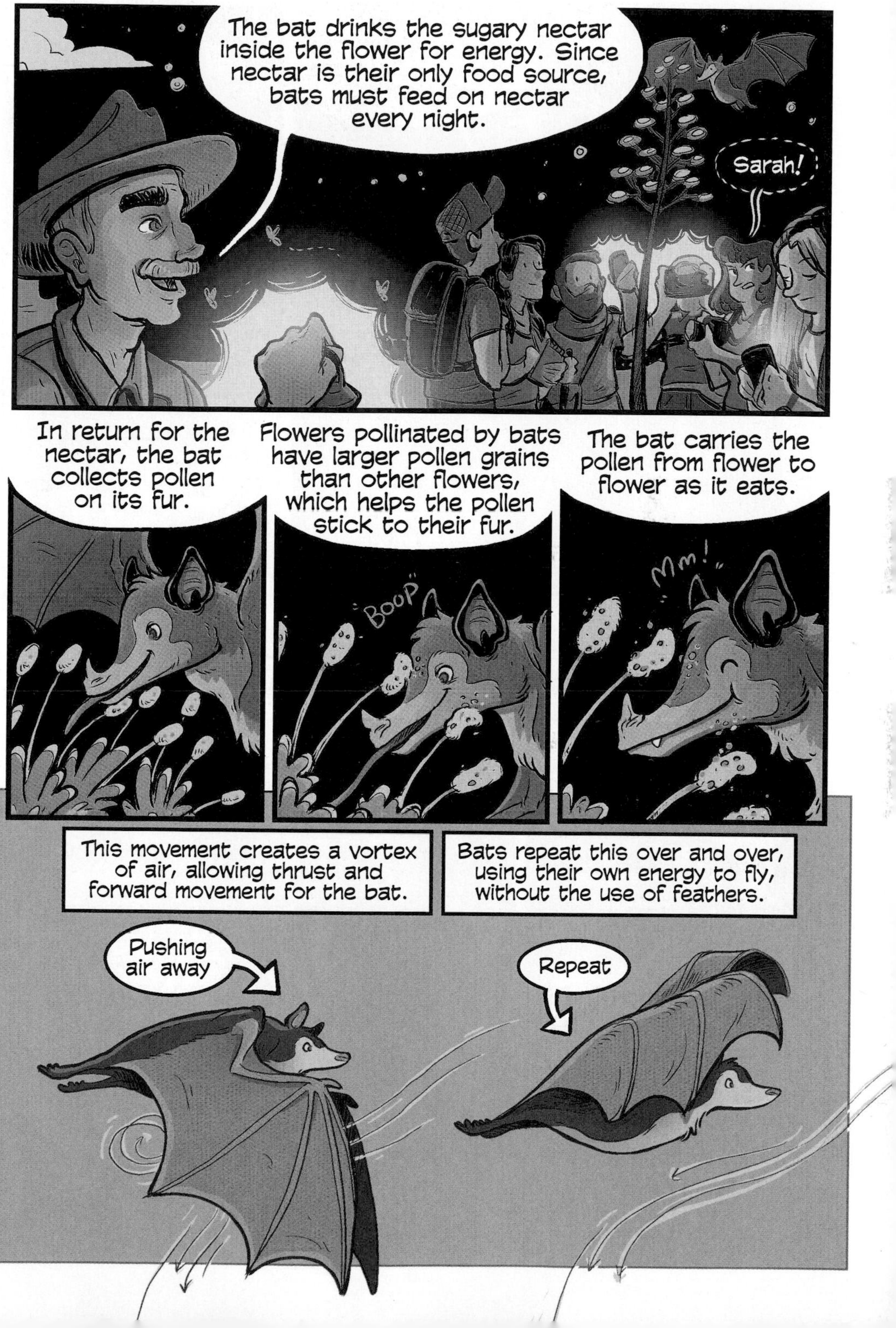
The bat drinks the sugary nectar inside the flower for energy. Since nectar is their only food source, bats must feed on nectar every night.
Sarah!
In return for the nectar, the bat collects pollen on its fur.
Flowers pollinated by bats have larger pollen grains than other flowers, which helps the pollen stick to their fur.
BOOP
The bat carries the pollen from flower to flower as it eats.
Mm!
This movement creates a vortex of air, allowing thrust and forward movement for the bat.
Bats repeat this over and over, using their own energy to fly, without the use of feathers.
Pushing air away
Repeat

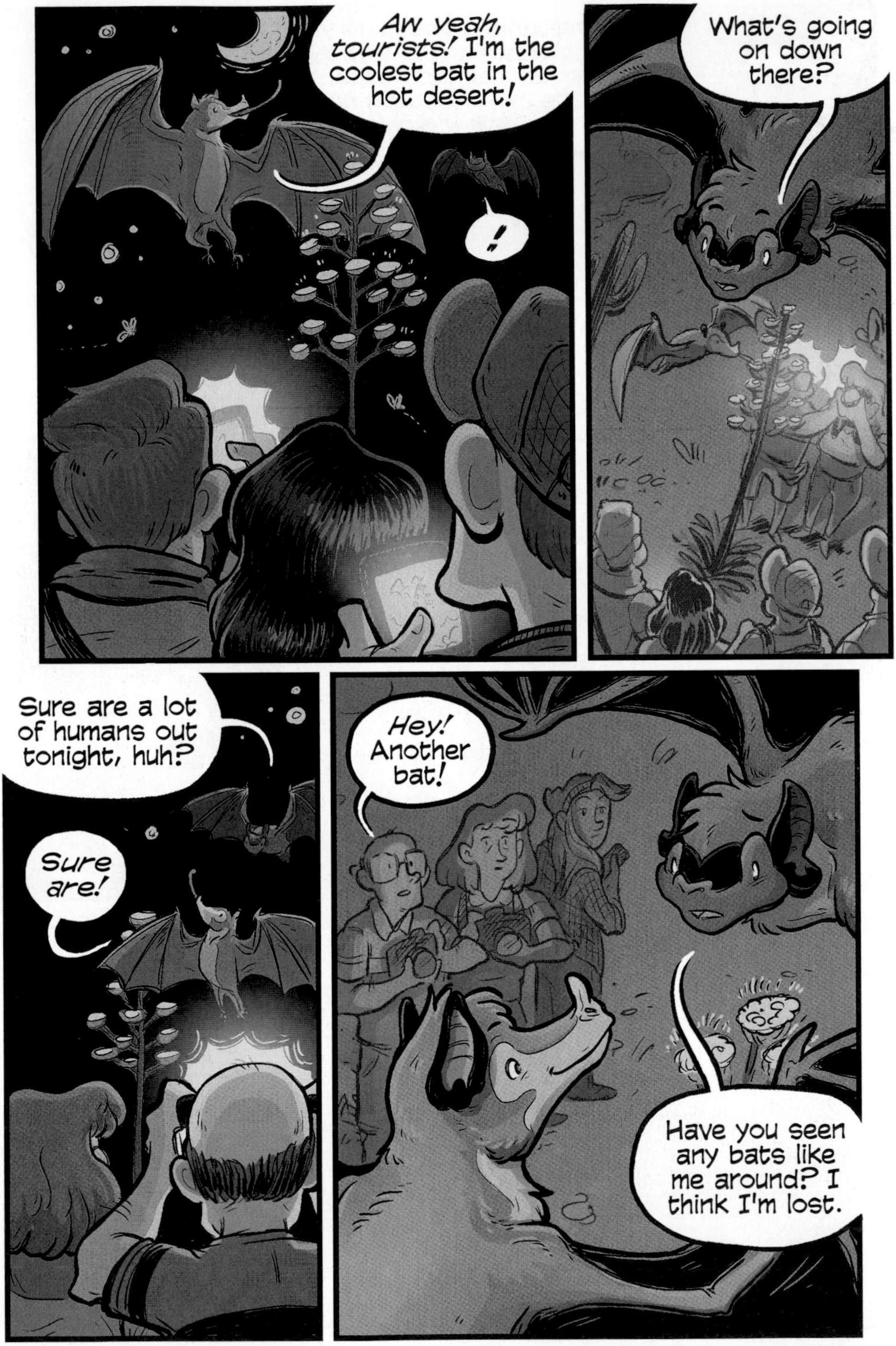
Aw yeah, tourists! I'm the coolest bat in the hot desert!
!
What's going on down there?
Sure are a lot of humans out tonight, huh?
Sure are!
Hey! Another bat!
Have you seen any bats like me around? I think I'm lost.

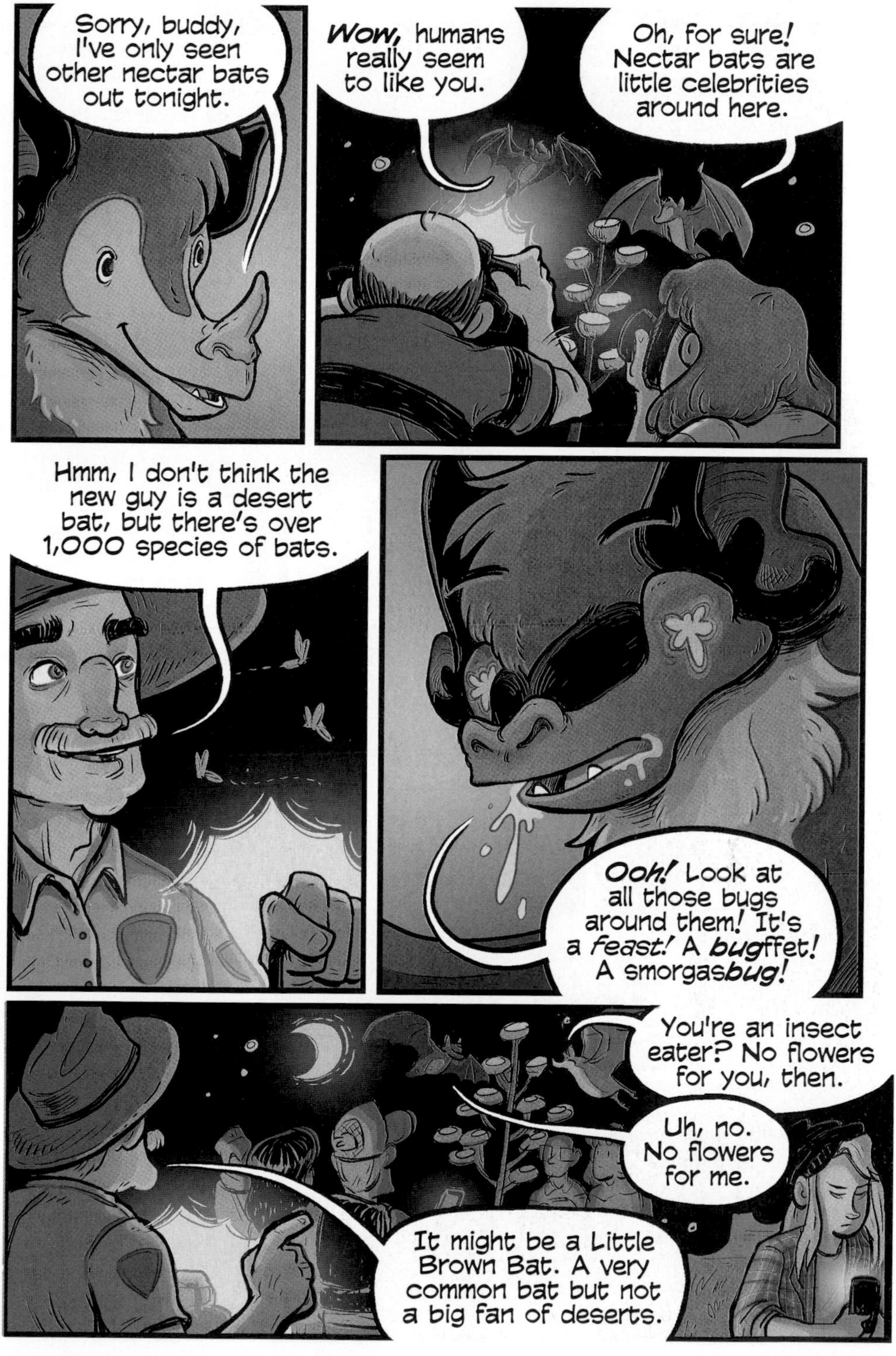
Sorry, buddy, I've only seen other nectar bats out tonight.
Wow, humans really seem to like you.
Oh, for sure! Nectar bats are little celebrities around here.
Hmm, I don't think the new guy is a desert bat, but there's over 1,000 species of bats.
Ooh! Look at all those bugs around them! It's a feast! A bugffet! A smorgasbug!
You're an insect eater? No flowers for you, then.
Uh, no. No flowers for me.
It might be a Little Brown Bat. A very common bat but not a big fan of deserts.

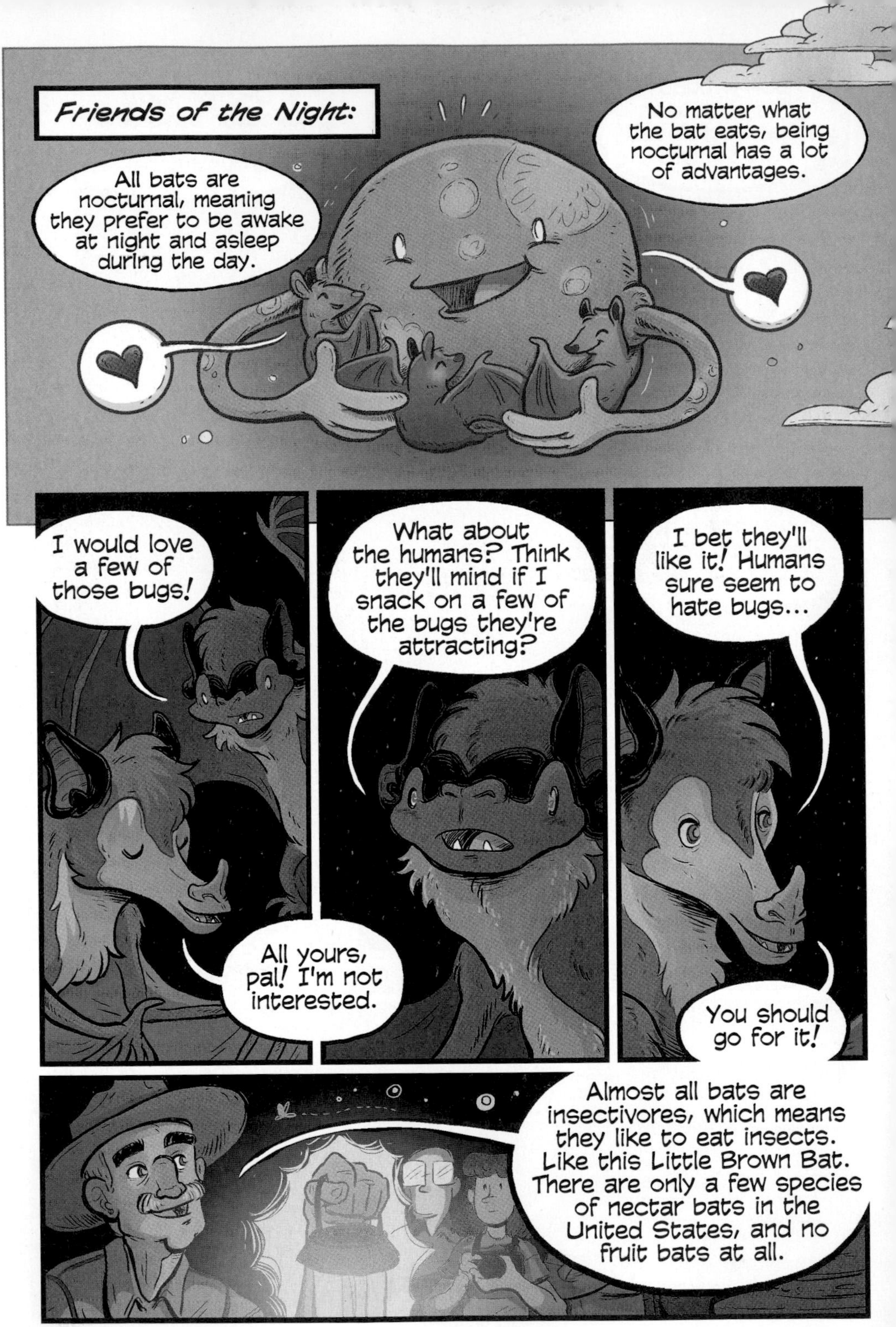
Friends of the Night:
All bats are nocturnal, meaning they prefer to be awake at night and asleep during the day.
No matter what the bat eats, being nocturnal has a lot of advantages.
I would love a few of those bugs!
All yours, pal! I'm not interested.
What about the humans? Think they'll mind if I snack on a few of the bugs they're attracting?
I bet they'll like it! Humans sure seem to hate bugs...
You should go for it!
Almost all bats are insectivores, which means they like to eat insects. Like this Little Brown Bat. There are only a few species of nectar bats in the United States, and no fruit bats at all.

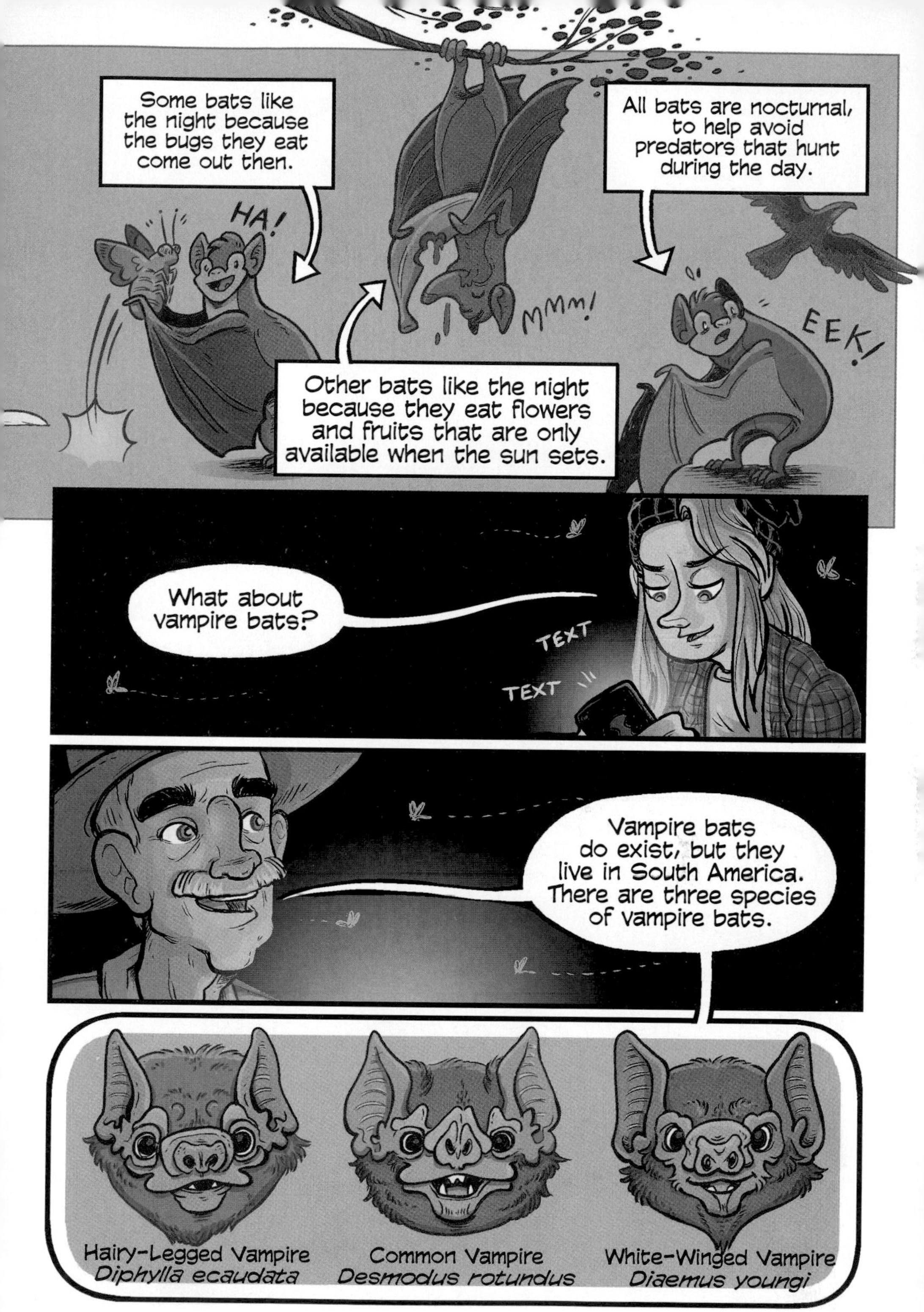

Some bats like the night because the bugs they eat come out then.
HA!
Other bats like the night because they eat flowers and fruits that are only available when the sun sets.
MMM!
All bats are nocturnal, to help avoid predators that hunt during the day.
EEK!
What about vampire bats?
TEXT
TEXT
Vampire bats do exist, but they live in South America. There are three species of vampire bats.
Hairy-Legged Vampire
Diphylla ecaudata
Common Vampire
Desmodus rotundus
White-Winged Vampire
Diaemus youngi

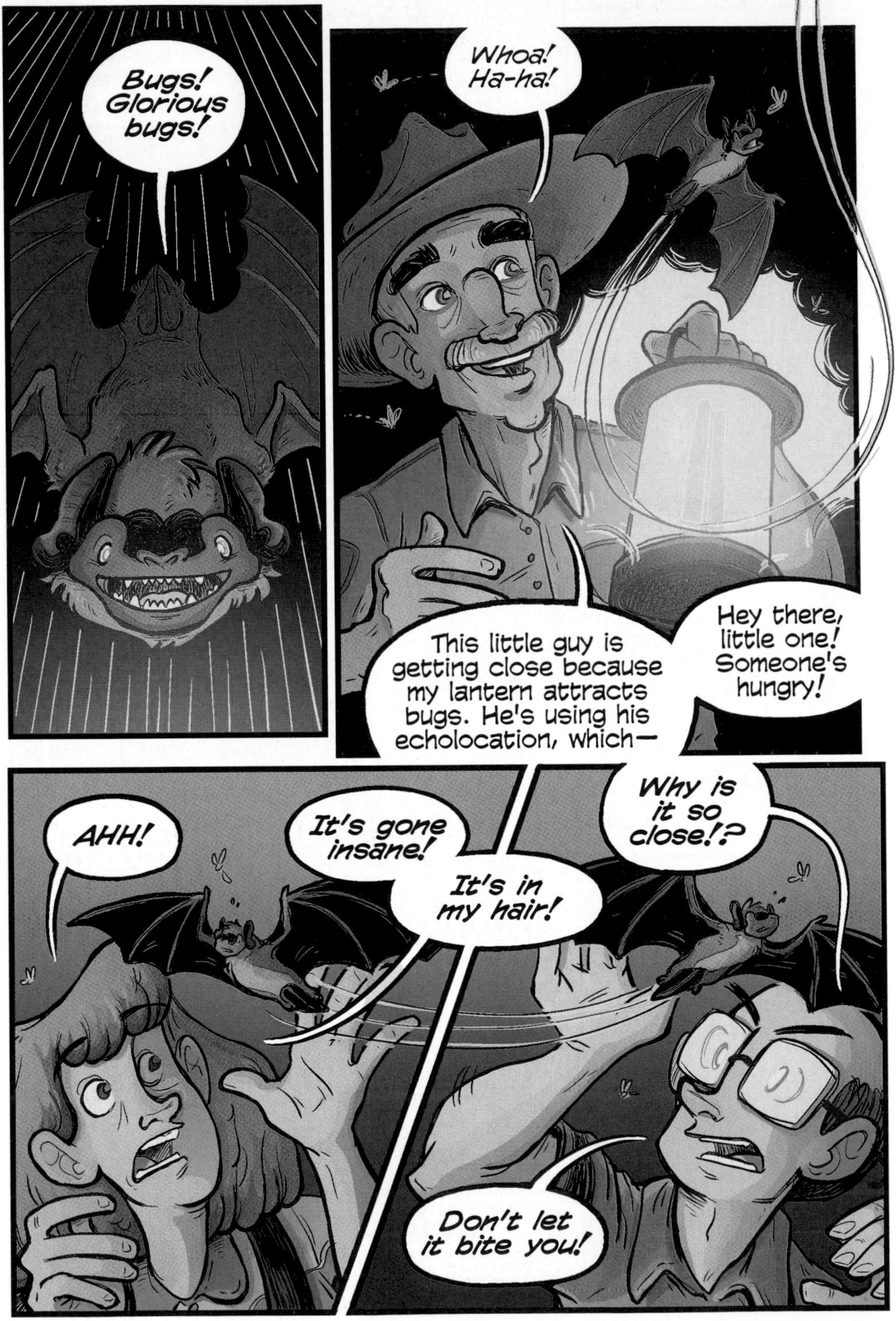
Bugs! Glorious bugs!
Whoa! Ha-ha!
This little guy is getting close because my lantern attracts bugs. He's using his echolocation, which—
Hey there, little one! Someone's hungry!
AHH!
It's gone insane!
It's in my hair!
Why is it so close!?
Don't let it bite you!

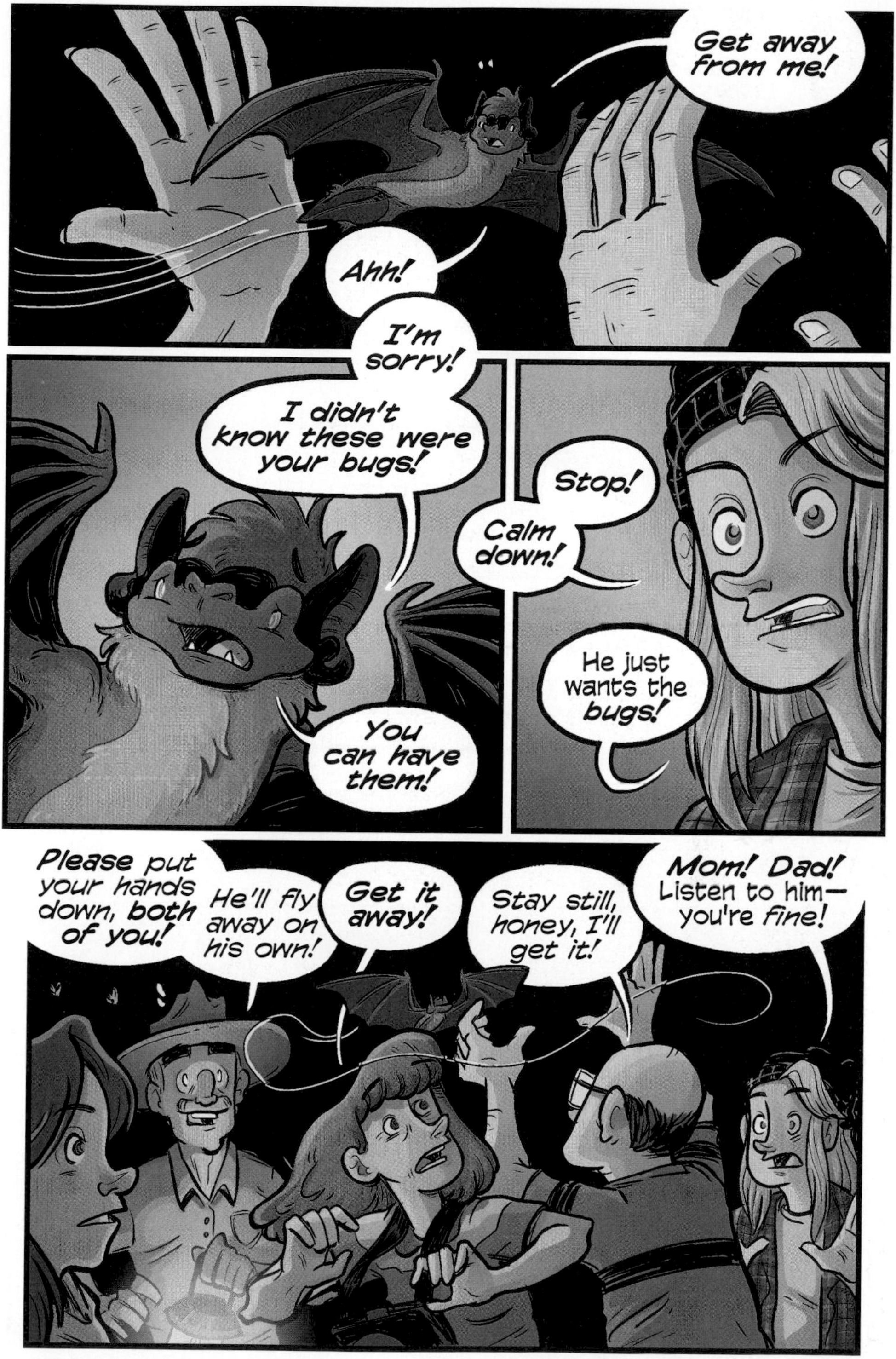

Get away from me!
Ahh!
I'm sorry!
I didn't know these were your bugs!
You can have them!
Stop!
Calm down!
He just wants the bugs!
Please put your hands down, both of you!
He'll fly away on his own!
Get it away!
Stay still, honey, I'll get it!
Mom! Dad! Listen to him—you're fine!

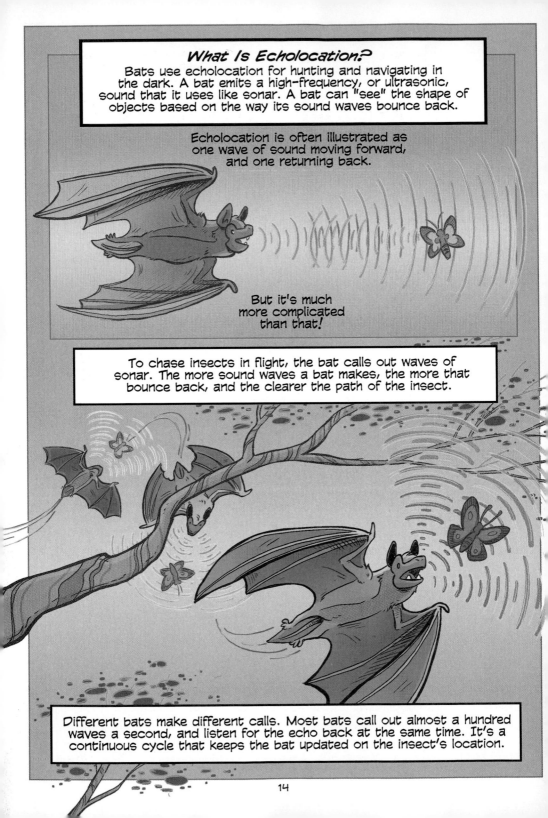

What Is Echolocation?

Bats use echolocation for hunting and navigating in the dark. A bat emits a high-frequency, or ultrasonic, sound that it uses like sonar. A bat can "see" the shape of objects based on the way its sound waves bounce back.

Echolocation is often illustrated as one wave of sound moving forward, and one returning back.

But it's much more complicated than that!

To chase insects in flight, the bat calls out waves of sonar. The more sound waves a bat makes, the more that bounce back, and the clearer the path of the insect.

Different bats make different calls. Most bats call out almost a hundred waves a second, and listen for the echo back at the same time. It's a continuous cycle that keeps the bat updated on the insect's location.

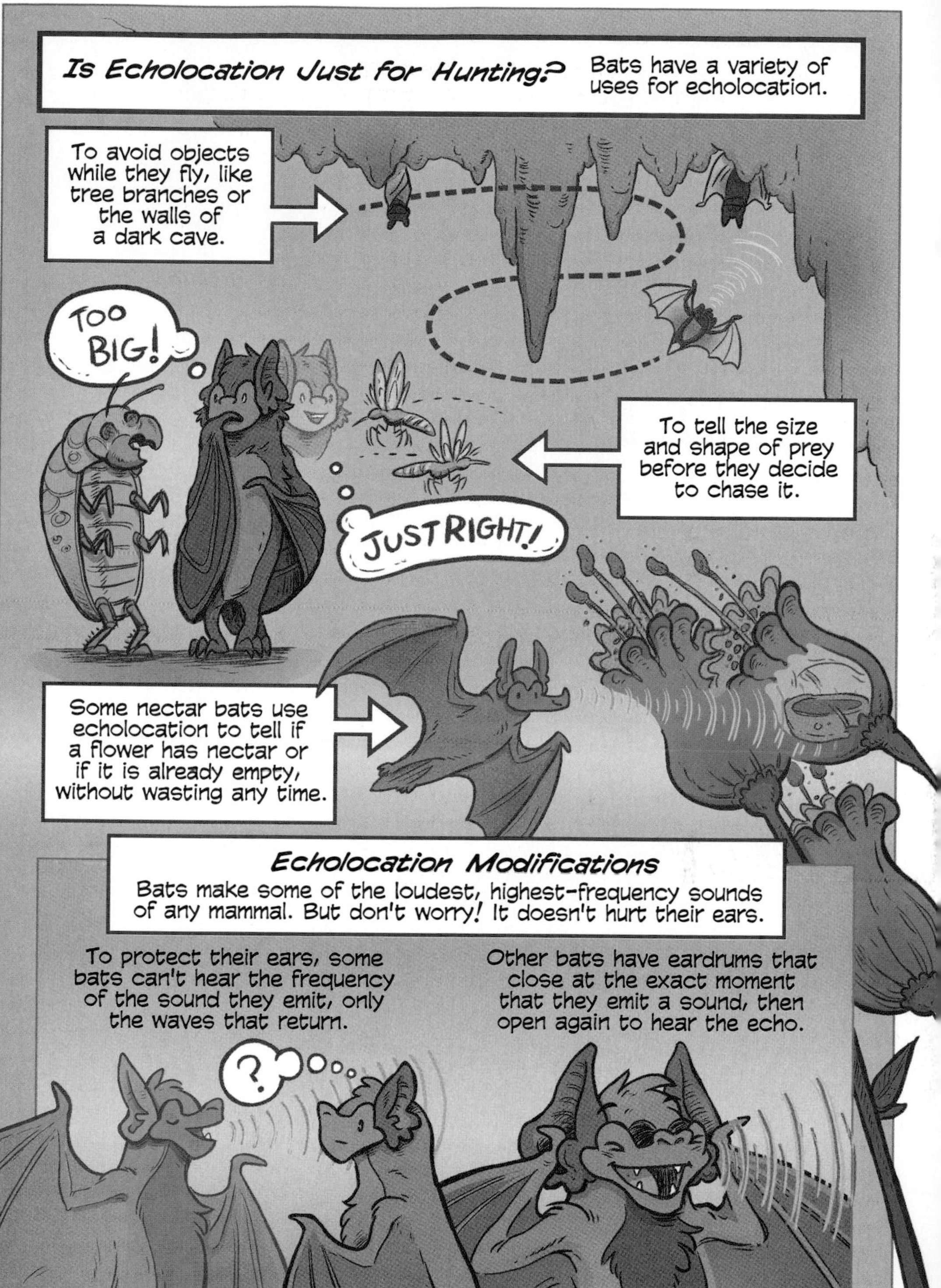
Is Echolocation Just for Hunting?
Bats have a variety of uses for echolocation.
To avoid objects while they fly, like tree branches or the walls of a dark cave.
TOO BIG!
JUST RIGHT!
To tell the size and shape of prey before they decide to chase it.
Some nectar bats use echolocation to tell if a flower has nectar or if it is already empty, without wasting any time.
Echolocation Modifications
Bats make some of the loudest, highest-frequency sounds of any mammal. But don't worry! It doesn't hurt their ears.
To protect their ears, some bats can't hear the frequency of the sound they emit, only the waves that return.
?
Other bats have eardrums that close at the exact moment that they emit a sound, then open again to hear the echo.

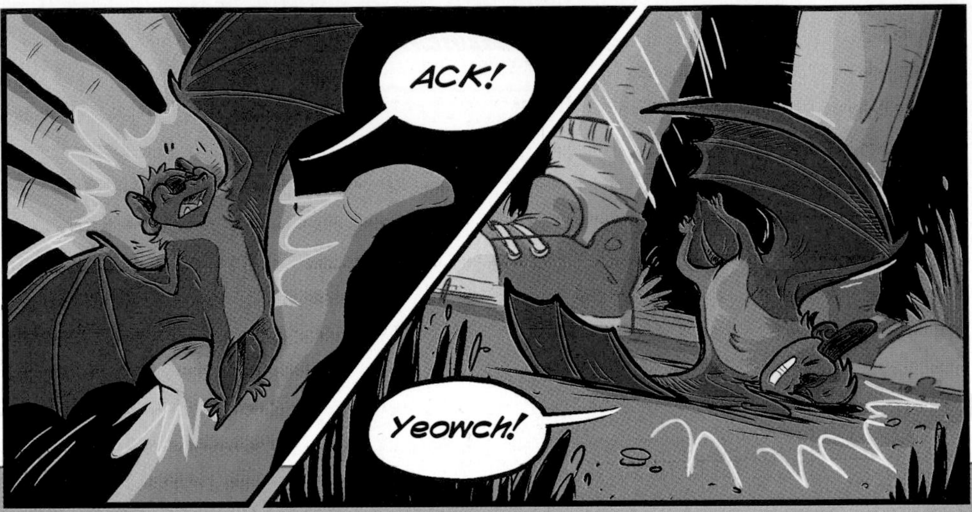
ACK!
Yeowch!

What Are the Parts of a Bat's Wing?

If a bat was human size, it might call the wing a hand because that's exactly what it is.

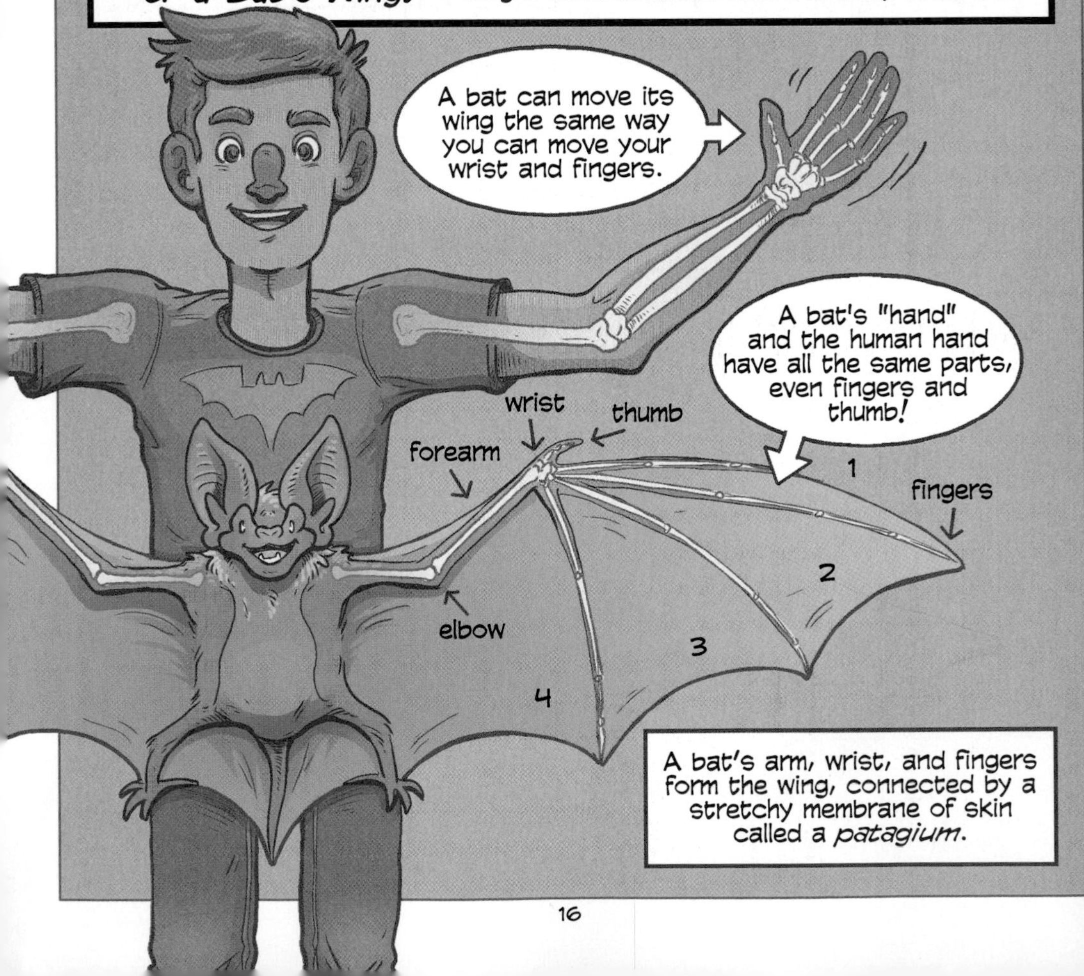
A bat can move its wing the same way you can move your wrist and fingers.
A bat's "hand" and the human hand have all the same parts, even fingers and thumb!
wrist
thumb
forearm
1
fingers
2
elbow
3
4
A bat's arm, wrist, and fingers form the wing, connected by a stretchy membrane of skin called a *patagium*.

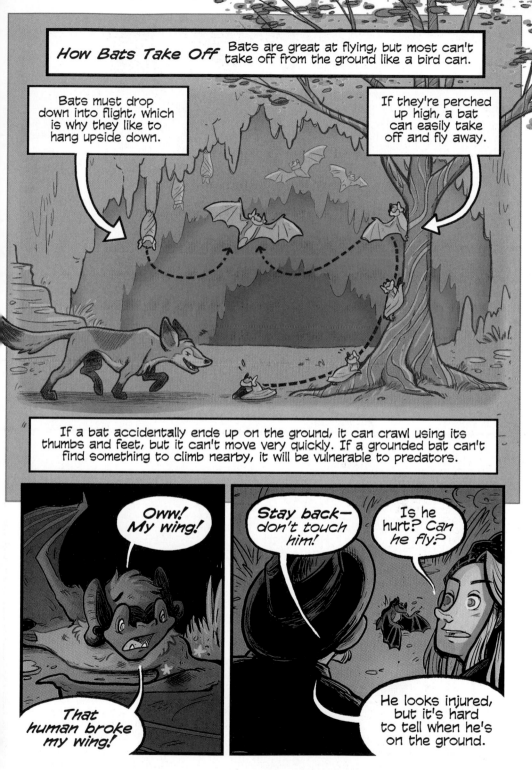

How Bats Take Off Bats are great at flying, but most can't take off from the ground like a bird can.

Bats must drop down into flight, which is why they like to hang upside down.

If they're perched up high, a bat can easily take off and fly away.

If a bat accidentally ends up on the ground, it can crawl using its thumbs and feet, but it can't move very quickly. If a grounded bat can't find something to climb nearby, it will be vulnerable to predators.

Oww! My wing!

That human broke my wing!

Stay back— don't touch him!

Is he hurt? Can he fly?

He looks injured, but it's hard to tell when he's on the ground.

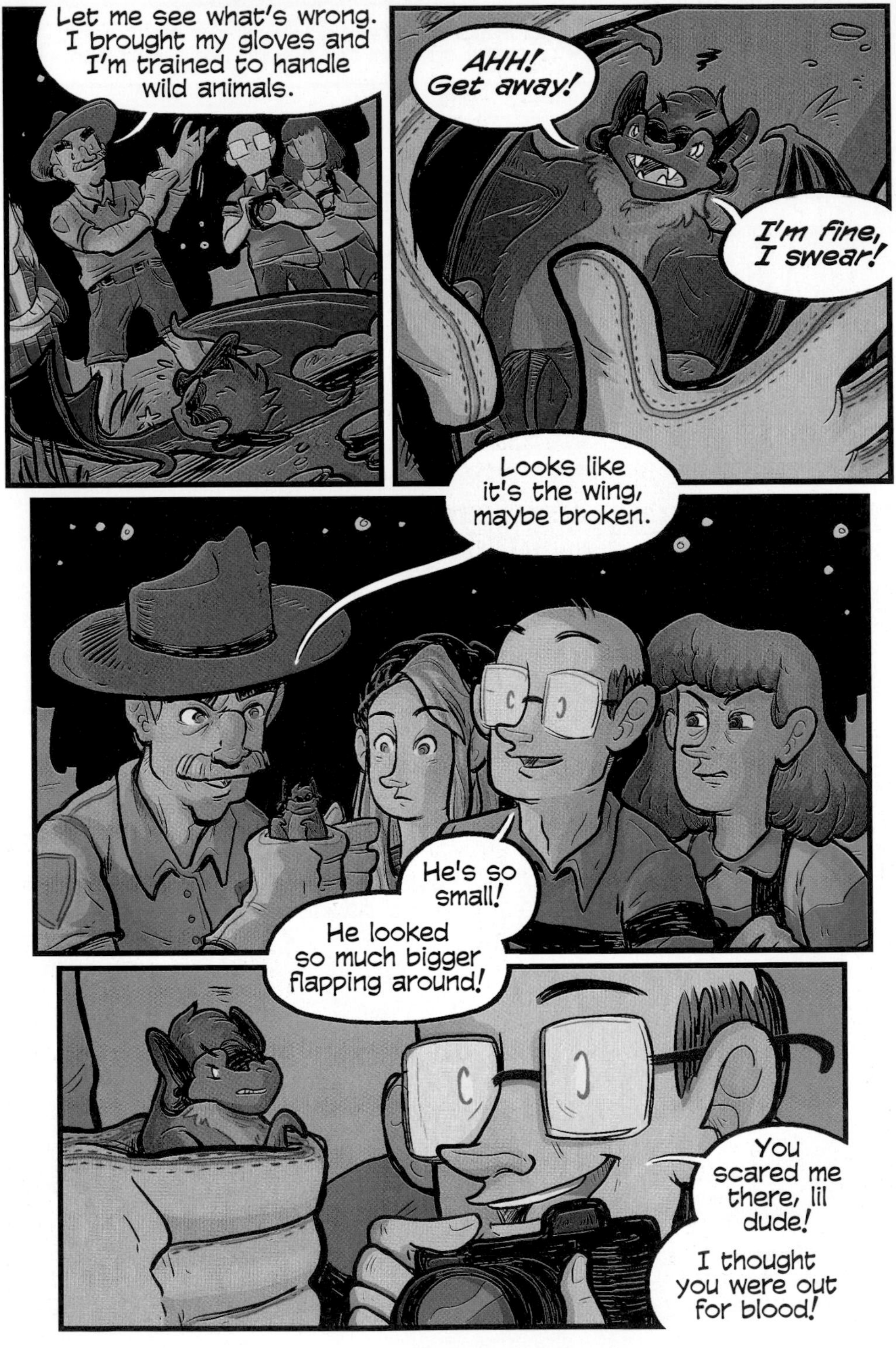
Let me see what's wrong. I brought my gloves and I'm trained to handle wild animals.
AHH! Get away!
I'm fine, I swear!
Looks like it's the wing, maybe broken.
He's so small!
He looked so much bigger flapping around!
You scared me there, lil dude!
I thought you were out for blood!

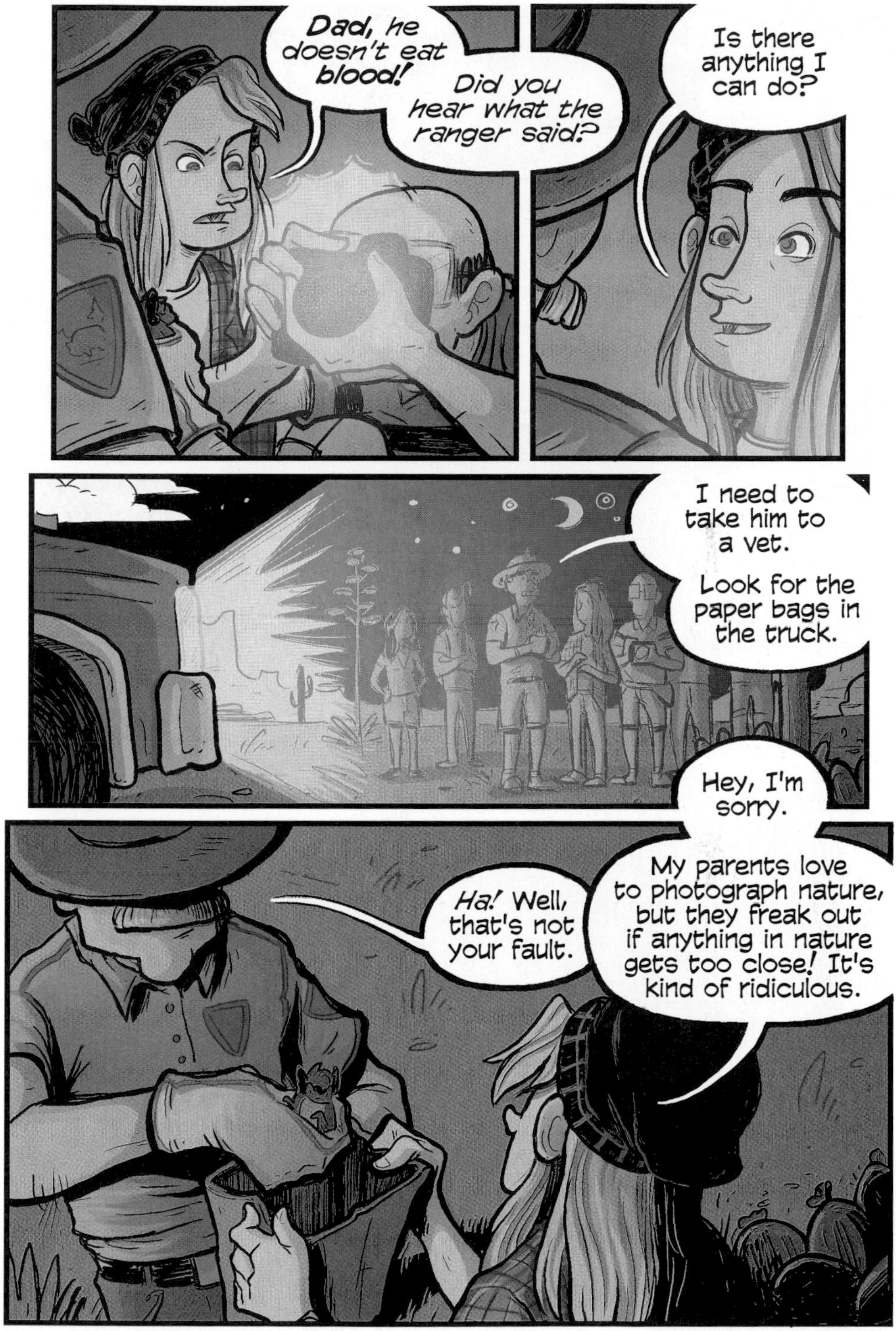

*Dad, he doesn't eat **blood!***
Did you hear what the ranger said?
Is there anything I can do?
I need to take him to a vet.
Look for the paper bags in the truck.
Hey, I'm sorry.
My parents love to photograph nature, but they freak out if anything in nature gets too close! It's kind of ridiculous.
Ha! Well, that's not your fault.

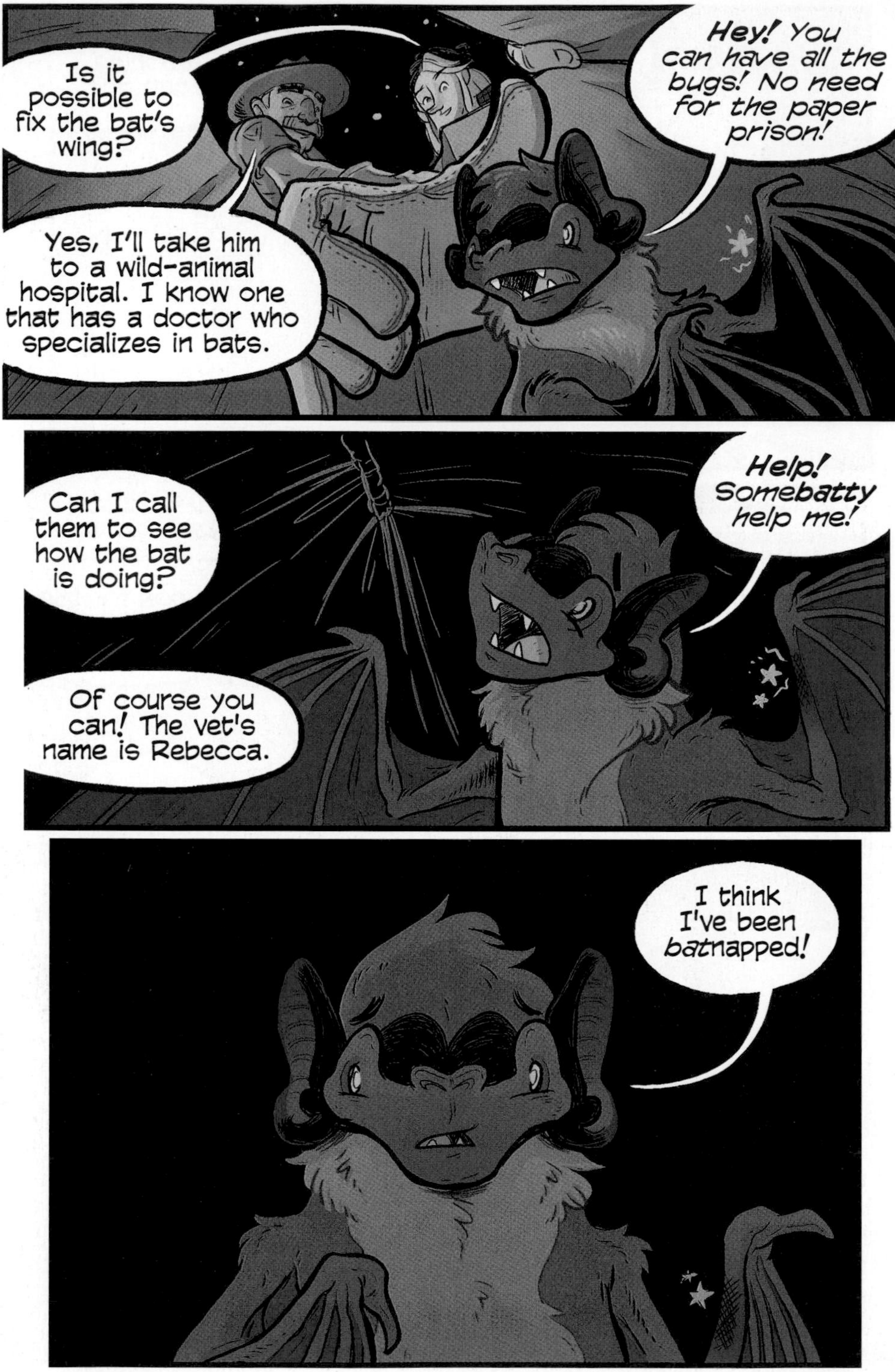
Is it possible to fix the bat's wing?
Hey! You can have all the bugs! No need for the paper prison!
Yes, I'll take him to a wild-animal hospital. I know one that has a doctor who specializes in bats.
Can I call them to see how the bat is doing?
Help! Somebatty help me!
Of course you can! The vet's name is Rebecca.
I think I've been batnapped!

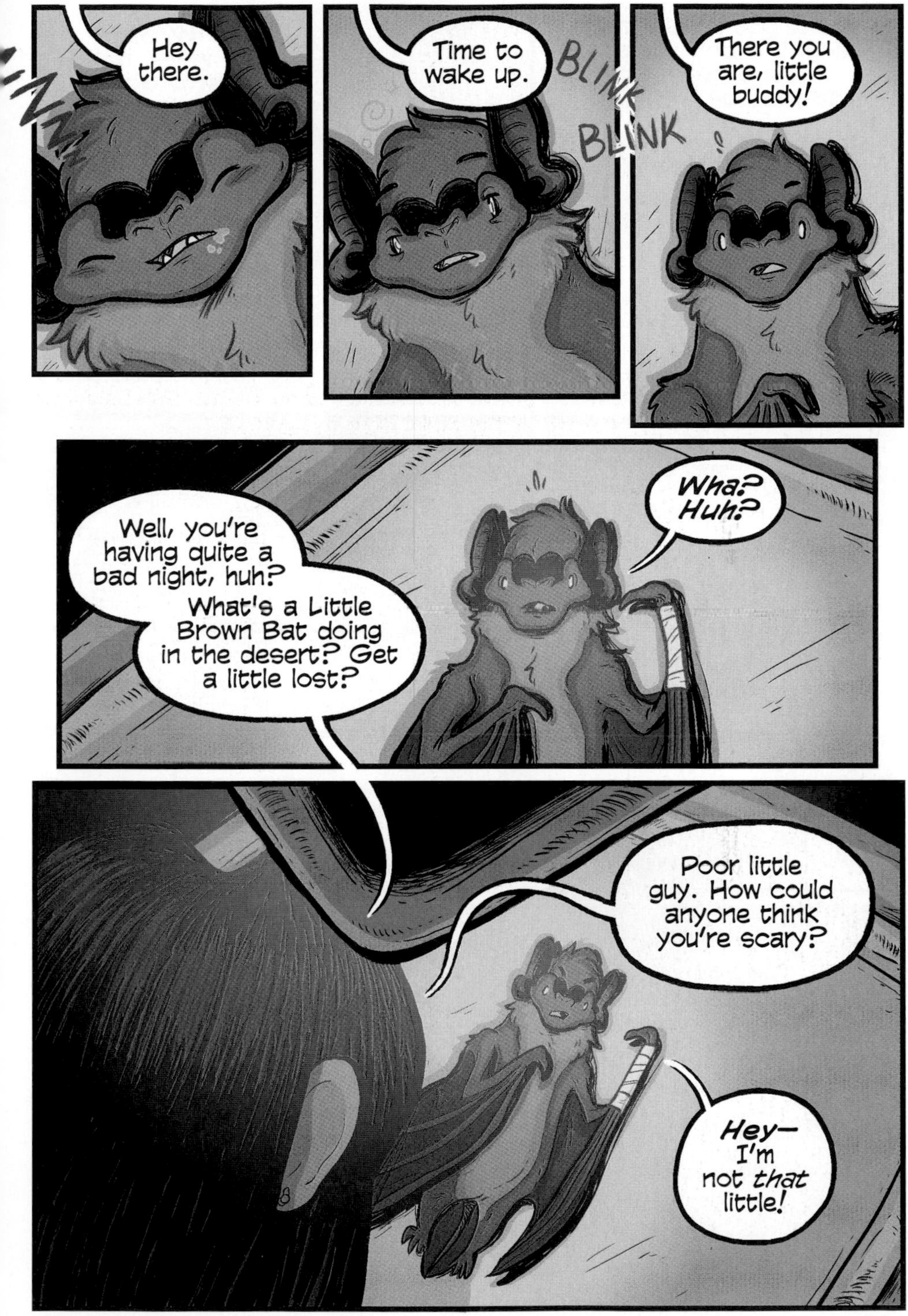
Hey there.
Time to wake up.
BLINK
BLINK
There you are, little buddy!
Wha? Huh?
Well, you're having quite a bad night, huh?
What's a Little Brown Bat doing in the desert? Get a little lost?
Poor little guy. How could anyone think you're scary?
Hey— I'm not *that* little!

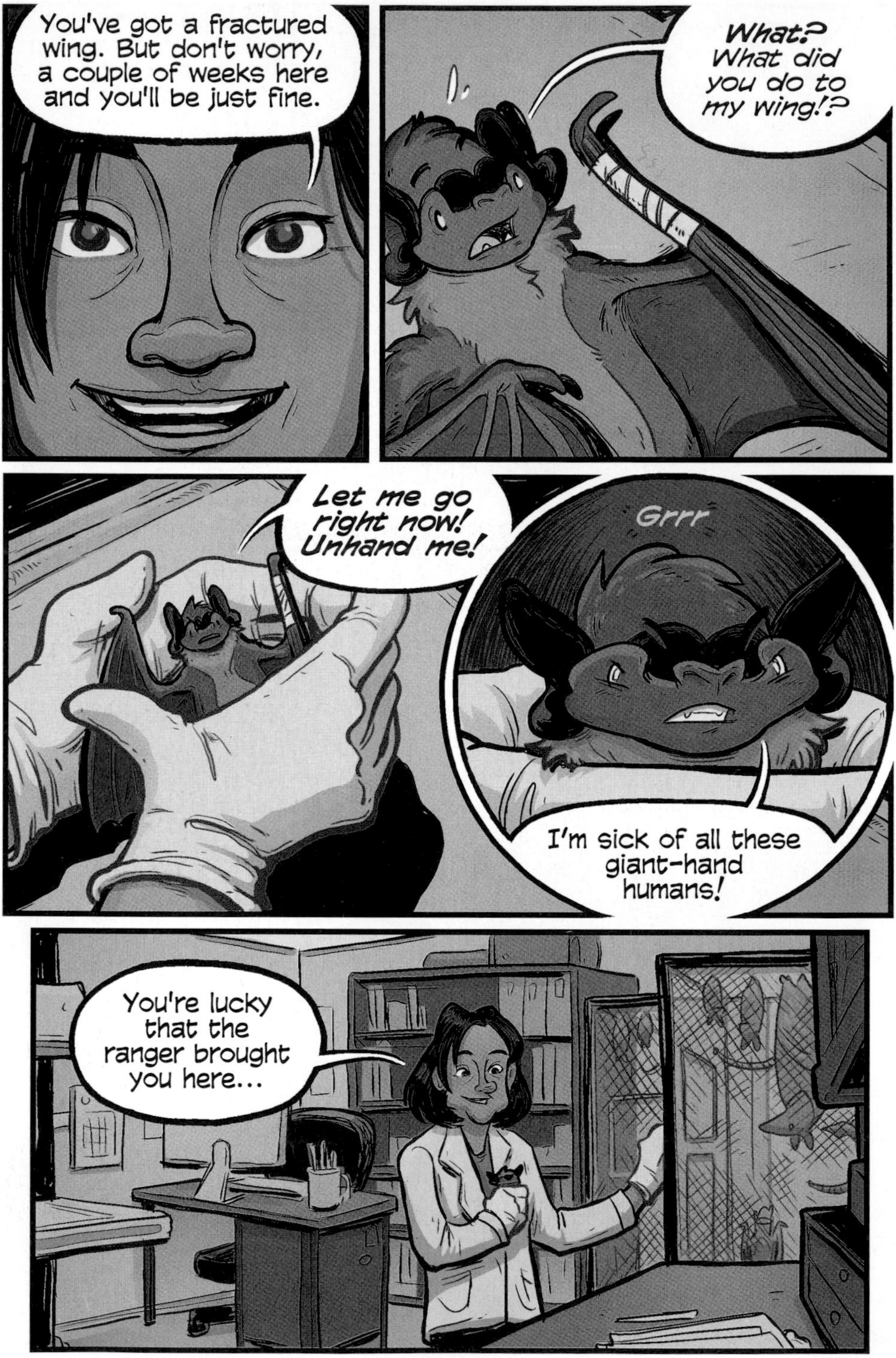
You've got a fractured wing. But don't worry, a couple of weeks here and you'll be just fine.
What? What did you do to my wing!?
Let me go right now! Unhand me!
Grrr
I'm sick of all these giant-hand humans!
You're lucky that the ranger brought you here...

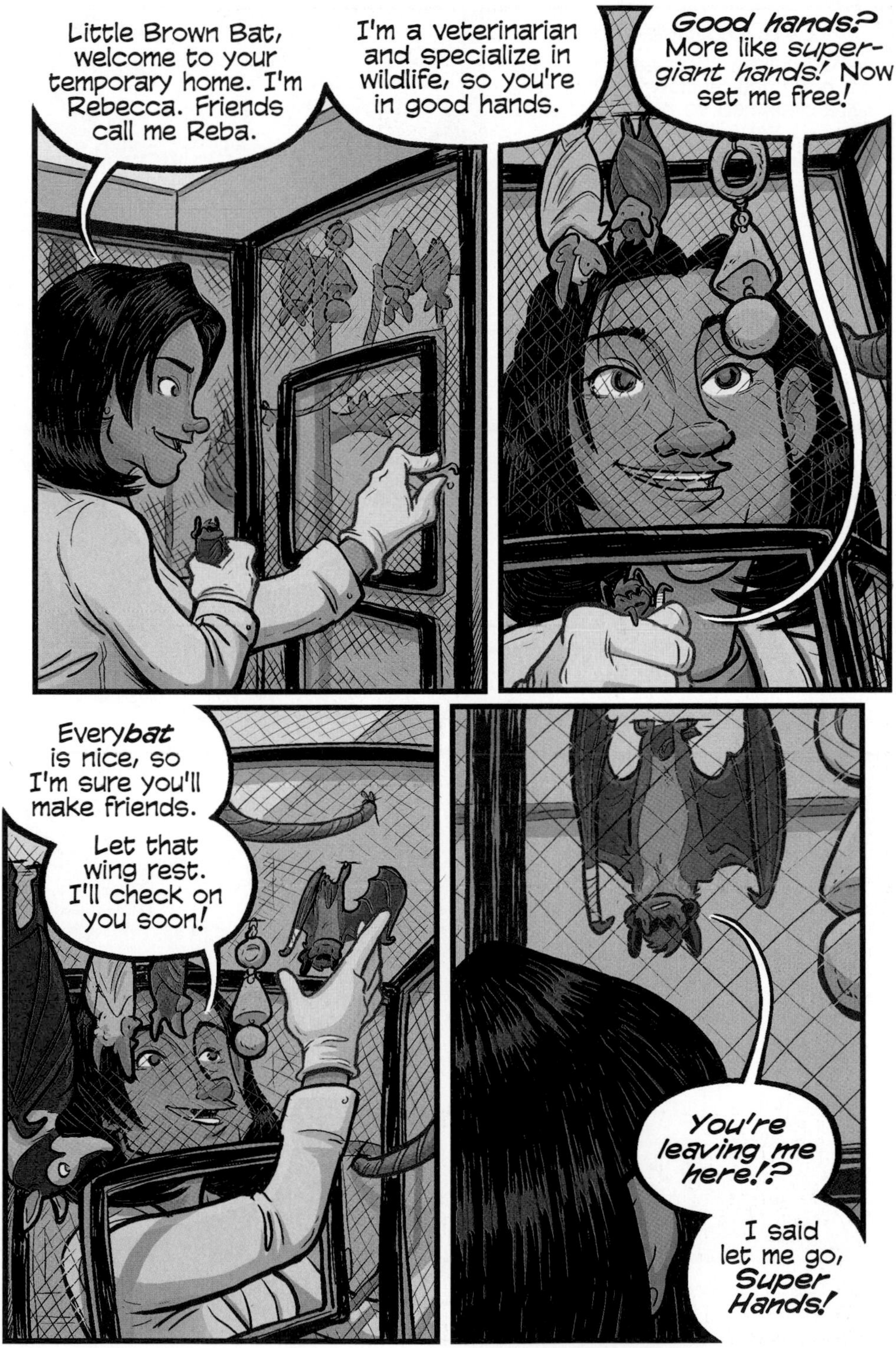

Little Brown Bat, welcome to your temporary home. I'm Rebecca. Friends call me Reba.
I'm a veterinarian and specialize in wildlife, so you're in good hands.
Good hands? More like *super-giant hands!* Now set me free!
Every**bat** is nice, so I'm sure you'll make friends.
Let that wing rest. I'll check on you soon!
You're leaving me here!?
I said let me go, ***Super Hands!***

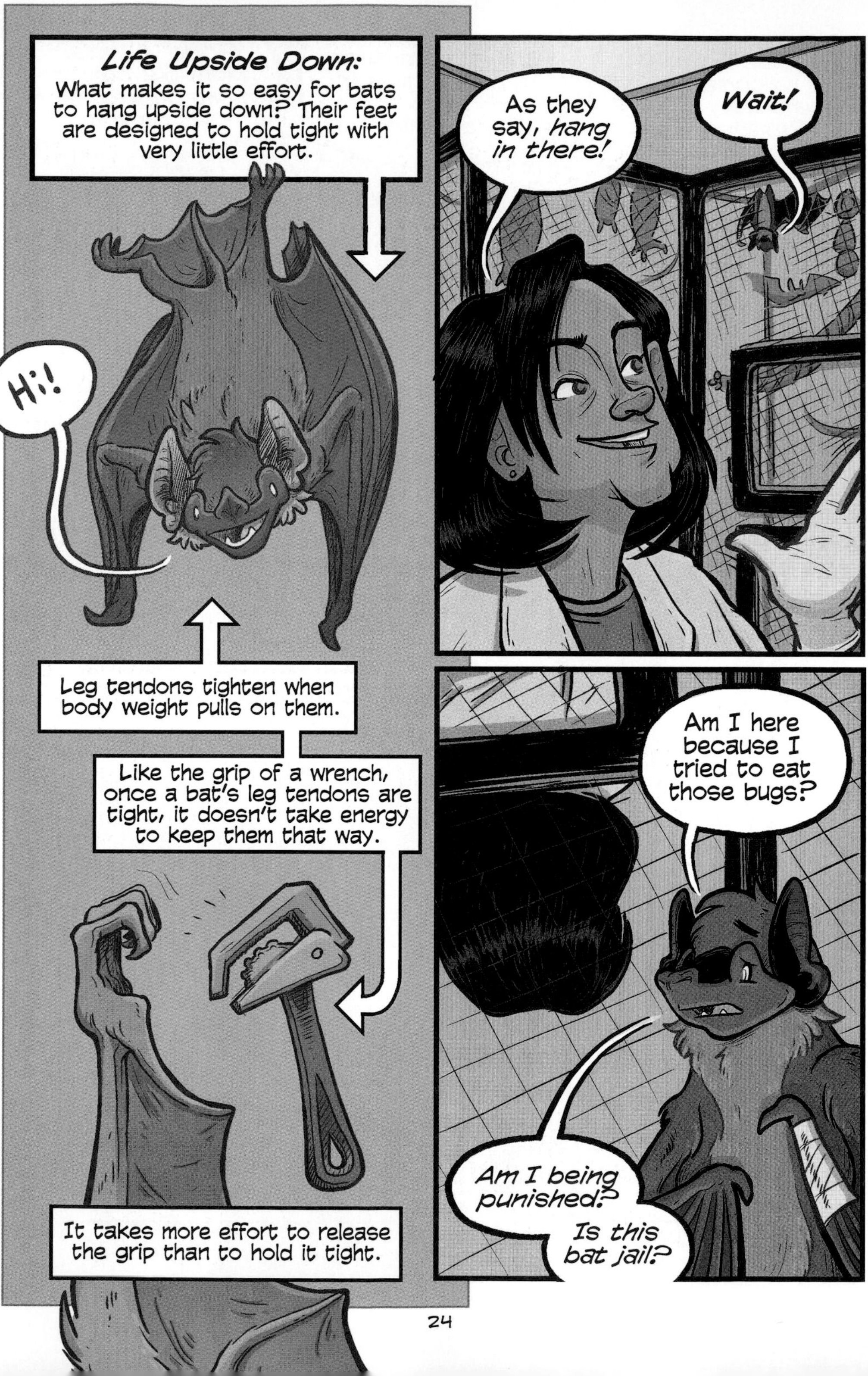

Life Upside Down:
What makes it so easy for bats to hang upside down? Their feet are designed to hold tight with very little effort.
Hi!
Leg tendons tighten when body weight pulls on them.
Like the grip of a wrench, once a bat's leg tendons are tight, it doesn't take energy to keep them that way.
It takes more effort to release the grip than to hold it tight.
As they say, *hang in there!*
Wait!
Am I here because I tried to eat those bugs?
Am I being punished?
Is this bat jail?

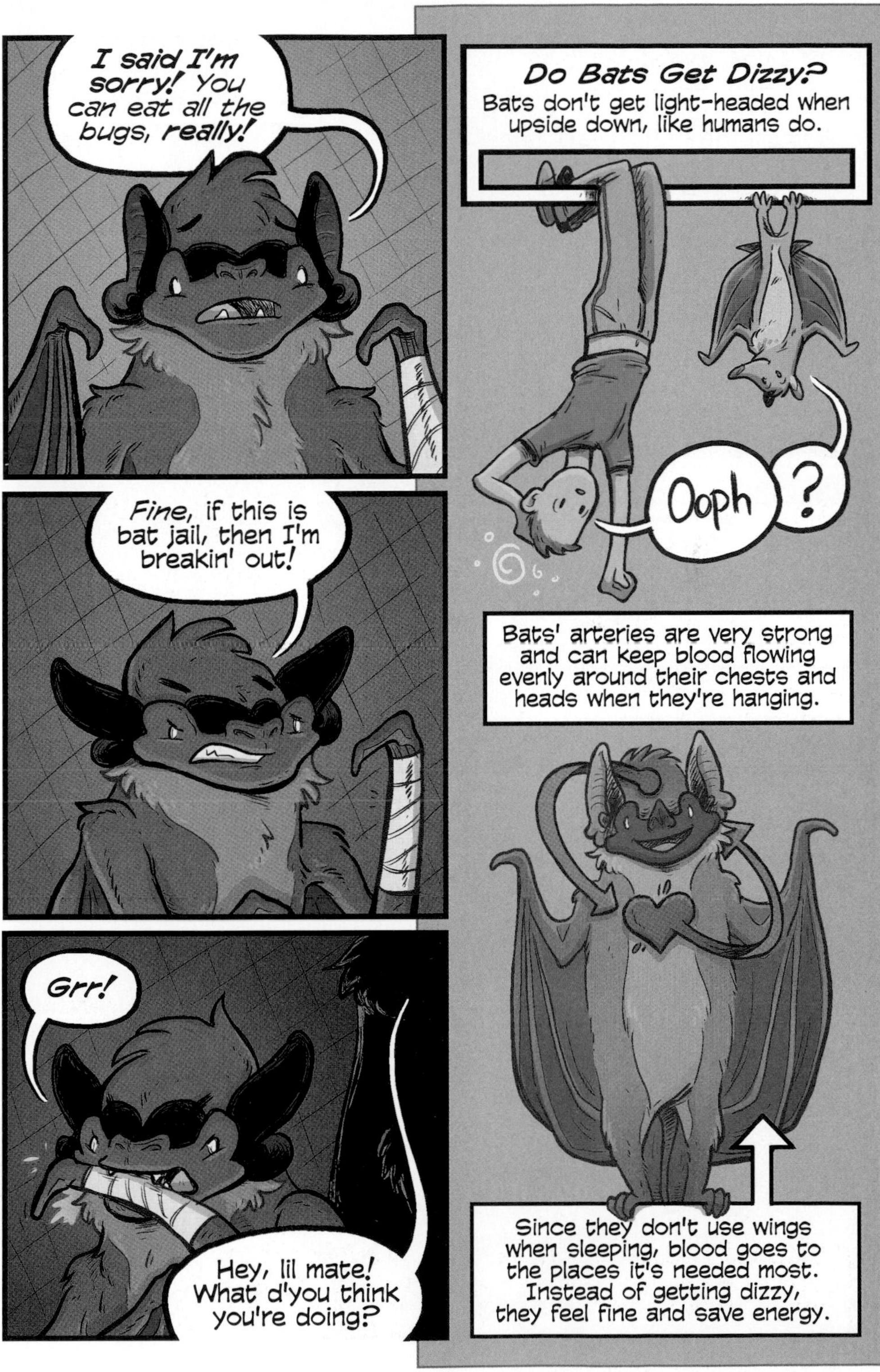
I said I'm sorry! You can eat all the bugs, really!
Fine, if this is bat jail, then I'm breakin' out!
Grr!
Hey, lil mate! What d'you think you're doing?
Do Bats Get Dizzy?
Bats don't get light-headed when upside down, like humans do.
Ooph
?
Bats' arteries are very strong and can keep blood flowing evenly around their chests and heads when they're hanging.
Since they don't use wings when sleeping, blood goes to the places it's needed most. Instead of getting dizzy, they feel fine and save energy.

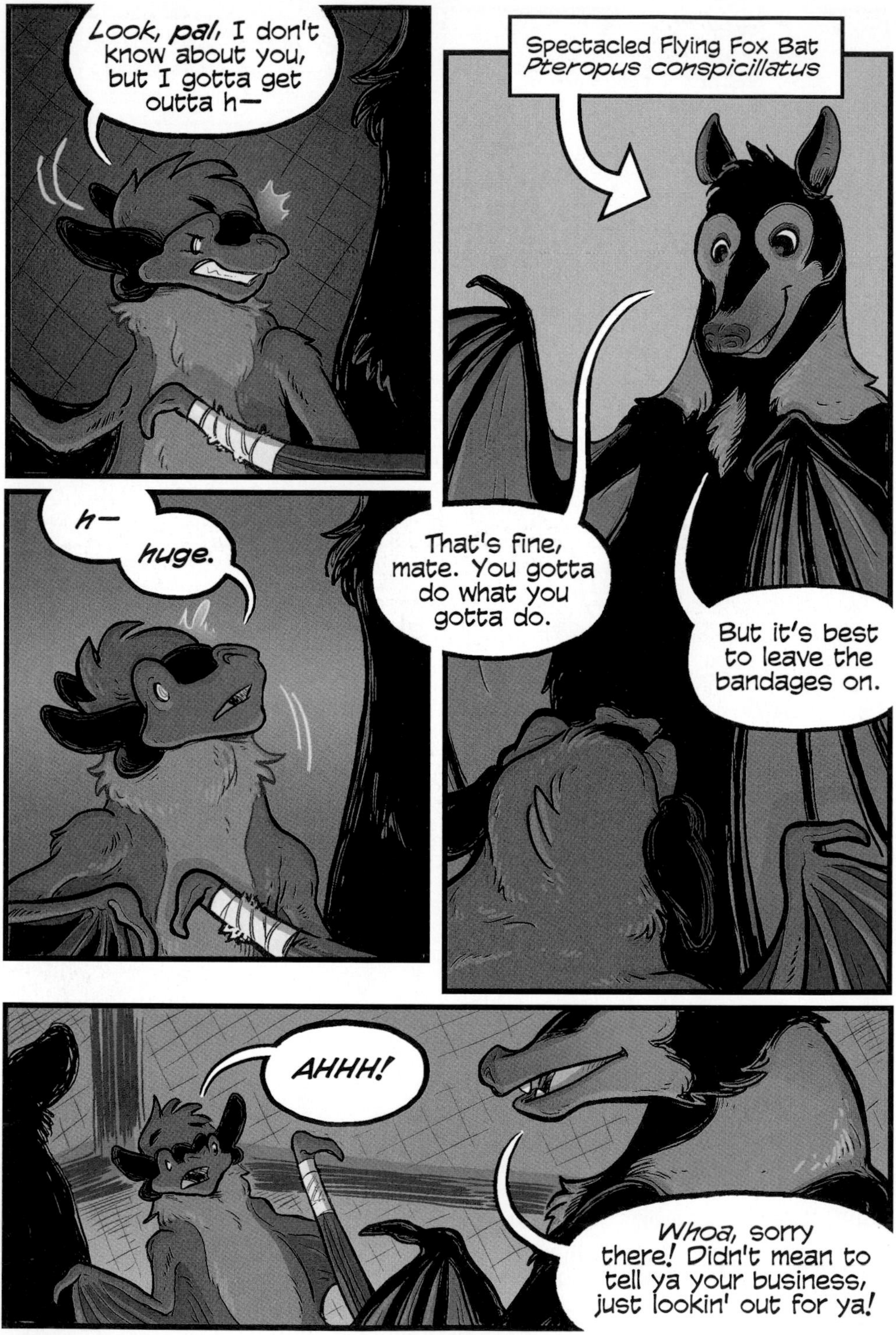
Look, pal, I don't know about you, but I gotta get outta h—
Spectacled Flying Fox Bat
Pteropus conspicillatus
h—
huge.
That's fine, mate. You gotta do what you gotta do.
But it's best to leave the bandages on.
AHHH!
Whoa, sorry there! Didn't mean to tell ya your business, just lookin' out for ya!

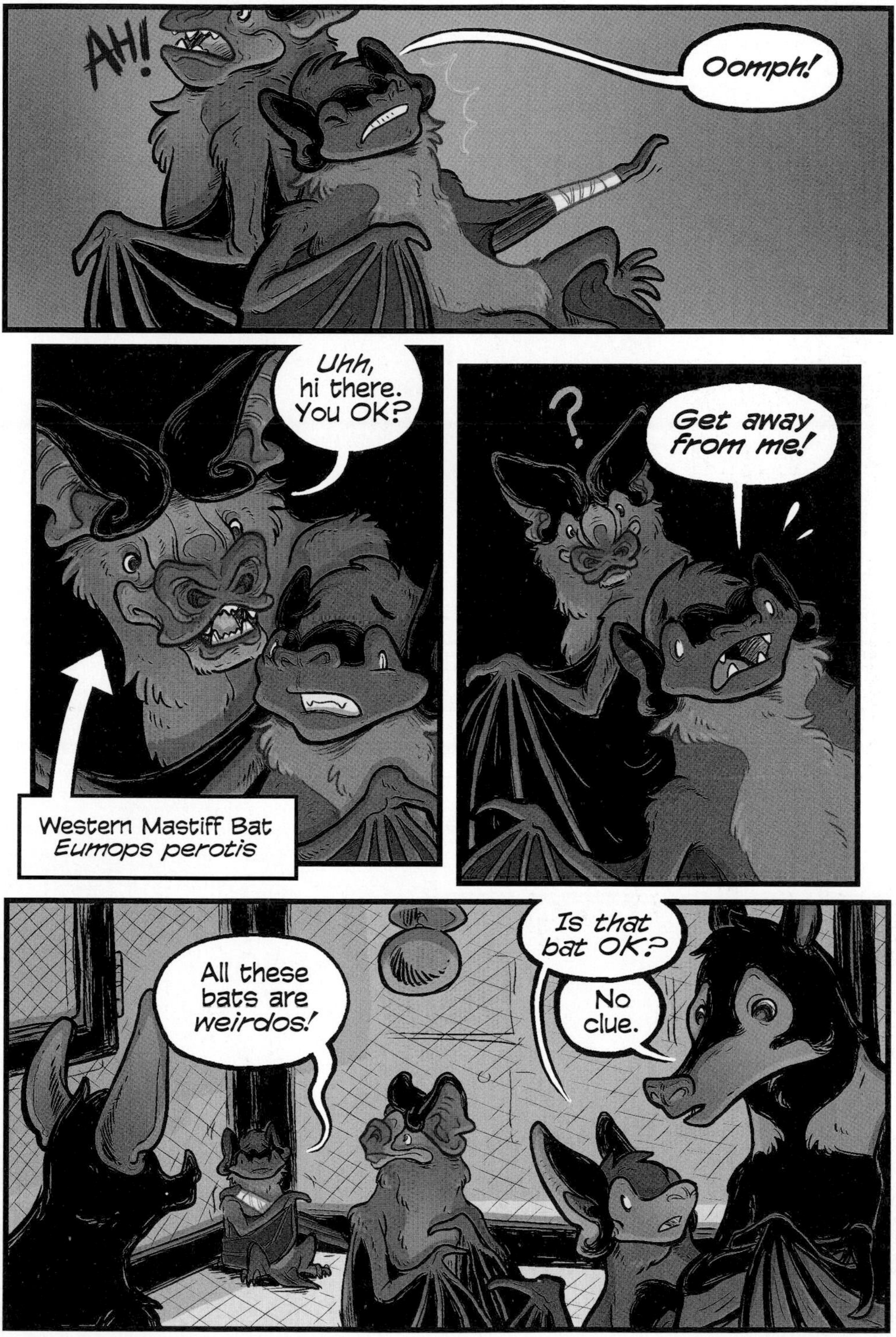
AH!
Oomph!
Uhh, hi there. You OK?
Western Mastiff Bat
Eumops perotis
?
Get away from me!
All these bats are *weirdos!*
Is that bat OK?
No clue.

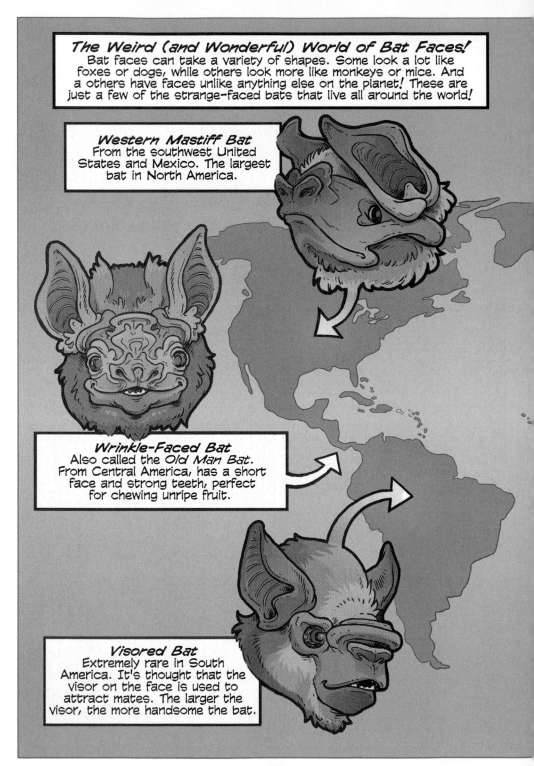

The Weird (and Wonderful) World of Bat Faces!
Bat faces can take a variety of shapes. Some look a lot like foxes or dogs, while others look more like monkeys or mice. And a others have faces unlike anything else on the planet! These are just a few of the strange-faced bats that live all around the world!

Western Mastiff Bat
From the southwest United States and Mexico. The largest bat in North America.

Wrinkle-Faced Bat
Also called the *Old Man Bat*. From Central America, has a short face and strong teeth, perfect for chewing unripe fruit.

Visored Bat
Extremely rare in South America. It's thought that the visor on the face is used to attract mates. The larger the visor, the more handsome the bat.

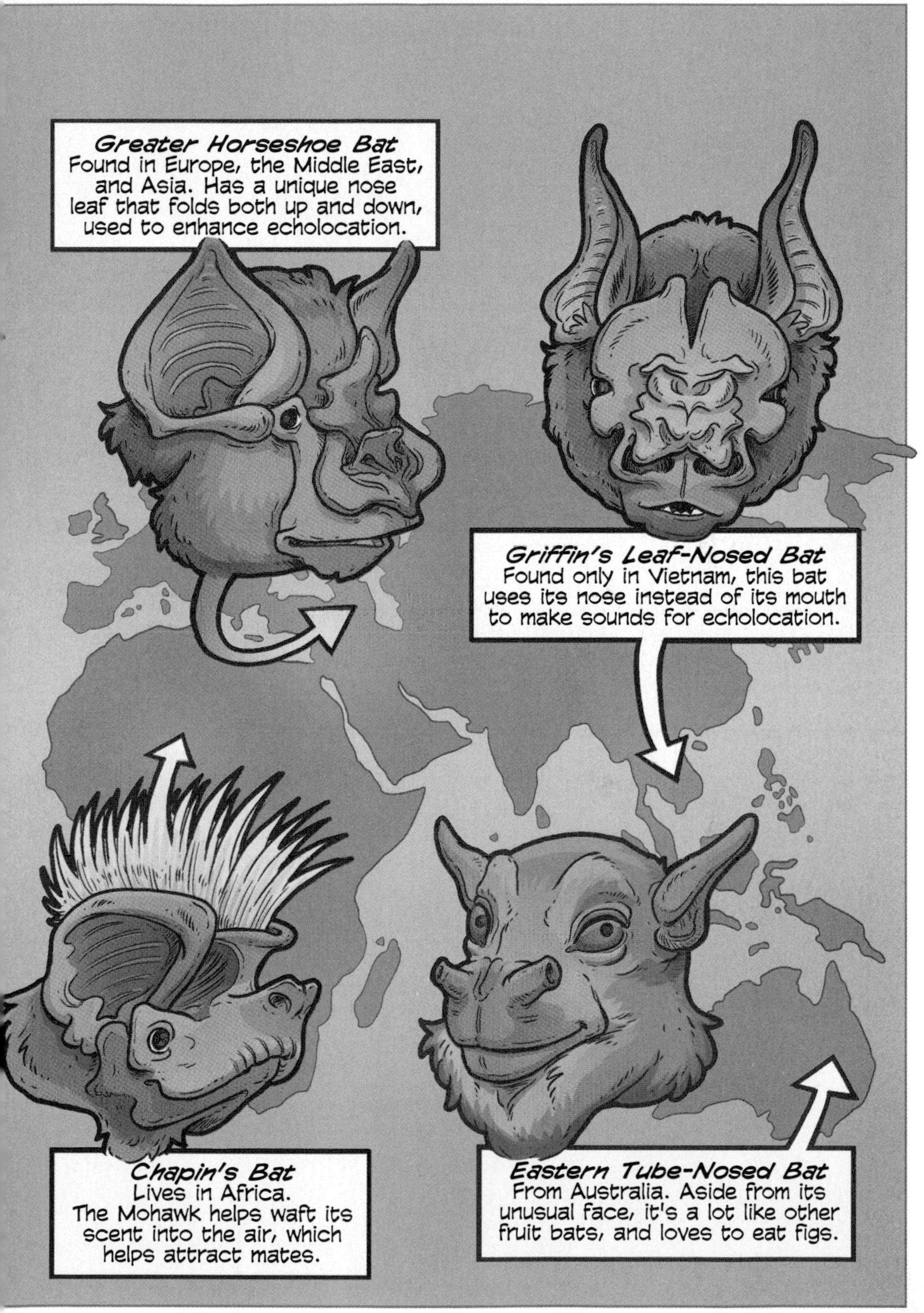
Greater Horseshoe Bat
Found in Europe, the Middle East, and Asia. Has a unique nose leaf that folds both up and down, used to enhance echolocation.
Griffin's Leaf-Nosed Bat
Found only in Vietnam, this bat uses its nose instead of its mouth to make sounds for echolocation.
Chapin's Bat
Lives in Africa.
The Mohawk helps waft its scent into the air, which helps attract mates.
Eastern Tube-Nosed Bat
From Australia. Aside from its unusual face, it's a lot like other fruit bats, and loves to eat figs.

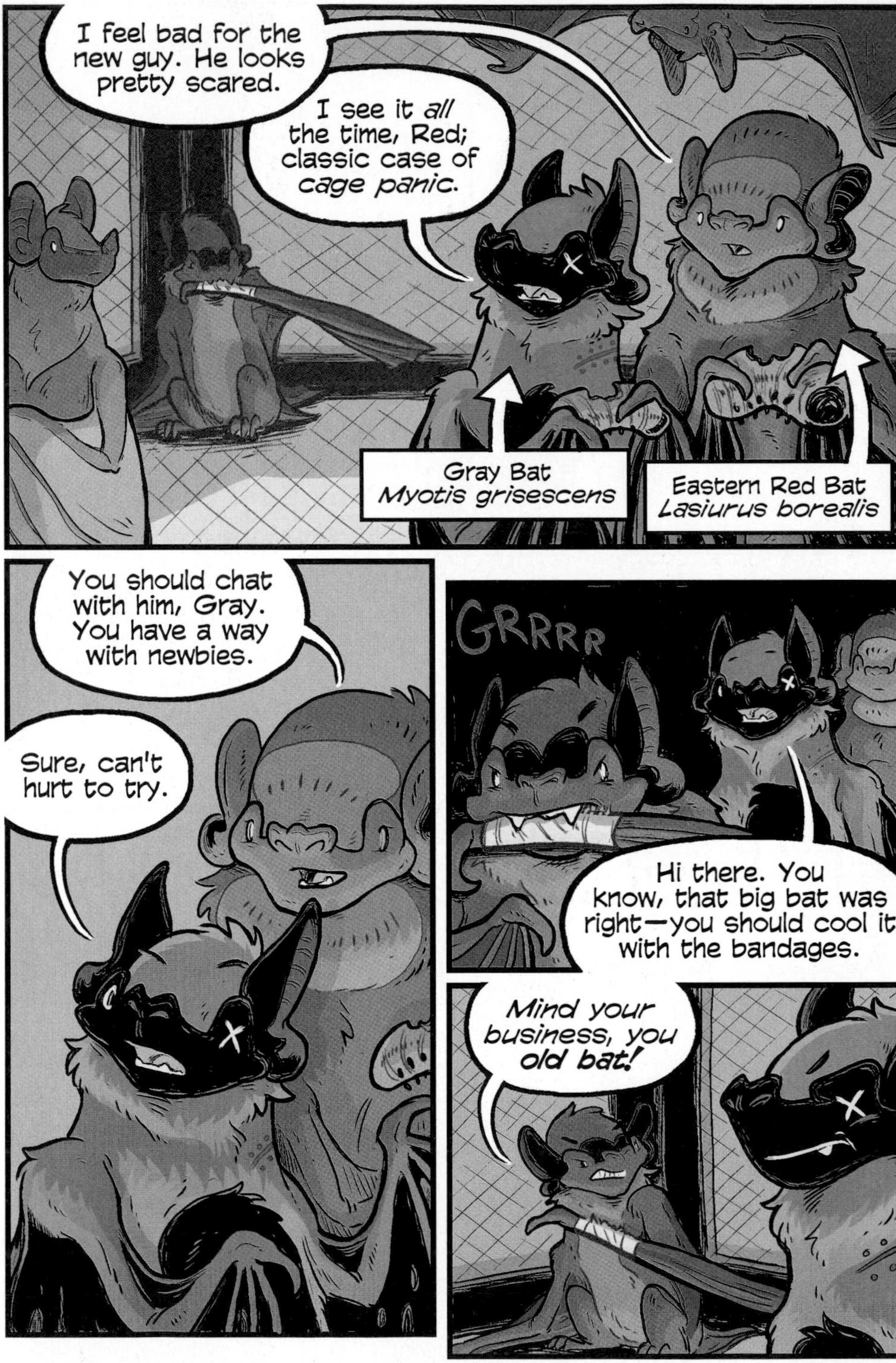
I feel bad for the new guy. He looks pretty scared.
I see it *all* the time, Red; classic case of *cage panic*.
Gray Bat *Myotis grisescens*
Eastern Red Bat *Lasiurus borealis*
You should chat with him, Gray. You have a way with newbies.
Sure, can't hurt to try.
GRRRR
Hi there. You know, that big bat was right—you should cool it with the bandages.
Mind your business, you ***old bat!***

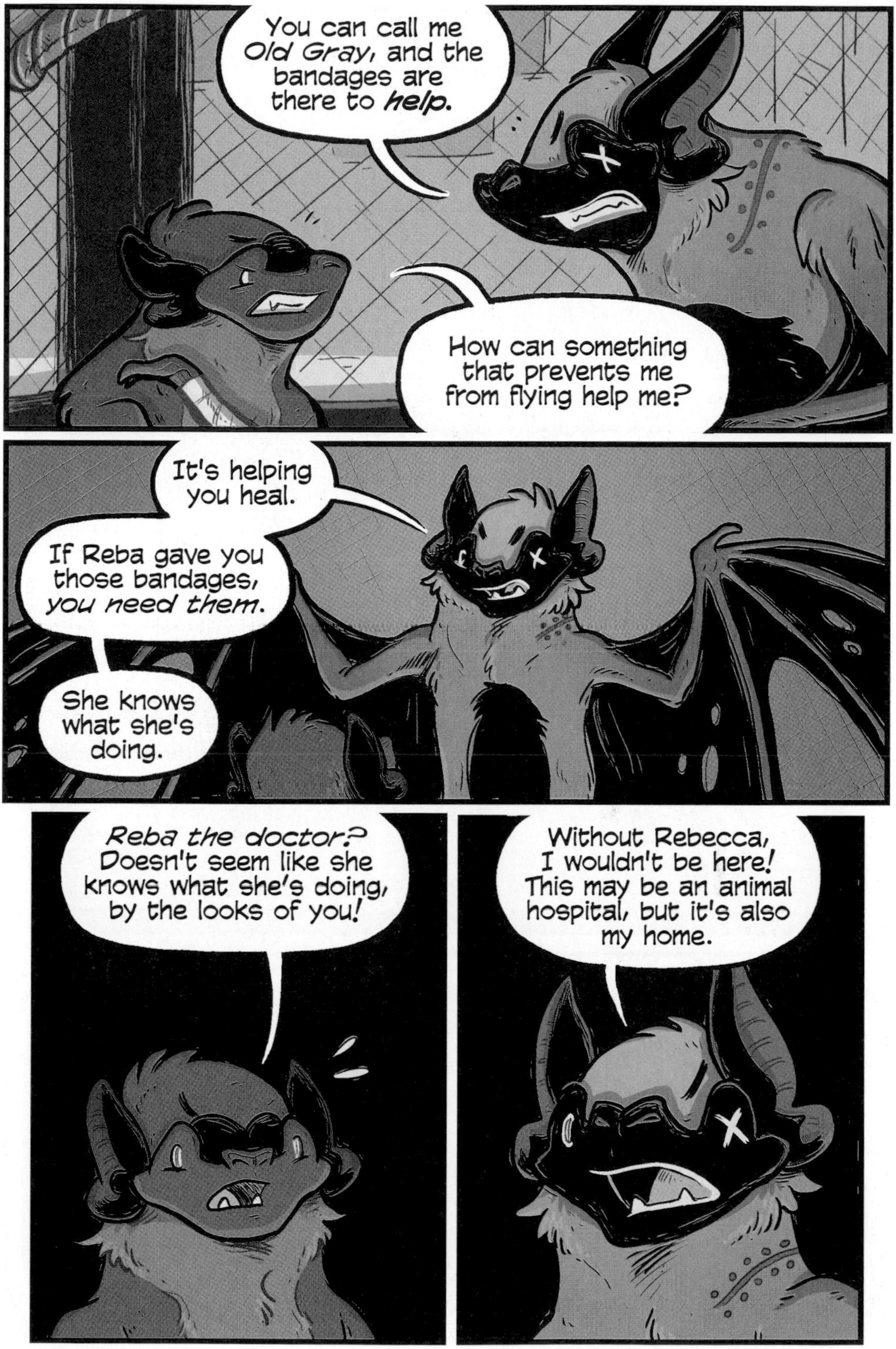
You can call me *Old Gray*, and the bandages are there to ***help***.
How can something that prevents me from flying help me?
It's helping you heal.
If Reba gave you those bandages, *you need them*.
She knows what she's doing.
Reba the doctor? Doesn't seem like she knows what she's doing, by the looks of you!
Without Rebecca, I wouldn't be here! This may be an animal hospital, but it's also my home.

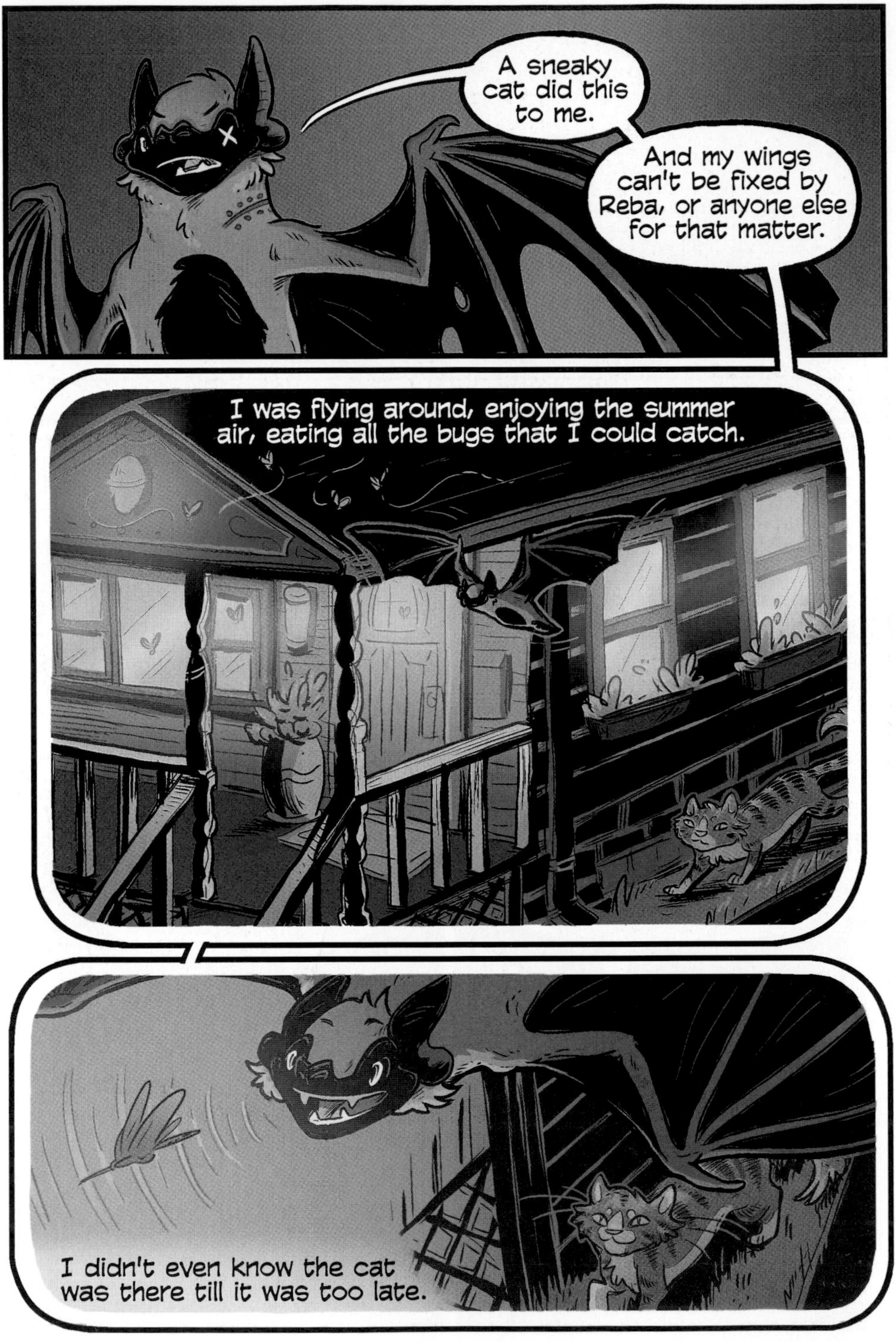
A sneaky cat did this to me.
And my wings can't be fixed by Reba, or anyone else for that matter.
I was flying around, enjoying the summer air, eating all the bugs that I could catch.
I didn't even know the cat was there till it was too late.

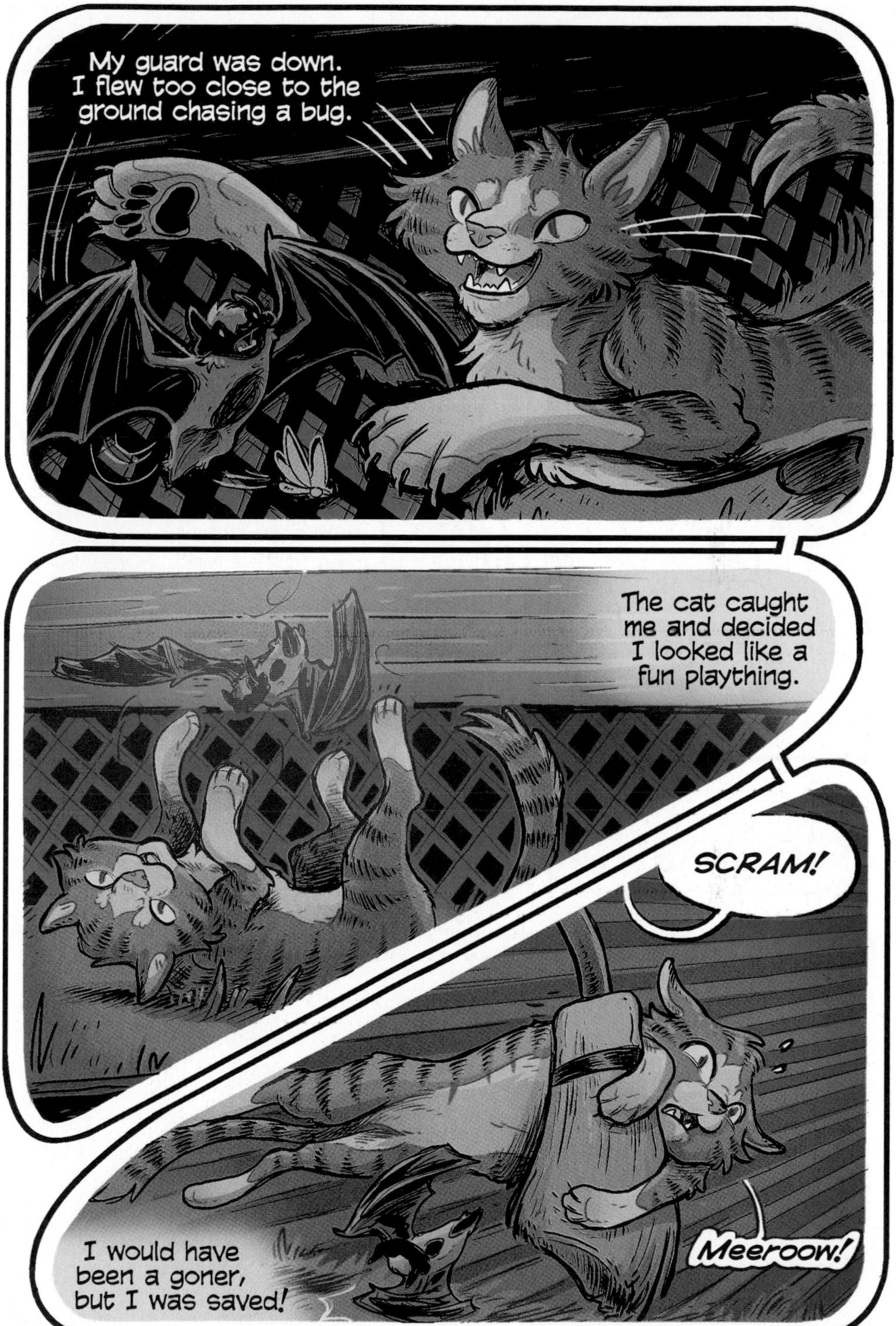
My guard was down. I flew too close to the ground chasing a bug.
The cat caught me and decided I looked like a fun plaything.
SCRAM!
Meeroow!
I would have been a goner, but I was saved!

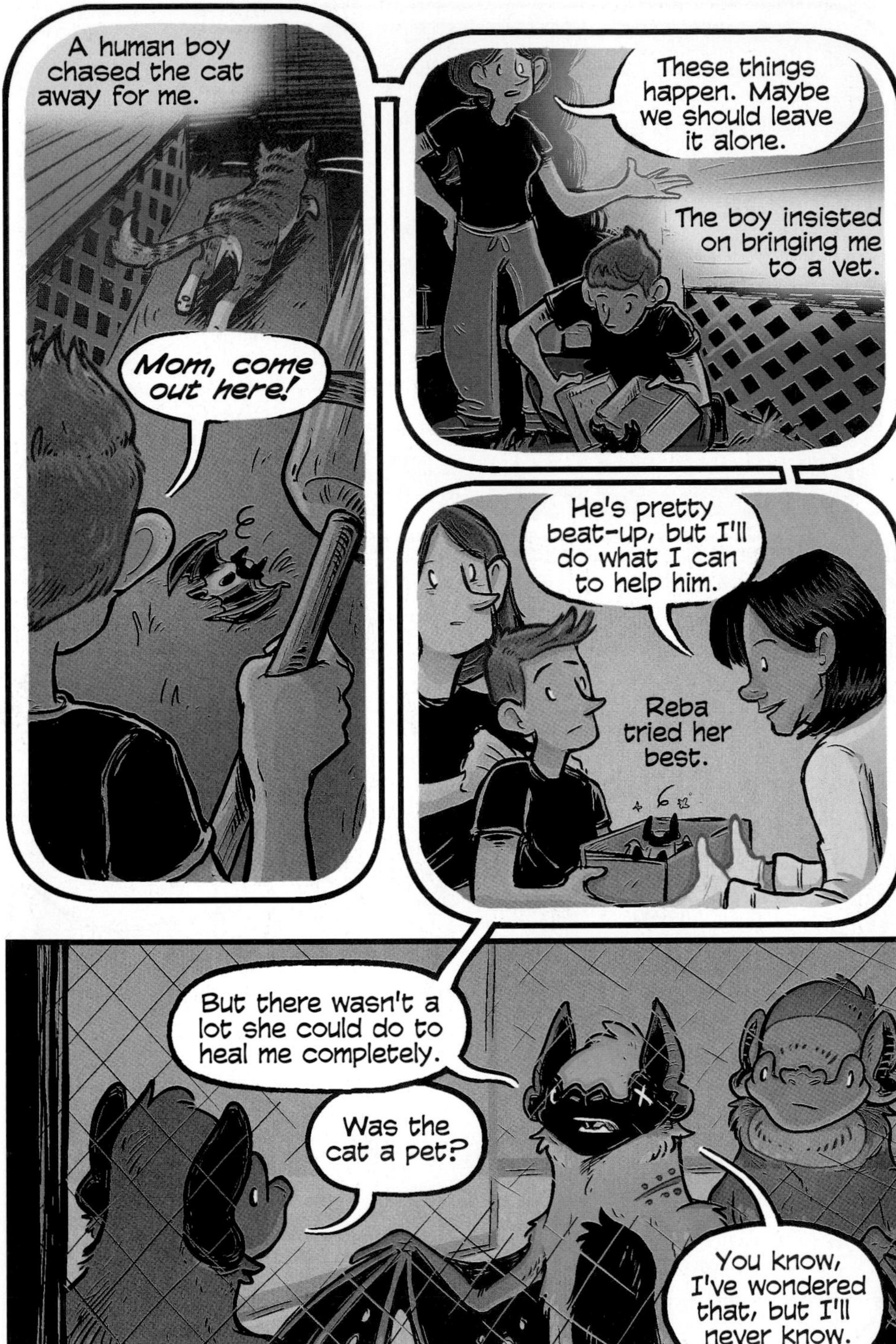
A human boy chased the cat away for me.
Mom, come out here!
These things happen. Maybe we should leave it alone.
The boy insisted on bringing me to a vet.
He's pretty beat-up, but I'll do what I can to help him.
Reba tried her best.
But there wasn't a lot she could do to heal me completely.
Was the cat a pet?
You know, I've wondered that, but I'll never know.

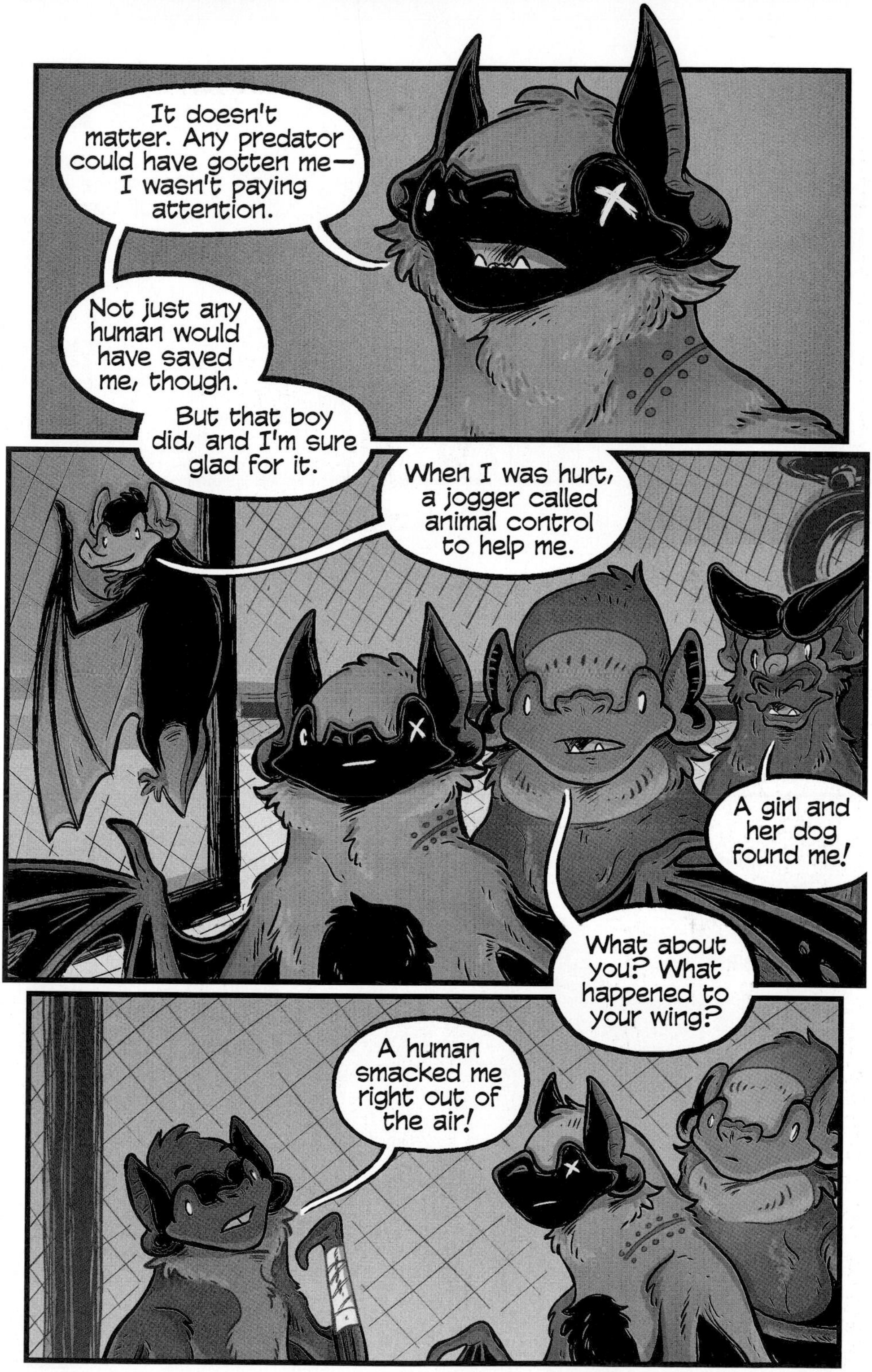
It doesn't matter. Any predator could have gotten me— I wasn't paying attention.
Not just any human would have saved me, though.
But that boy did, and I'm sure glad for it.
When I was hurt, a jogger called animal control to help me.
A girl and her dog found me!
What about you? What happened to your wing?
A human smacked me right out of the air!

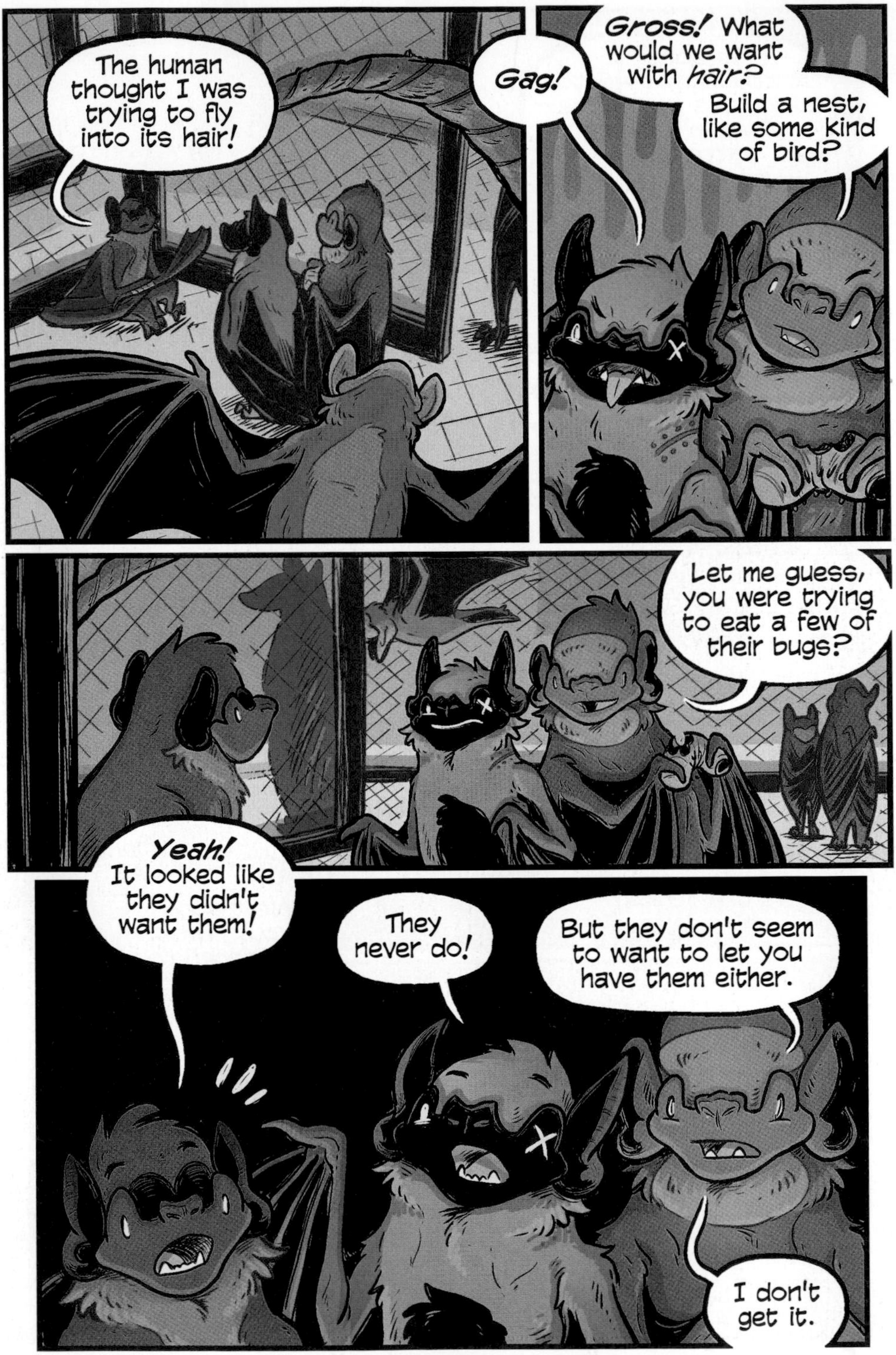
The human thought I was trying to fly into its hair!
Gag!
Gross! What would we want with hair?
Build a nest, like some kind of bird?
Let me guess, you were trying to eat a few of their bugs?
Yeah! It looked like they didn't want them!
They never do!
But they don't seem to want to let you have them either.
I don't get it.

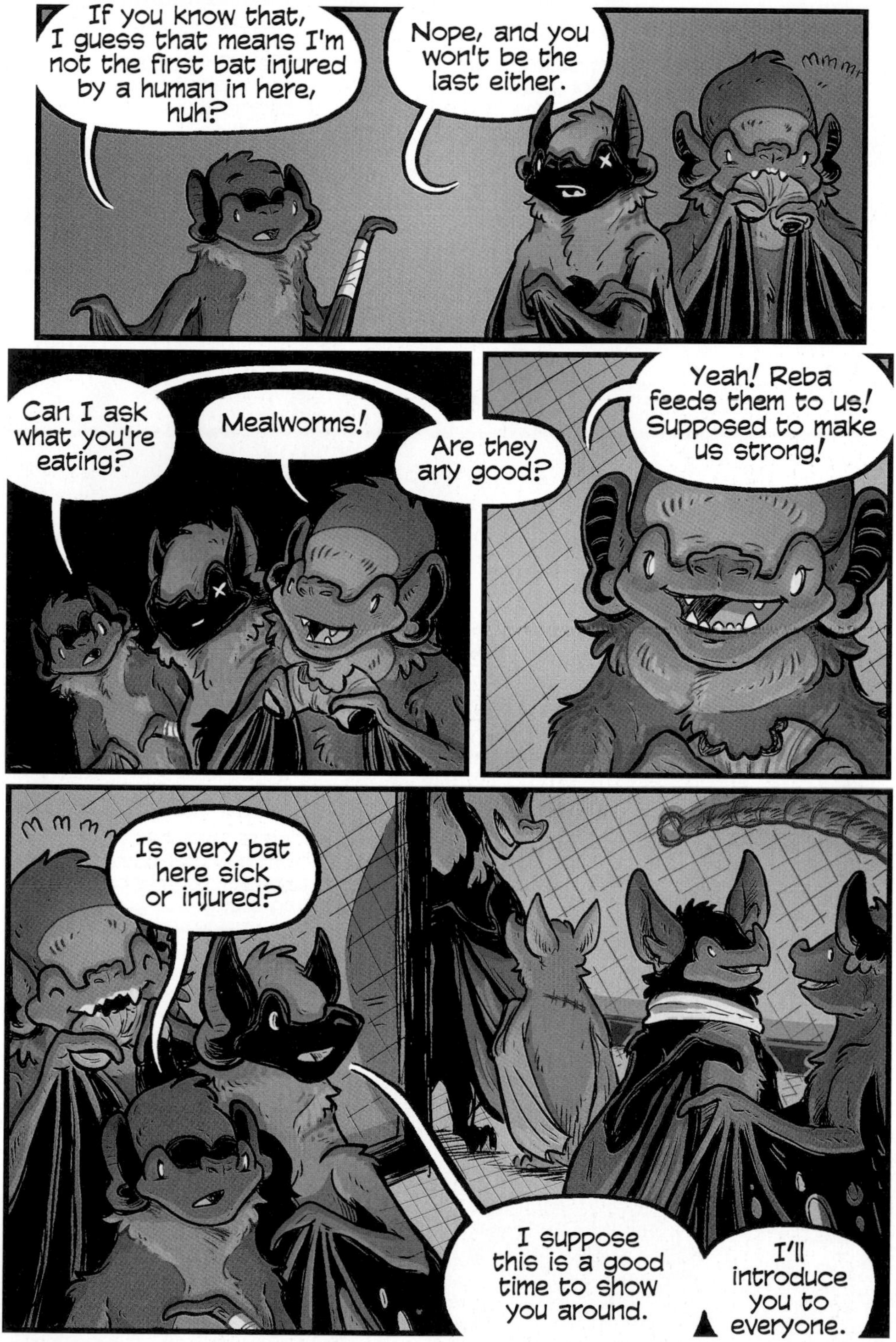
If you know that, I guess that means I'm not the first bat injured by a human in here, huh?
Nope, and you won't be the last either.
mmmm
Can I ask what you're eating?
Mealworms!
Are they any good?
Yeah! Reba feeds them to us! Supposed to make us strong!
mmmm
Is every bat here sick or injured?
I suppose this is a good time to show you around.
I'll introduce you to everyone.

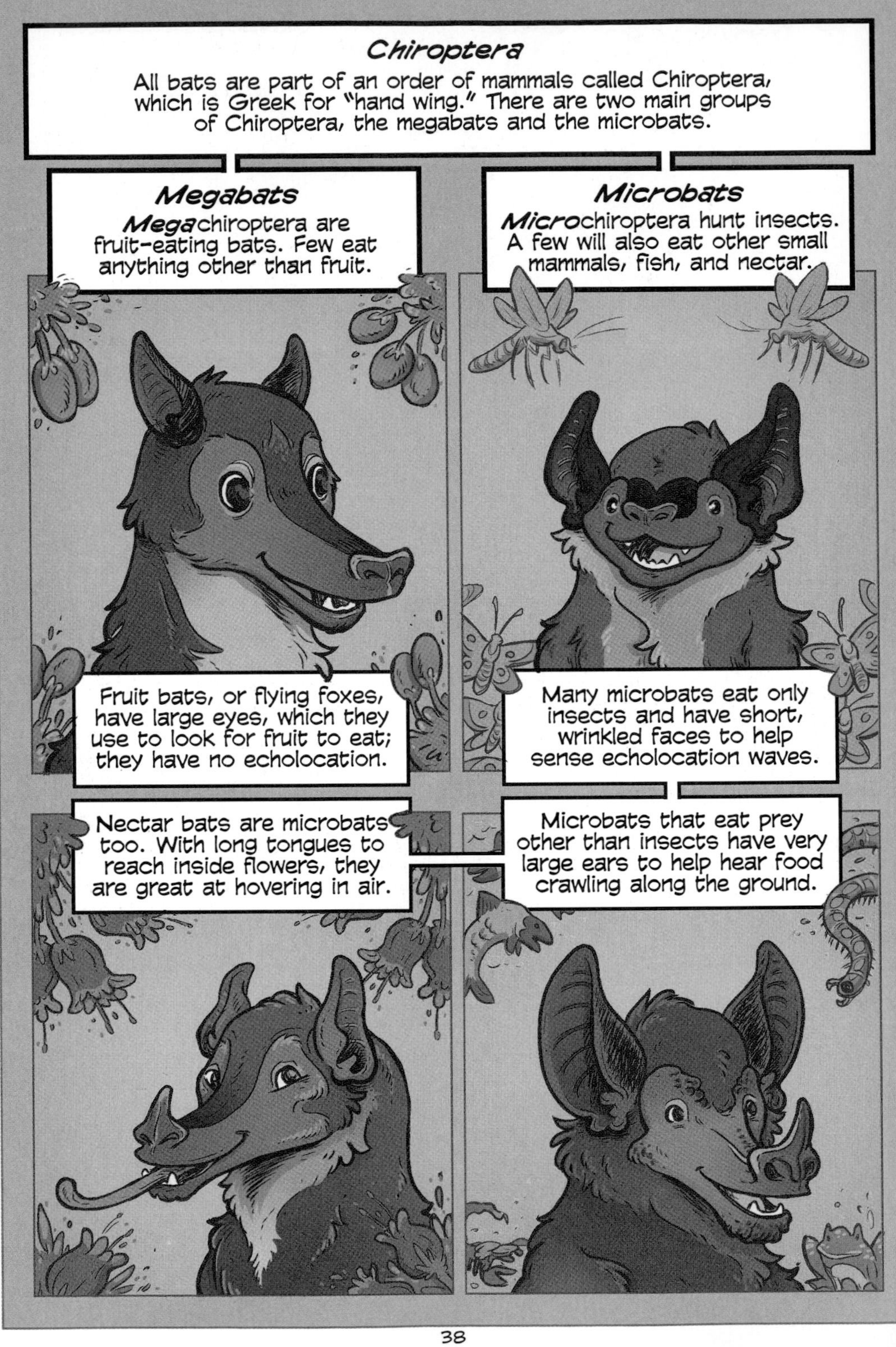
Chiroptera
All bats are part of an order of mammals called Chiroptera, which is Greek for "hand wing." There are two main groups of Chiroptera, the megabats and the microbats.
Megabats
Megachiroptera are fruit-eating bats. Few eat anything other than fruit.
Microbats
Microchiroptera hunt insects. A few will also eat other small mammals, fish, and nectar.
Fruit bats, or flying foxes, have large eyes, which they use to look for fruit to eat; they have no echolocation.
Many microbats eat only insects and have short, wrinkled faces to help sense echolocation waves.
Nectar bats are microbats too. With long tongues to reach inside flowers, they are great at hovering in air.
Microbats that eat prey other than insects have very large ears to help hear food crawling along the ground.

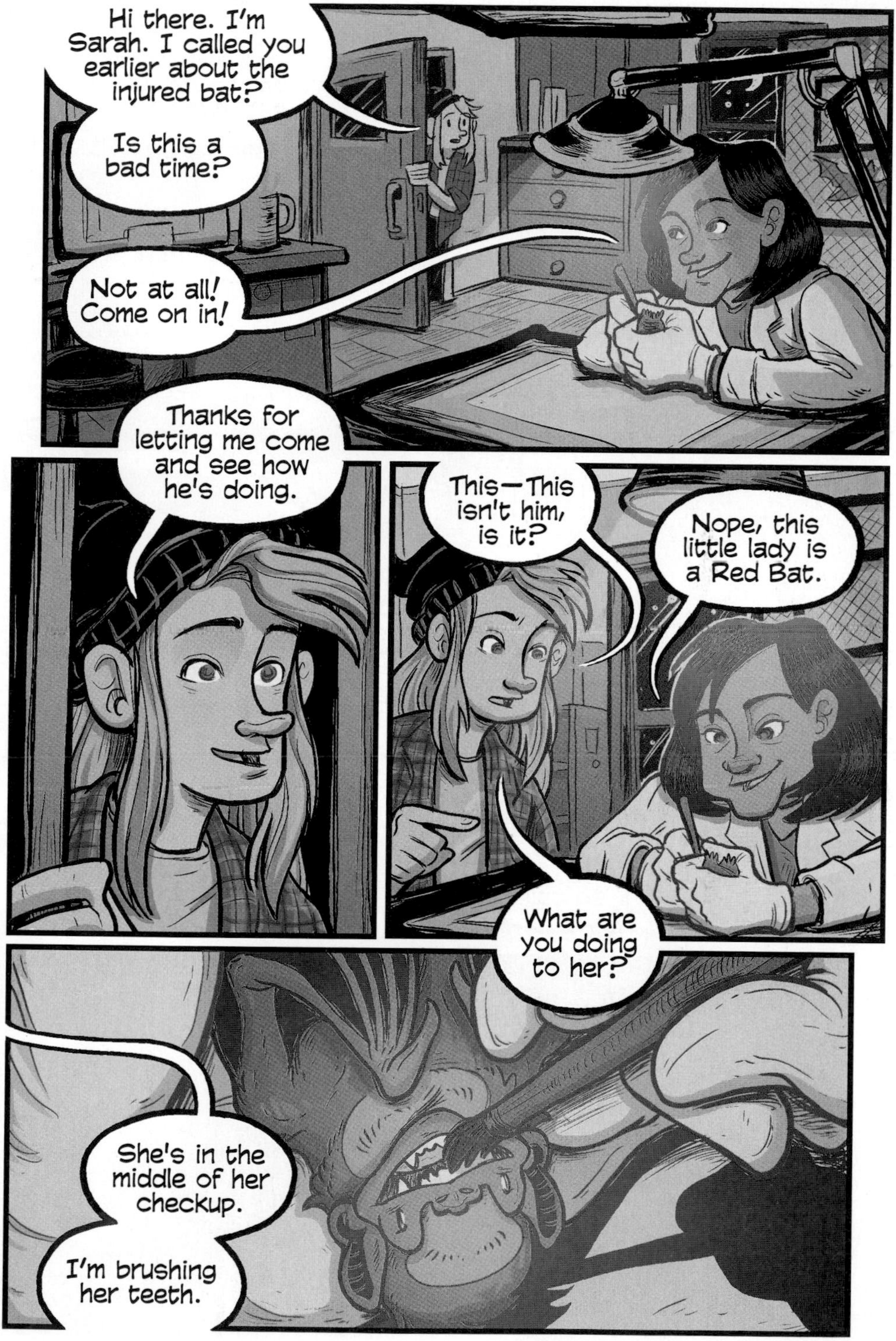
Hi there. I'm Sarah. I called you earlier about the injured bat?
Is this a bad time?
Not at all! Come on in!
Thanks for letting me come and see how he's doing.
This—This isn't him, is it?
Nope, this little lady is a Red Bat.
What are you doing to her?
She's in the middle of her checkup.
I'm brushing her teeth.

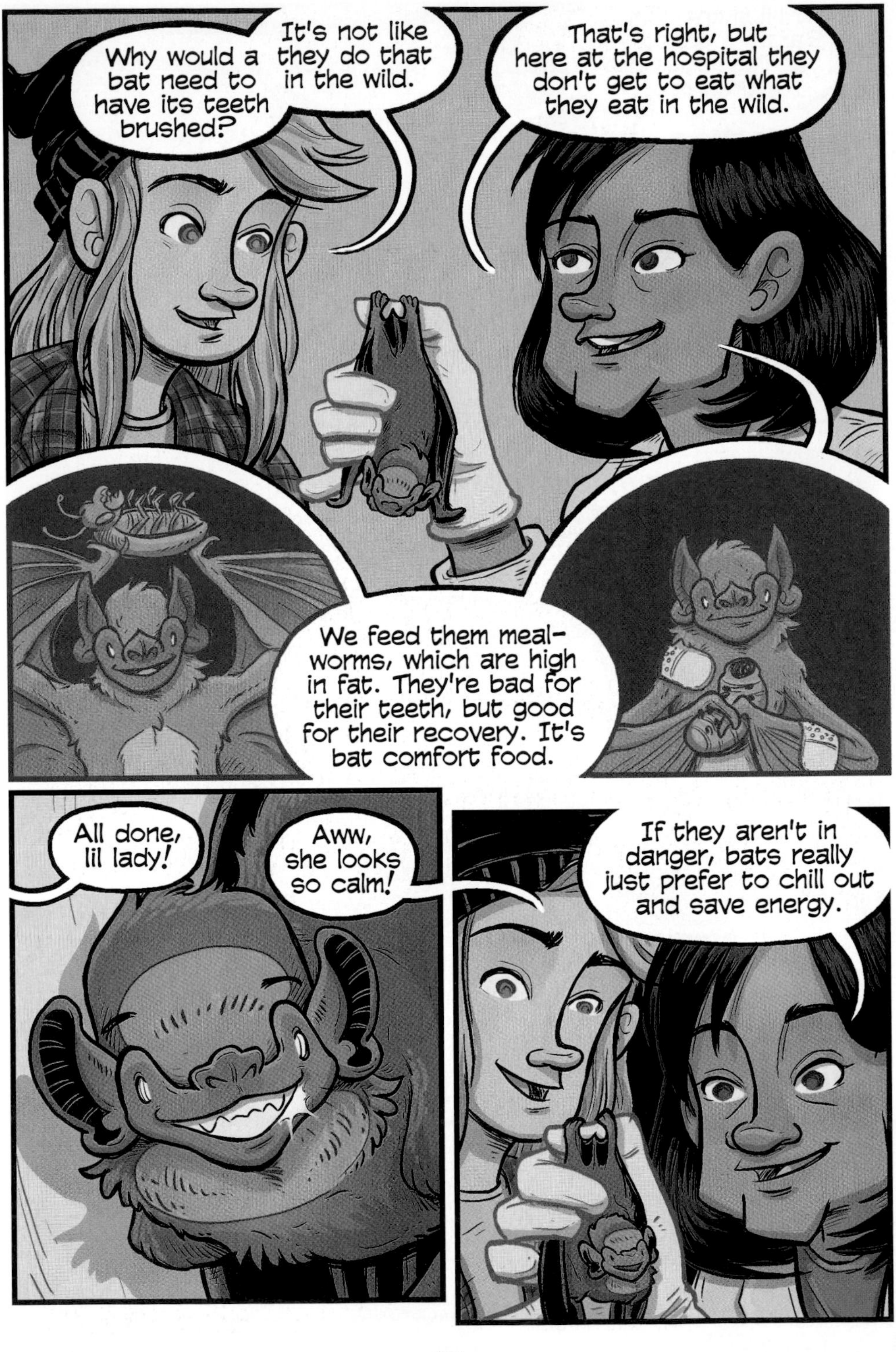
Why would a bat need to have its teeth brushed?
It's not like they do that in the wild.
That's right, but here at the hospital they don't get to eat what they eat in the wild.
We feed them meal-worms, which are high in fat. They're bad for their teeth, but good for their recovery. It's bat comfort food.
All done, lil lady!
Aww, she looks so calm!
If they aren't in danger, bats really just prefer to chill out and save energy.

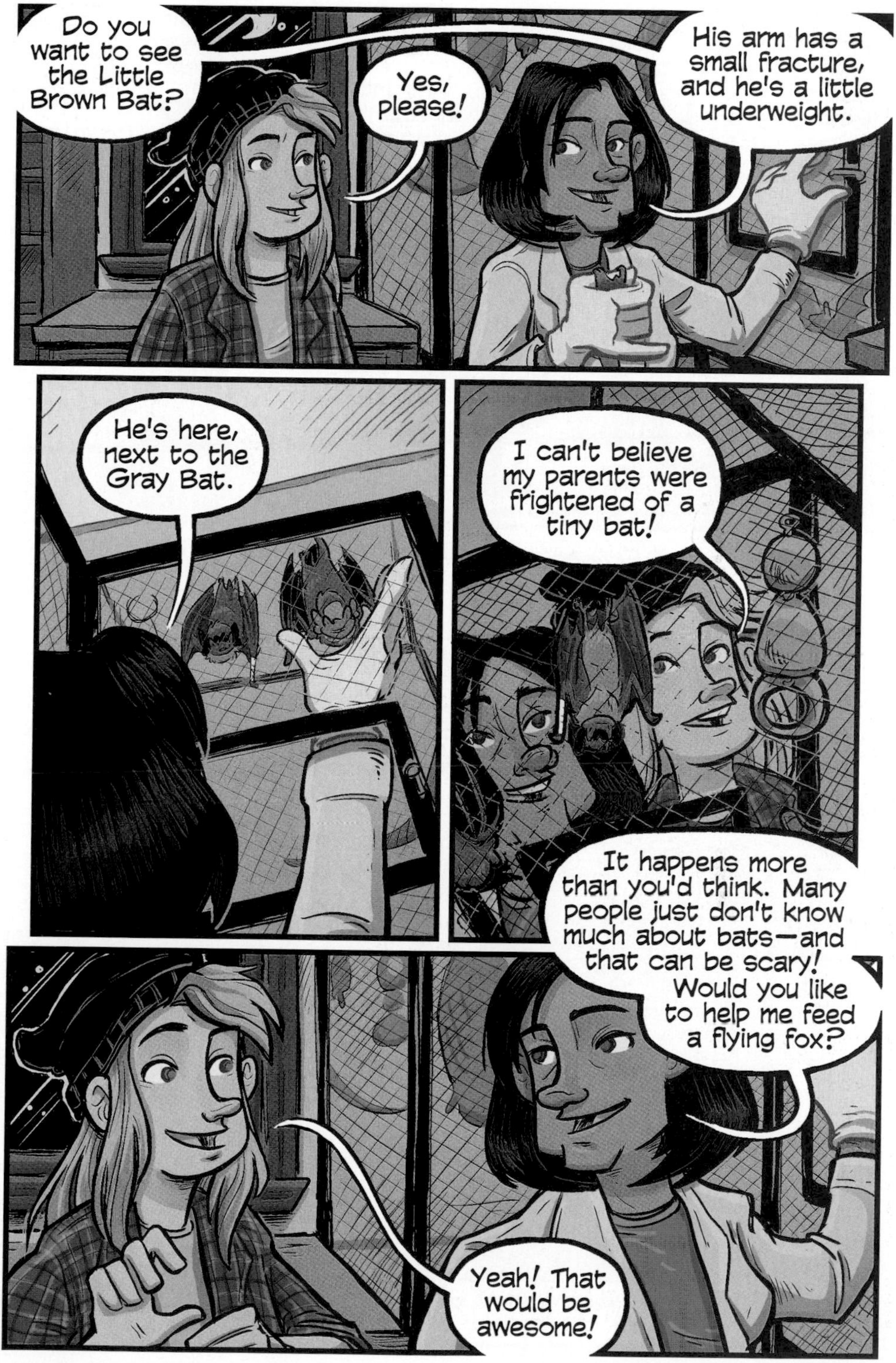
Do you want to see the Little Brown Bat?
Yes, please!
His arm has a small fracture, and he's a little underweight.
He's here, next to the Gray Bat.
I can't believe my parents were frightened of a tiny bat!
It happens more than you'd think. Many people just don't know much about bats—and that can be scary!
Would you like to help me feed a flying fox?
Yeah! That would be awesome!

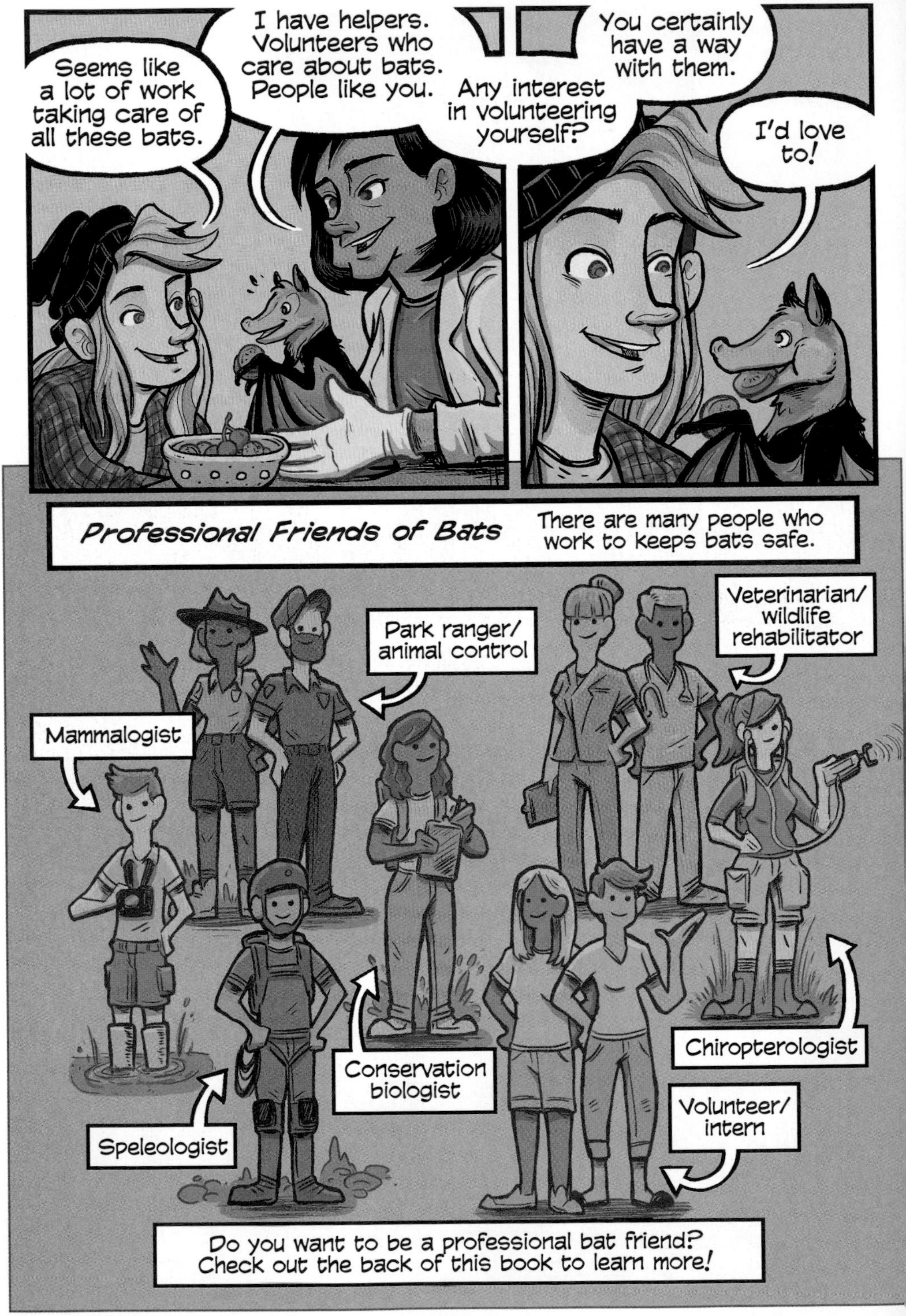

Seems like a lot of work taking care of all these bats.
I have helpers. Volunteers who care about bats. People like you.
You certainly have a way with them.
Any interest in volunteering yourself?
I'd love to!
Professional Friends of Bats
There are many people who work to keeps bats safe.
Park ranger/ animal control
Veterinarian/ wildlife rehabilitator
Mammalogist
Chiropterologist
Conservation biologist
Volunteer/ intern
Speleologist
Do you want to be a professional bat friend? Check out the back of this book to learn more!

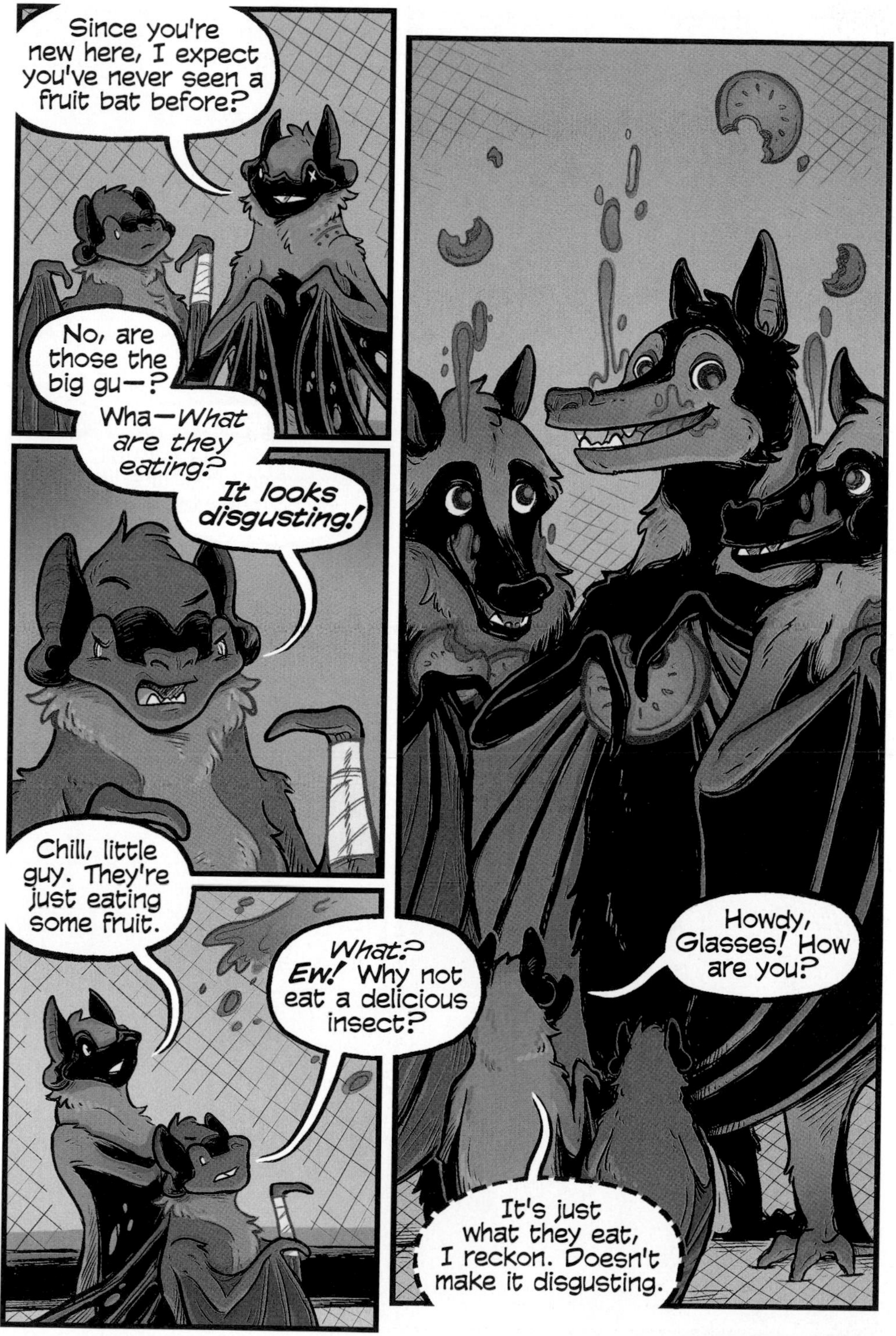

Since you're new here, I expect you've never seen a fruit bat before?
No, are those the big gu—?
Wha—*What* are they eating?
It looks disgusting!
Chill, little guy. They're just eating some fruit.
What? ***Ew!*** Why not eat a delicious insect?
Howdy, Glasses! How are you?
It's just what they eat, I reckon. Doesn't make it disgusting.

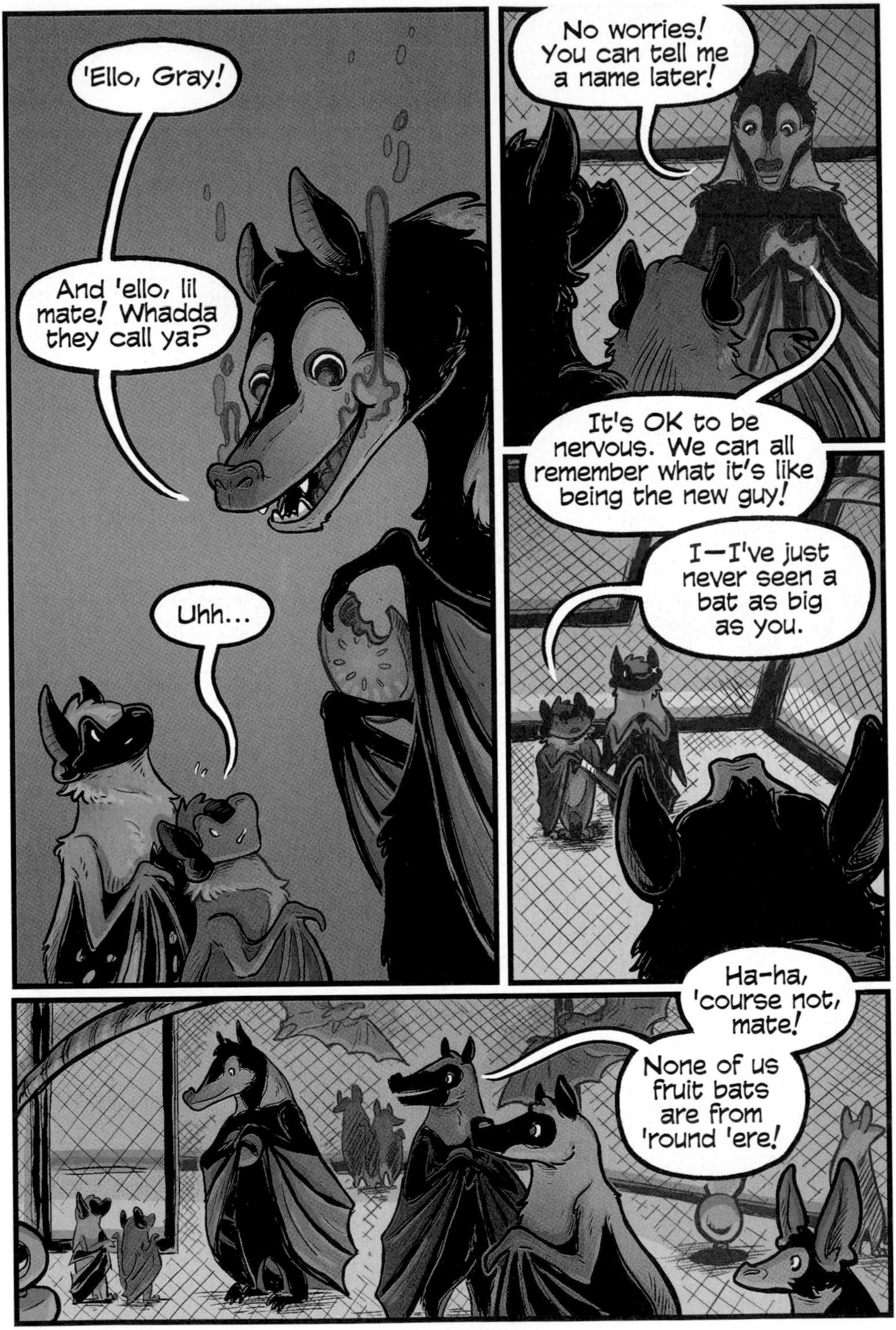
'Ello, Gray!
And 'ello, lil mate! Whadda they call ya?
Uhh...
No worries! You can tell me a name later!
It's OK to be nervous. We can all remember what it's like being the new guy!
I—I've just never seen a bat as big as you.
Ha-ha, 'course not, mate!
None of us fruit bats are from 'round 'ere!

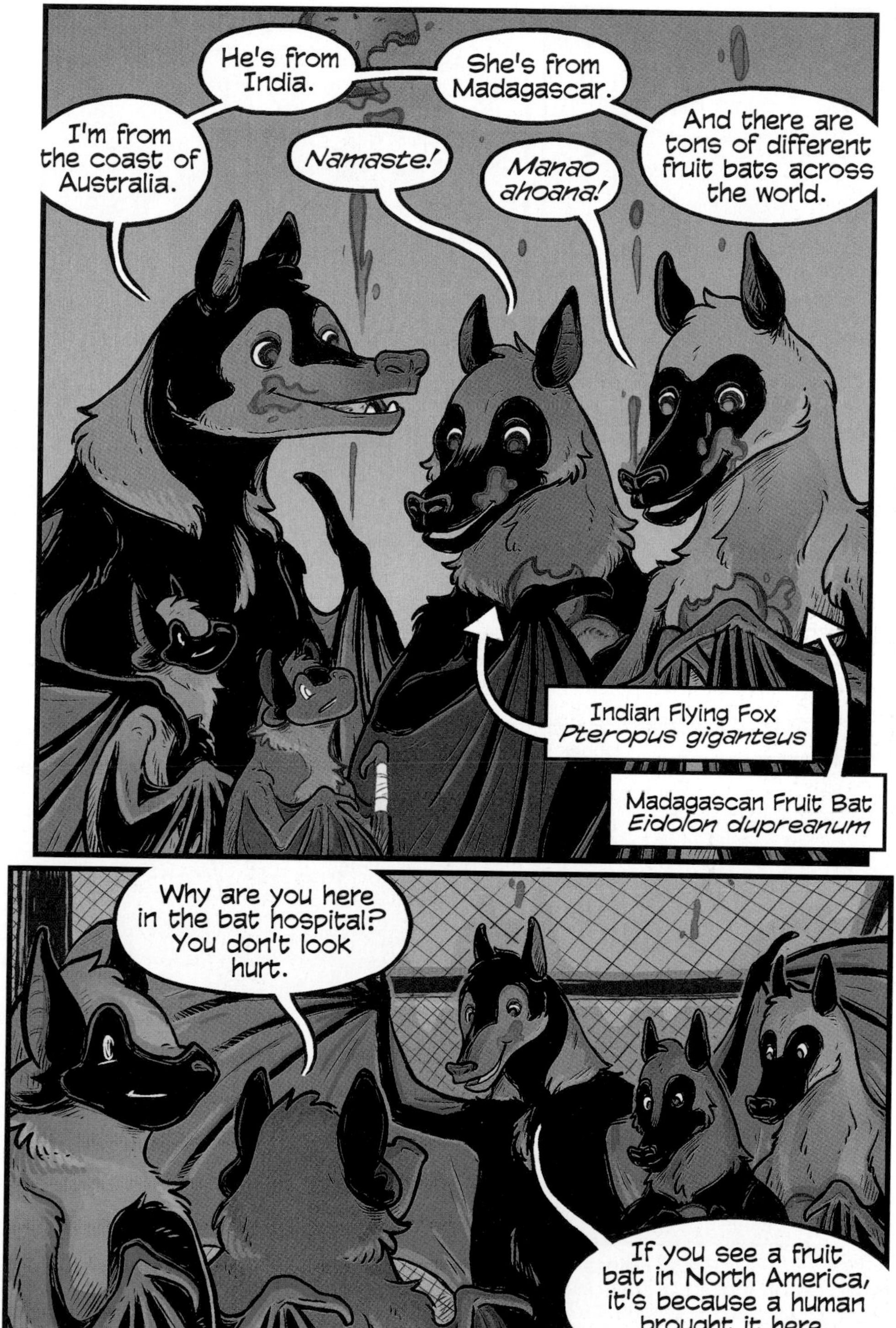
He's from India.
She's from Madagascar.
I'm from the coast of Australia.
Namaste!
Manao ahoana!
And there are tons of different fruit bats across the world.
Indian Flying Fox *Pteropus giganteus*
Madagascan Fruit Bat *Eidolon dupreanum*
Why are you here in the bat hospital? You don't look hurt.
If you see a fruit bat in North America, it's because a human brought it here.

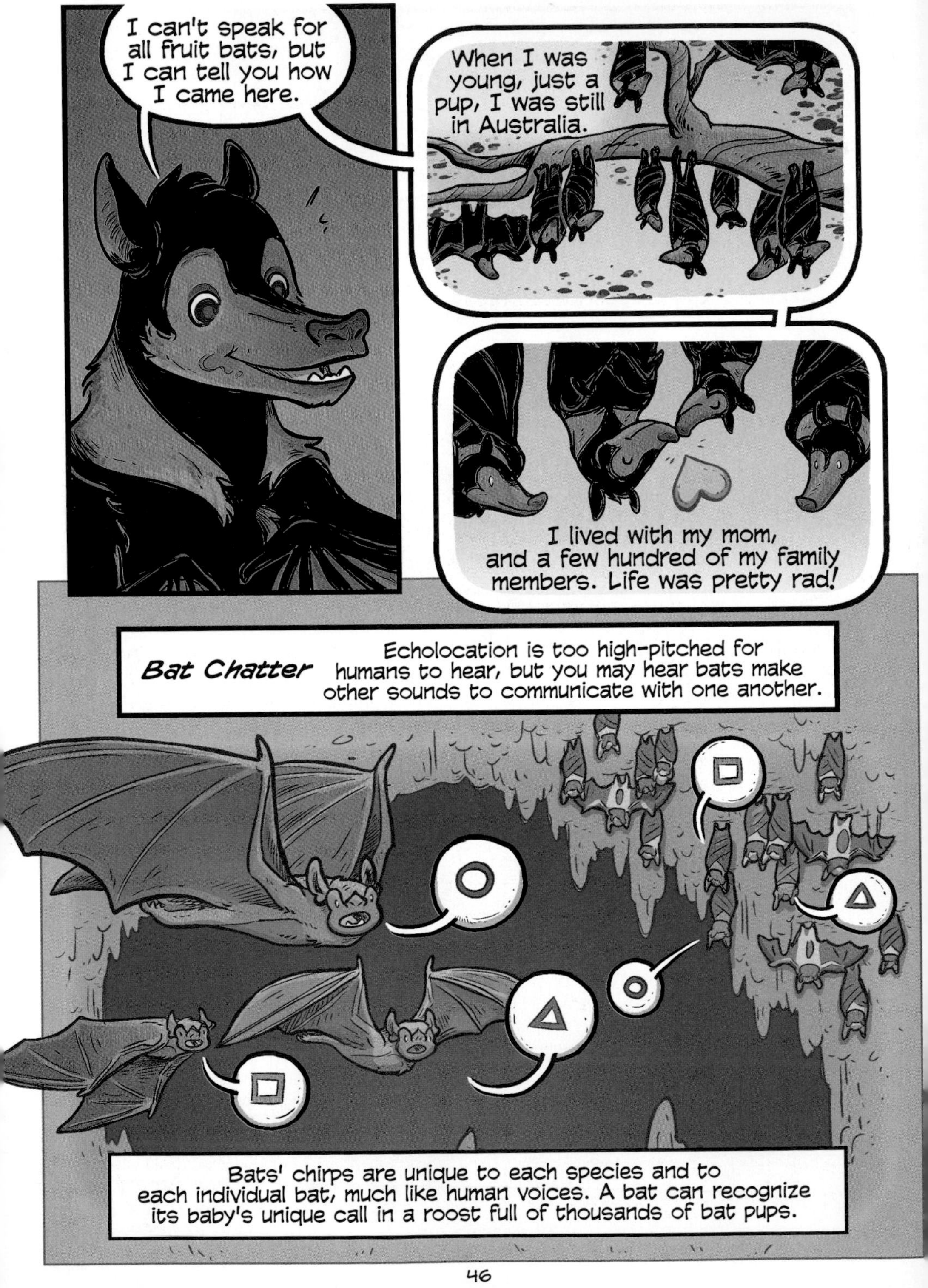
I can't speak for all fruit bats, but I can tell you how I came here.
When I was young, just a pup, I was still in Australia.
I lived with my mom, and a few hundred of my family members. Life was pretty rad!
Bat Chatter
Echolocation is too high-pitched for humans to hear, but you may hear bats make other sounds to communicate with one another.
Bats' chirps are unique to each species and to each individual bat, much like human voices. A bat can recognize its baby's unique call in a roost full of thousands of bat pups.

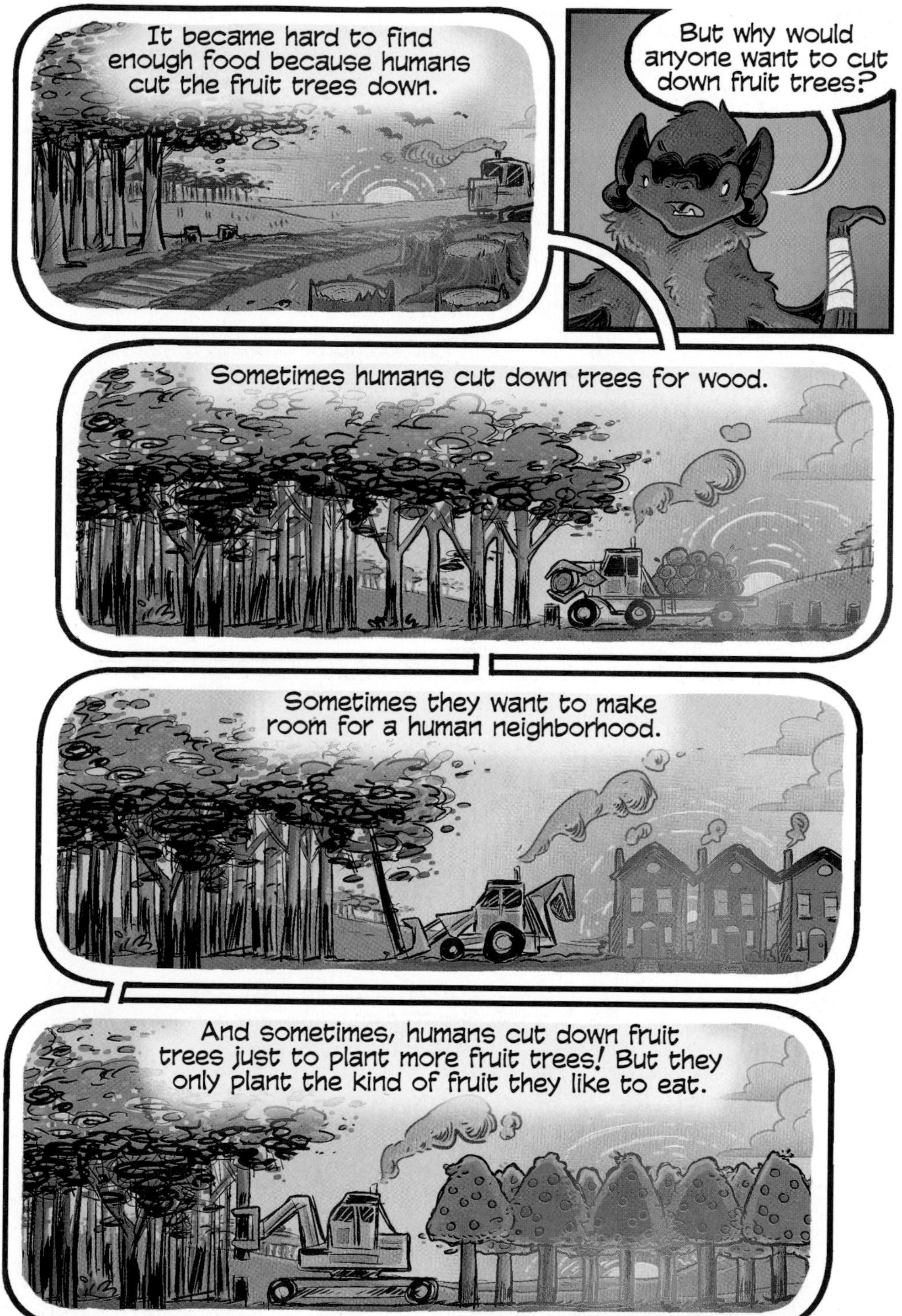
It became hard to find enough food because humans cut the fruit trees down.
But why would anyone want to cut down fruit trees?
Sometimes humans cut down trees for wood.
Sometimes they want to make room for a human neighborhood.
And sometimes, humans cut down fruit trees just to plant more fruit trees! But they only plant the kind of fruit they like to eat.

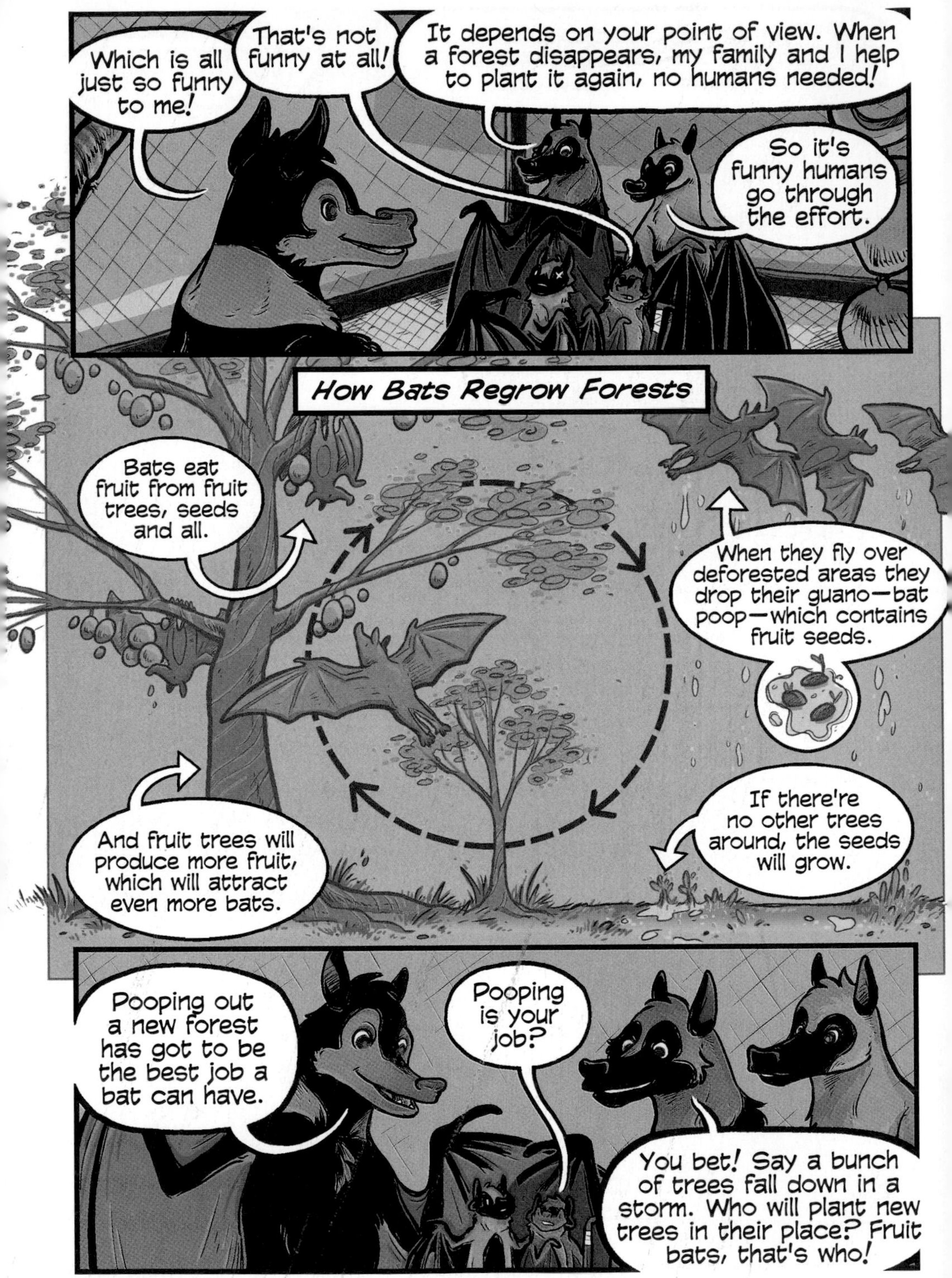
Which is all just so funny to me!
That's not funny at all!
It depends on your point of view. When a forest disappears, my family and I help to plant it again, no humans needed!
So it's funny humans go through the effort.
How Bats Regrow Forests
Bats eat fruit from fruit trees, seeds and all.
When they fly over deforested areas they drop their guano—bat poop—which contains fruit seeds.
If there're no other trees around, the seeds will grow.
And fruit trees will produce more fruit, which will attract even more bats.
Pooping out a new forest has got to be the best job a bat can have.
Pooping is your job?
You bet! Say a bunch of trees fall down in a storm. Who will plant new trees in their place? Fruit bats, that's who!

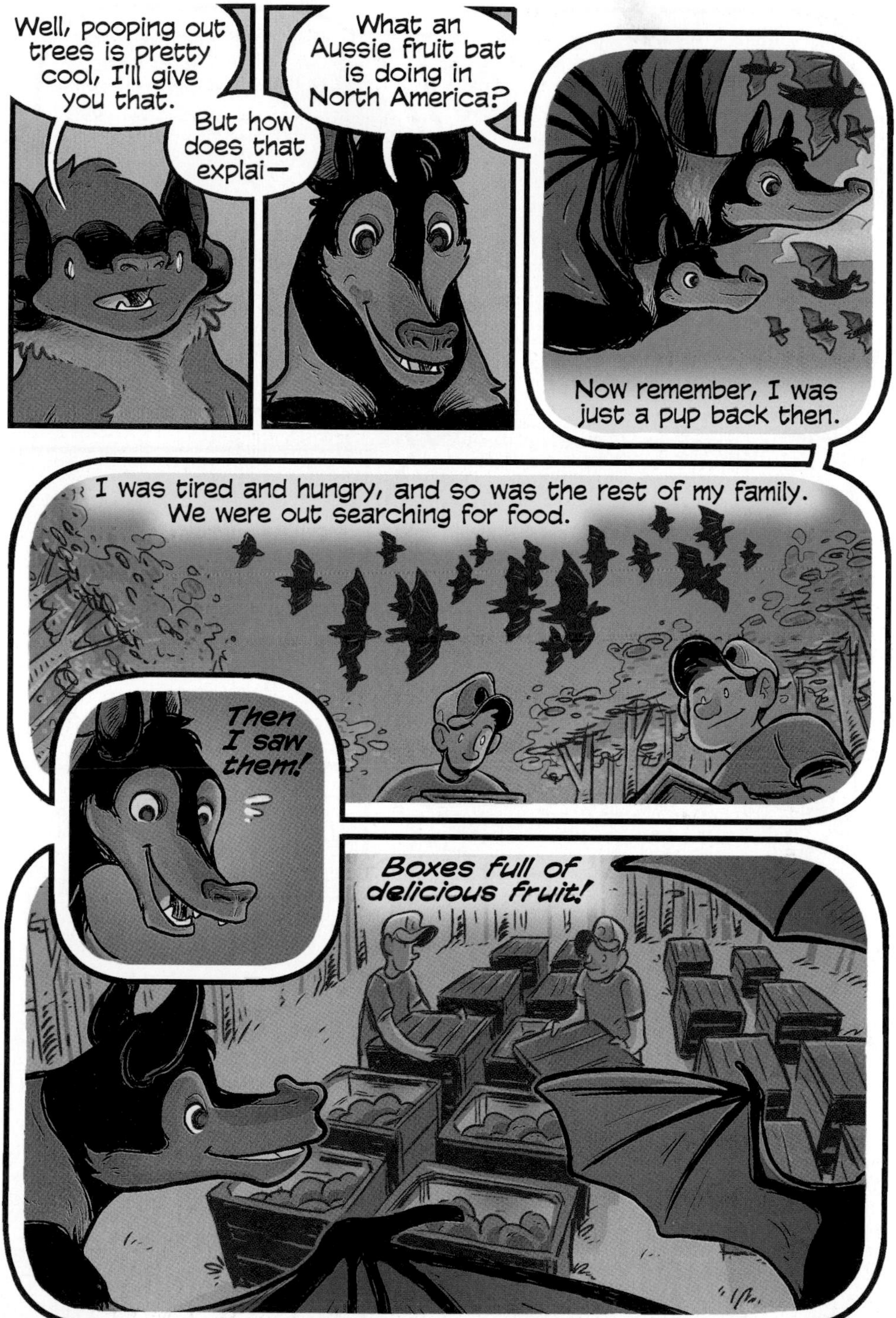

Well, pooping out trees is pretty cool, I'll give you that.
But how does that explai—
What an Aussie fruit bat is doing in North America?
Now remember, I was just a pup back then.
I was tired and hungry, and so was the rest of my family. We were out searching for food.
Then I saw them!
Boxes full of delicious fruit!

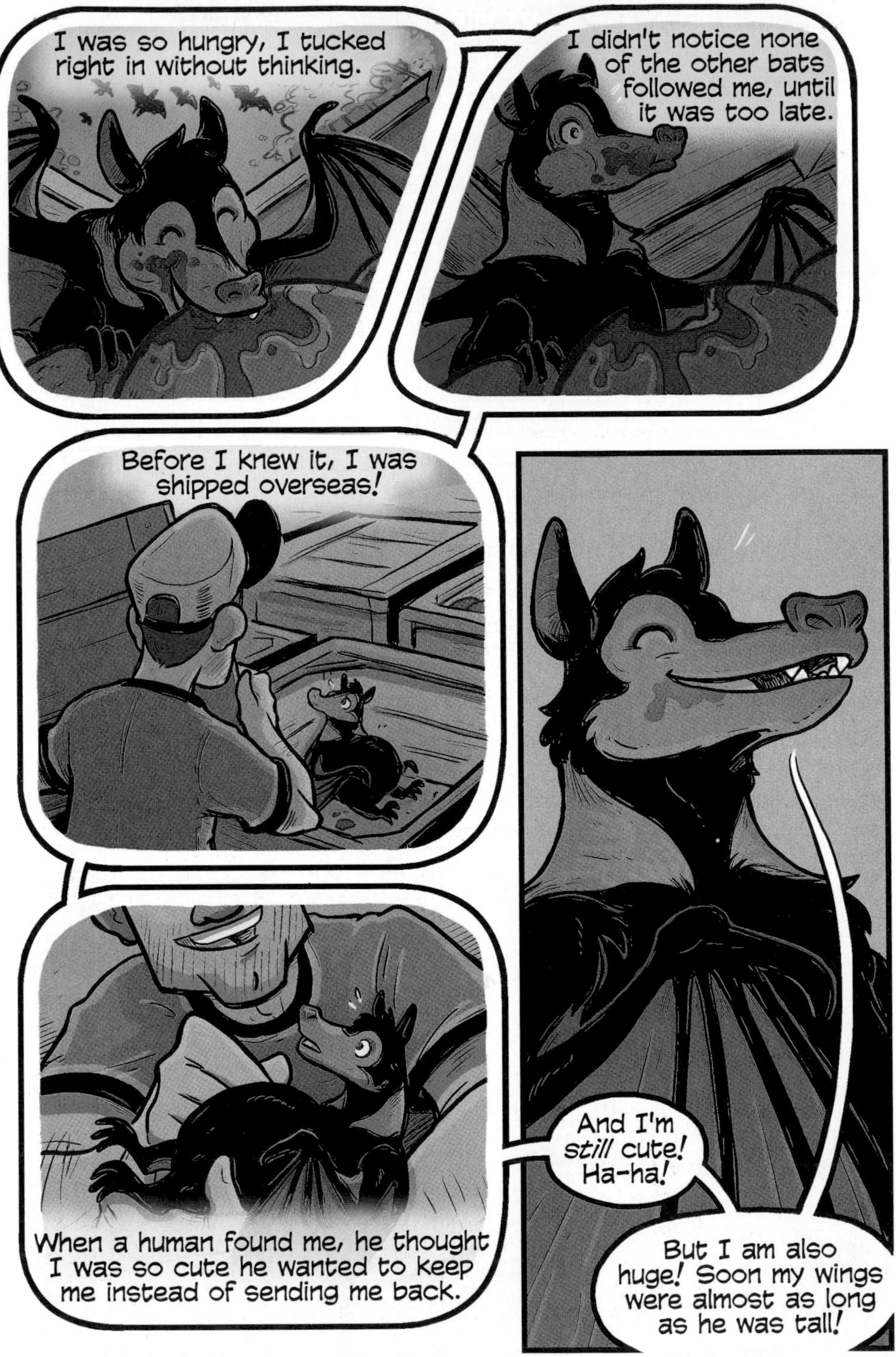

I was so hungry, I tucked right in without thinking.
I didn't notice none of the other bats followed me, until it was too late.
Before I knew it, I was shipped overseas!
When a human found me, he thought I was so cute he wanted to keep me instead of sending me back.
And I'm *still* cute! Ha-ha!
But I am also huge! Soon my wings were almost as long as he was tall!

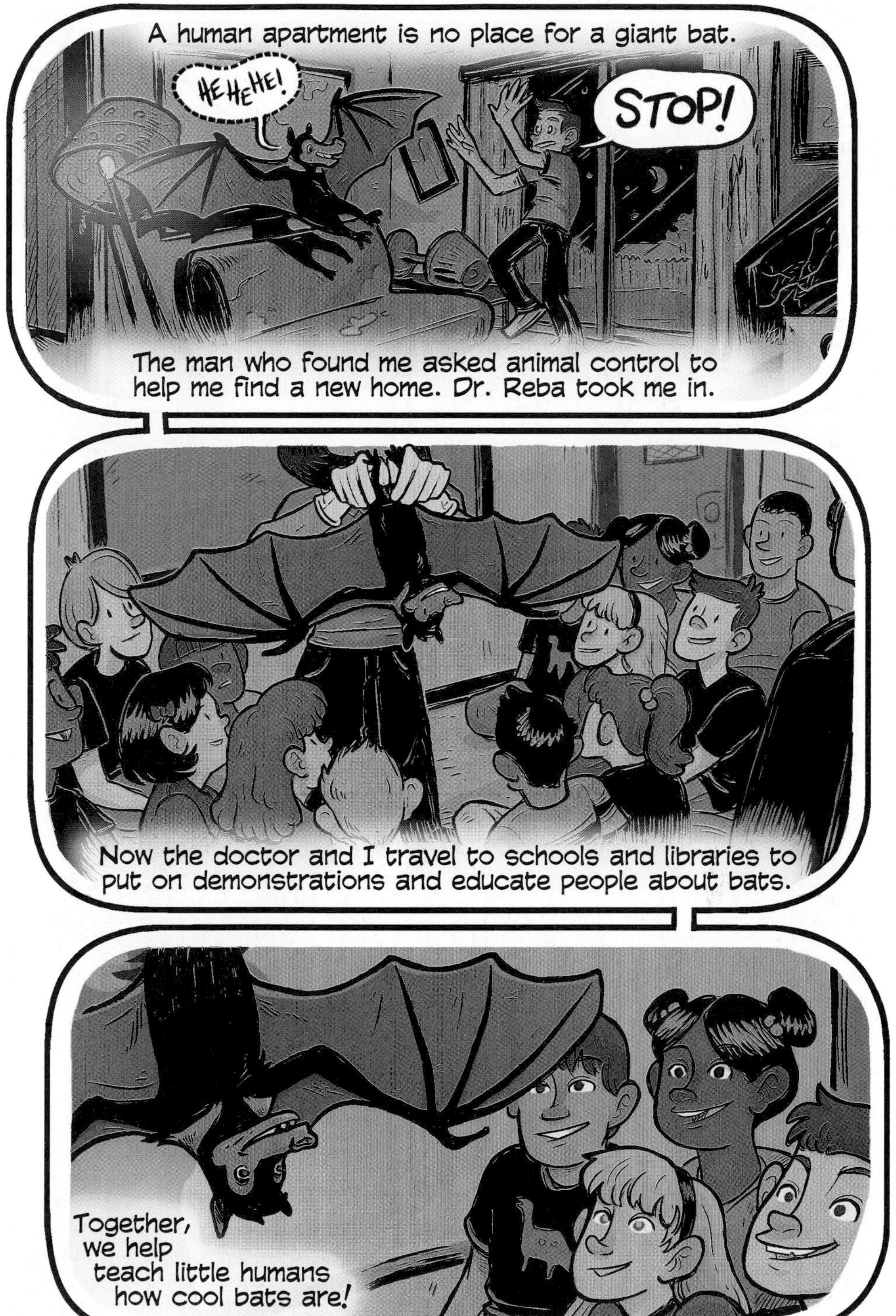
A human apartment is no place for a giant bat.
HE HE HE!
STOP!
The man who found me asked animal control to help me find a new home. Dr. Reba took me in.
Now the doctor and I travel to schools and libraries to put on demonstrations and educate people about bats.
Together, we help teach little humans how cool bats are!

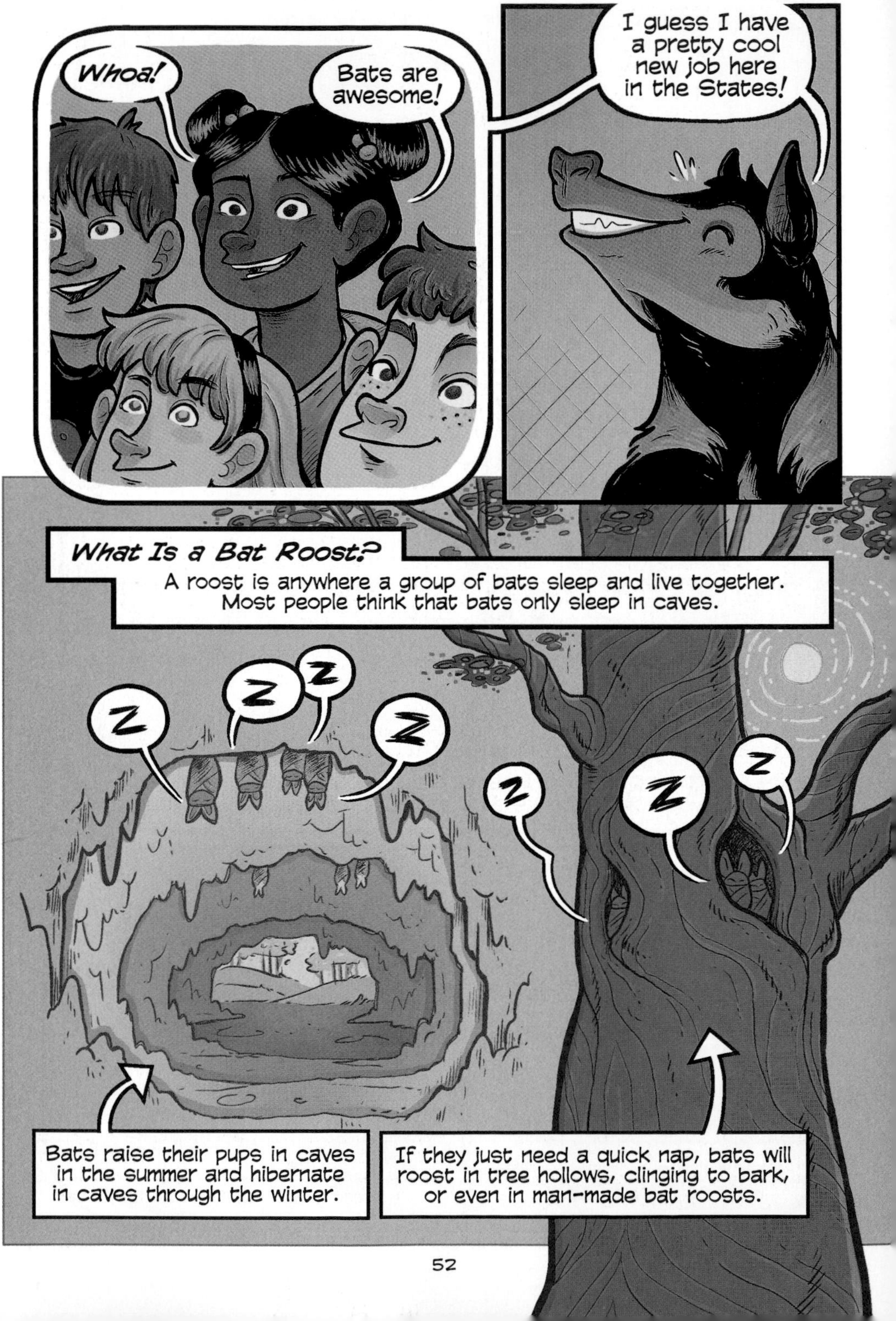
Whoa!
Bats are awesome!
I guess I have a pretty cool new job here in the States!
What Is a Bat Roost?
A roost is anywhere a group of bats sleep and live together. Most people think that bats only sleep in caves.
Z
Z
Z
Z
Z
Z
Z
Bats raise their pups in caves in the summer and hibernate in caves through the winter.
If they just need a quick nap, bats will roost in tree hollows, clinging to bark, or even in man-made bat roosts.

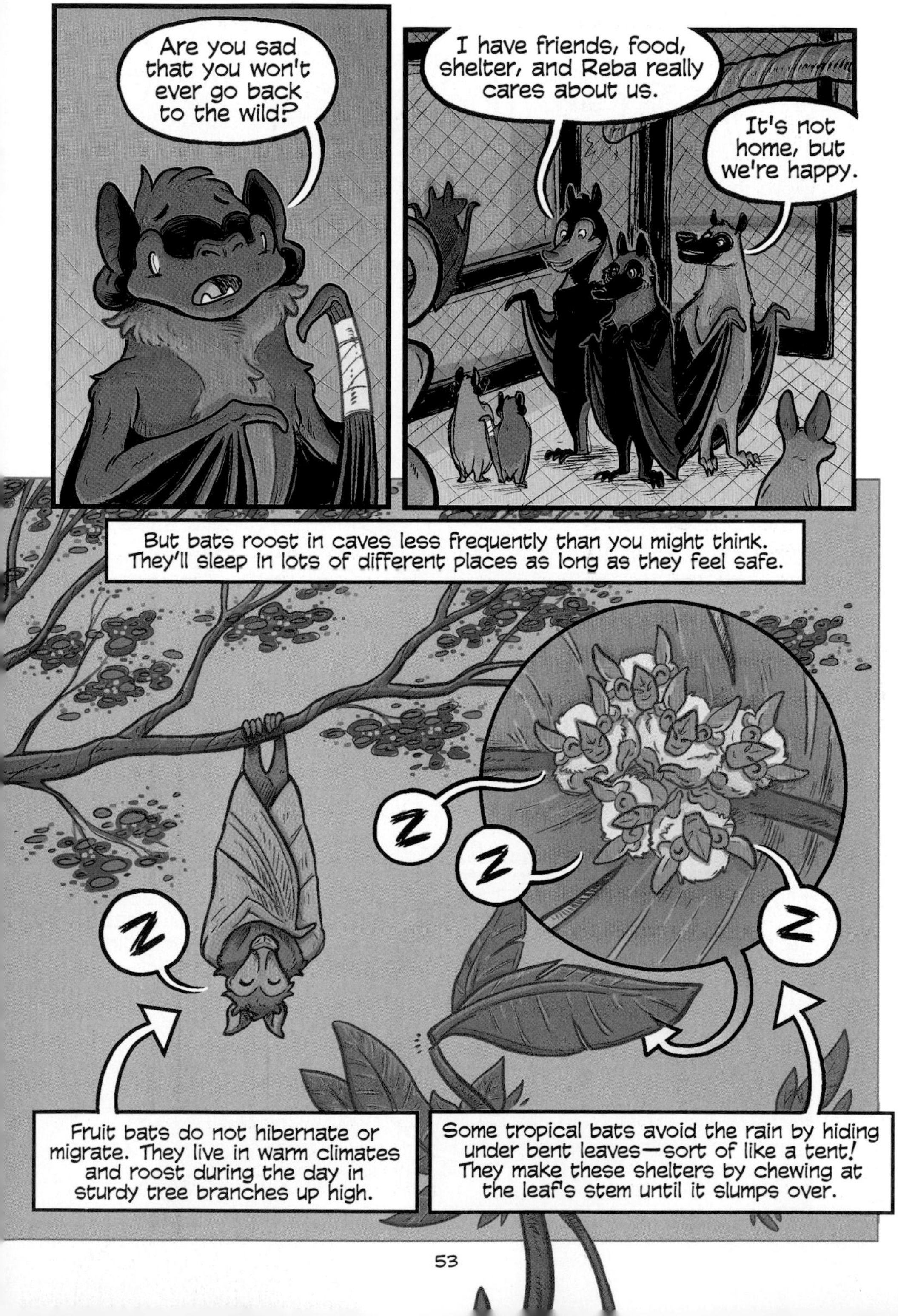
Are you sad that you won't ever go back to the wild?
I have friends, food, shelter, and Reba really cares about us.
It's not home, but we're happy.
But bats roost in caves less frequently than you might think. They'll sleep in lots of different places as long as they feel safe.
Z
Z
Z
Z
Fruit bats do not hibernate or migrate. They live in warm climates and roost during the day in sturdy tree branches up high.
Some tropical bats avoid the rain by hiding under bent leaves—sort of like a tent! They make these shelters by chewing at the leaf's stem until it slumps over.

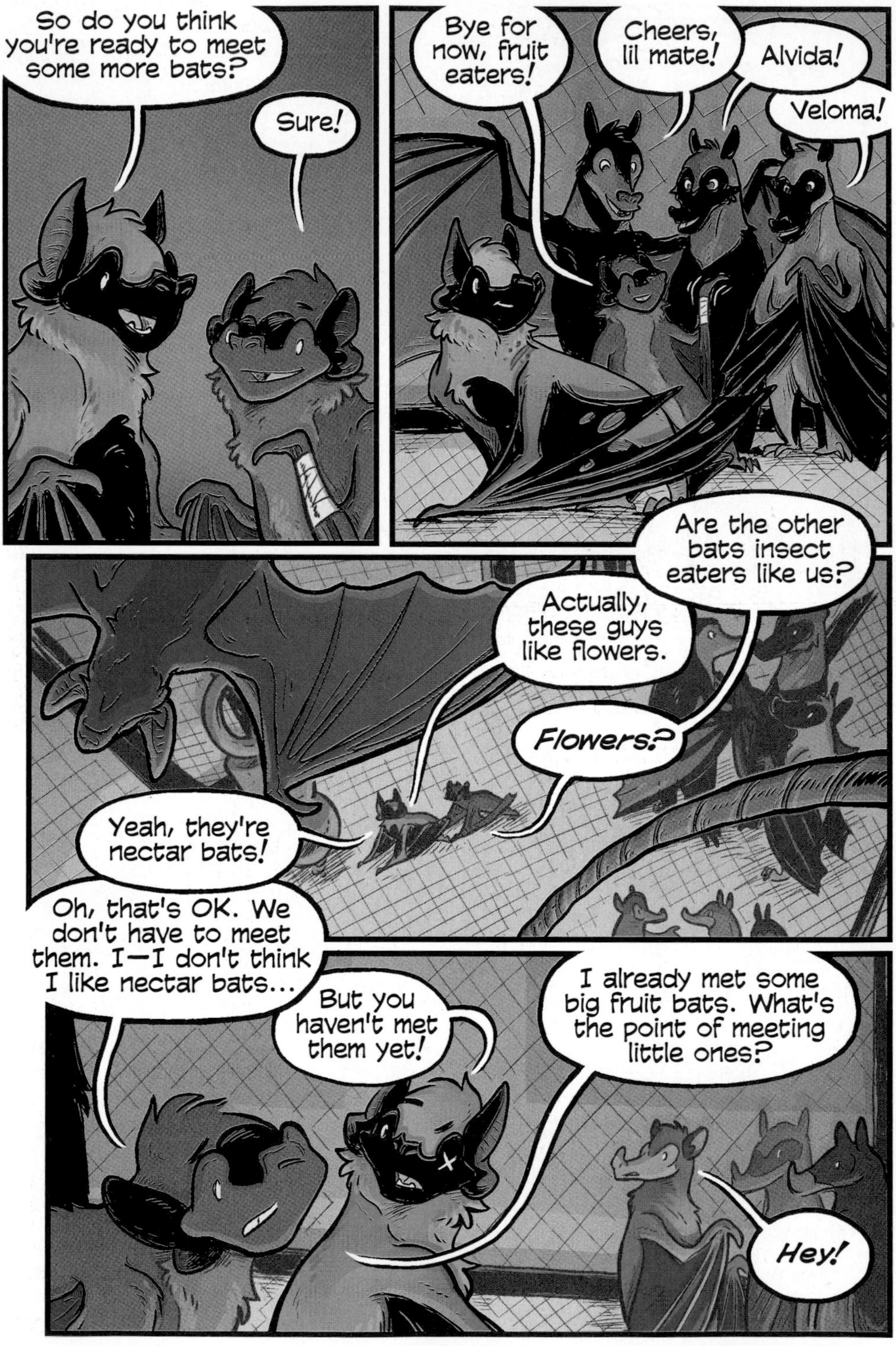
So do you think you're ready to meet some more bats?
Sure!
Bye for now, fruit eaters!
Cheers, lil mate!
Alvida!
Veloma!
Are the other bats insect eaters like us?
Actually, these guys like flowers.
Flowers?
Yeah, they're nectar bats!
Oh, that's OK. We don't have to meet them. I—I don't think I like nectar bats...
But you haven't met them yet!
I already met some big fruit bats. What's the point of meeting little ones?
Hey!

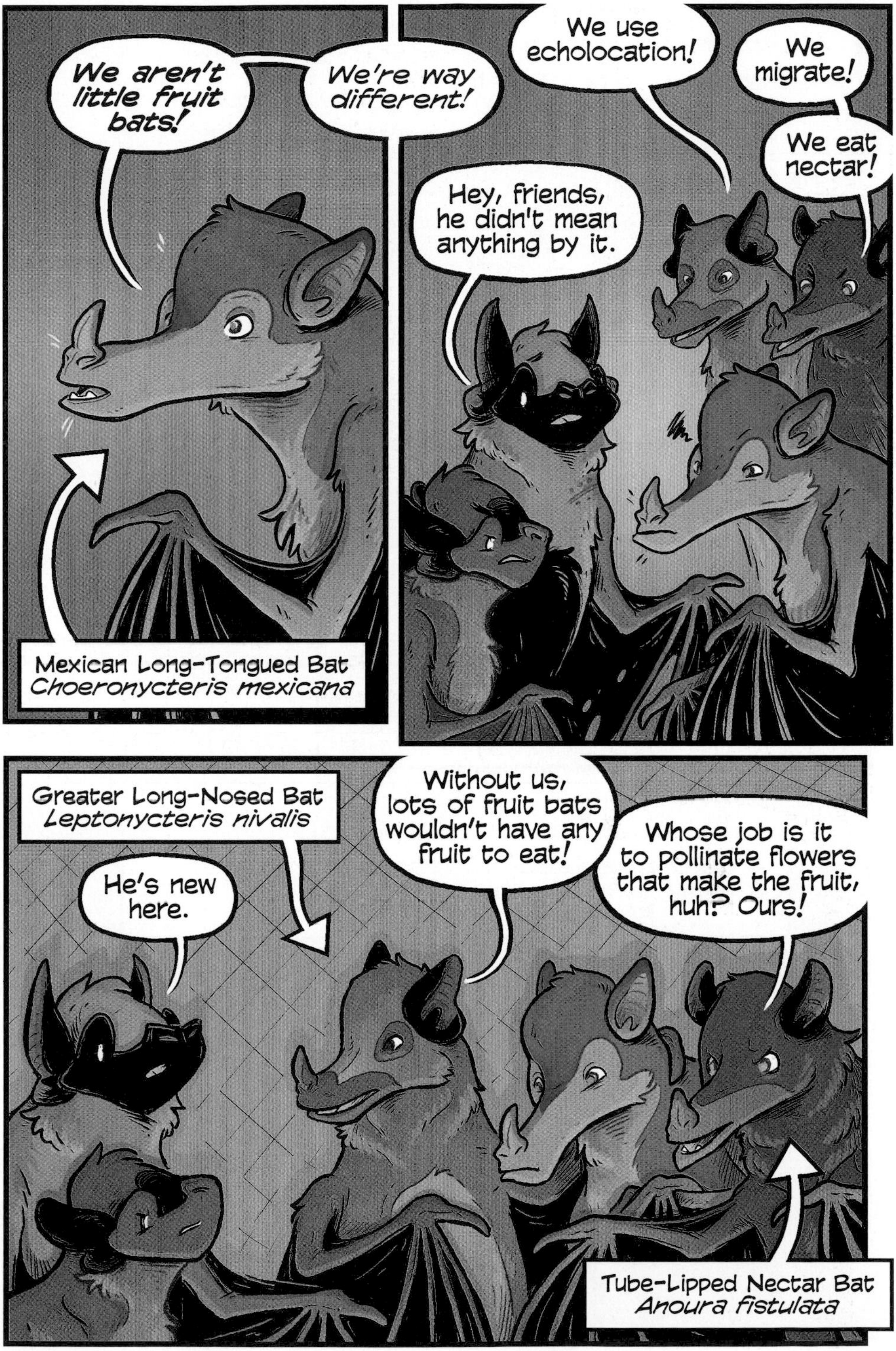
We aren't little fruit bats!
We're way different!
Mexican Long-Tongued Bat
Choeronycteris mexicana
We use echolocation!
We migrate!
We eat nectar!
Hey, friends, he didn't mean anything by it.
Greater Long-Nosed Bat
Leptonycteris nivalis
He's new here.
Without us, lots of fruit bats wouldn't have any fruit to eat!
Whose job is it to pollinate flowers that make the fruit, huh? Ours!
Tube-Lipped Nectar Bat
Anoura fistulata

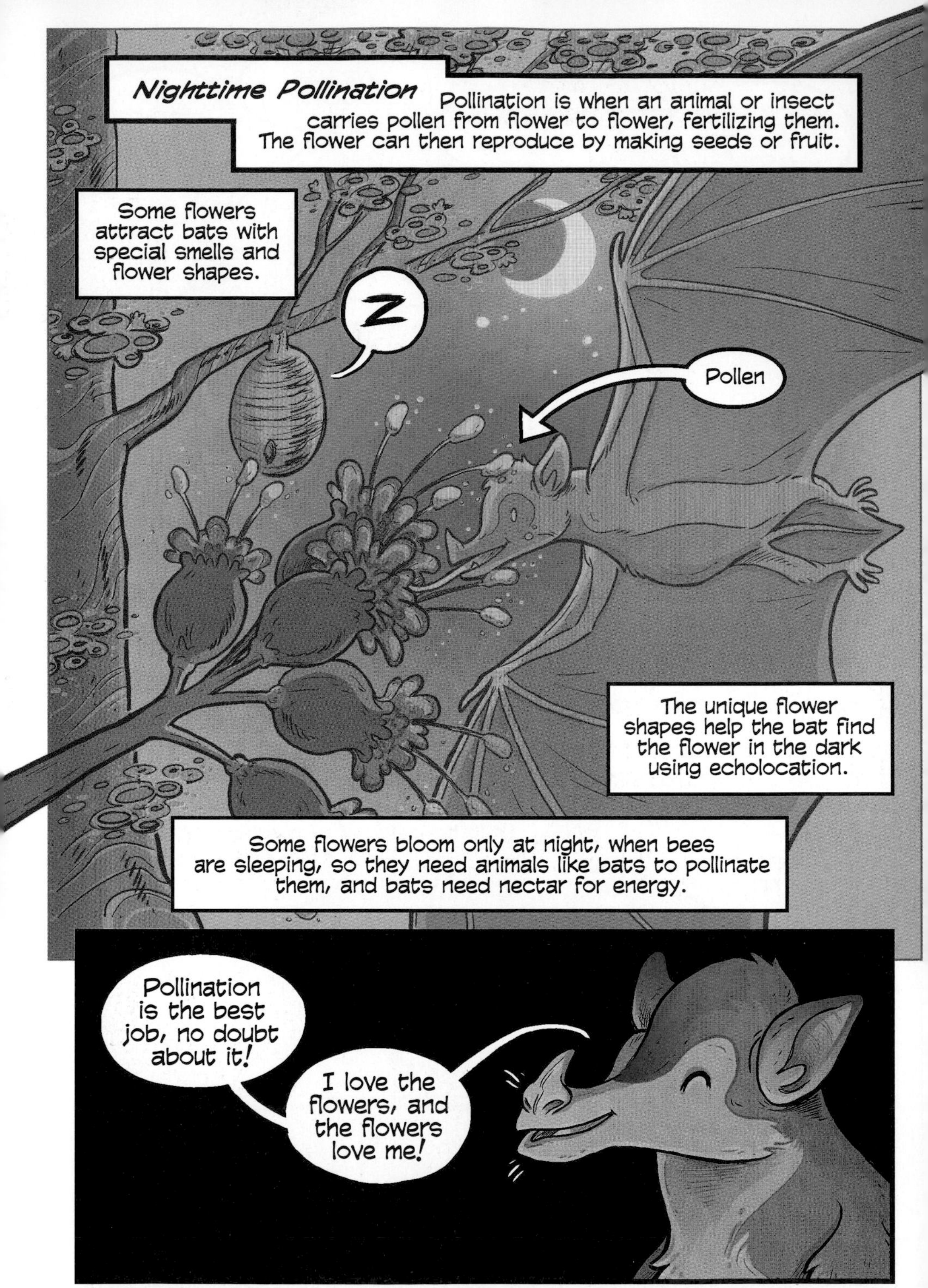
Nighttime Pollination
Pollination is when an animal or insect carries pollen from flower to flower, fertilizing them. The flower can then reproduce by making seeds or fruit.
Some flowers attract bats with special smells and flower shapes.
Z
Pollen
The unique flower shapes help the bat find the flower in the dark using echolocation.
Some flowers bloom only at night, when bees are sleeping, so they need animals like bats to pollinate them, and bats need nectar for energy.
Pollination is the best job, no doubt about it!
I love the flowers, and the flowers love me!

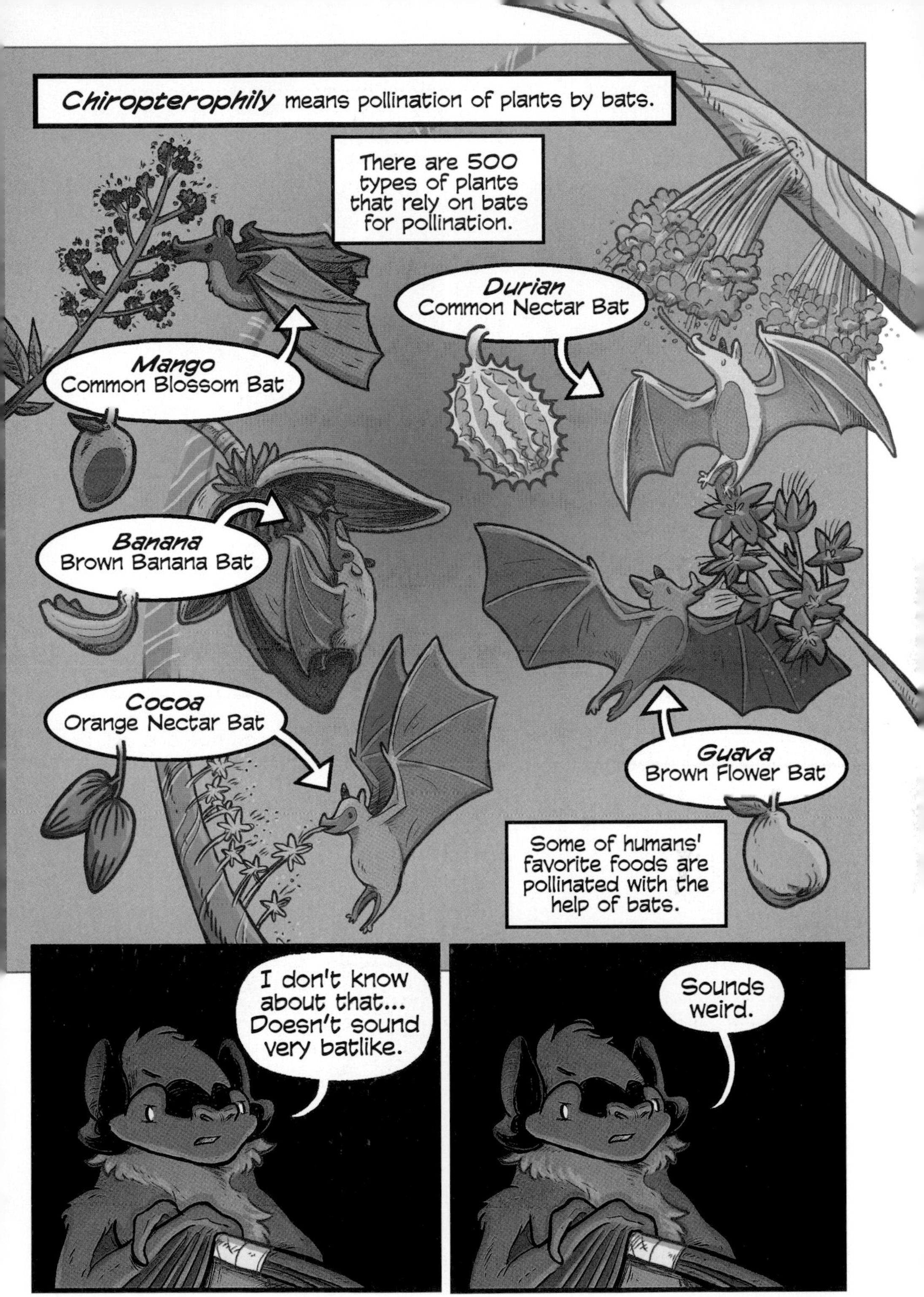
Chiropterophily means pollination of plants by bats.
There are 500 types of plants that rely on bats for pollination.
Mango
Common Blossom Bat
Durian
Common Nectar Bat
Banana
Brown Banana Bat
Cocoa
Orange Nectar Bat
Guava
Brown Flower Bat
Some of humans' favorite foods are pollinated with the help of bats.
I don't know about that... Doesn't sound very batlike.
Sounds weird.

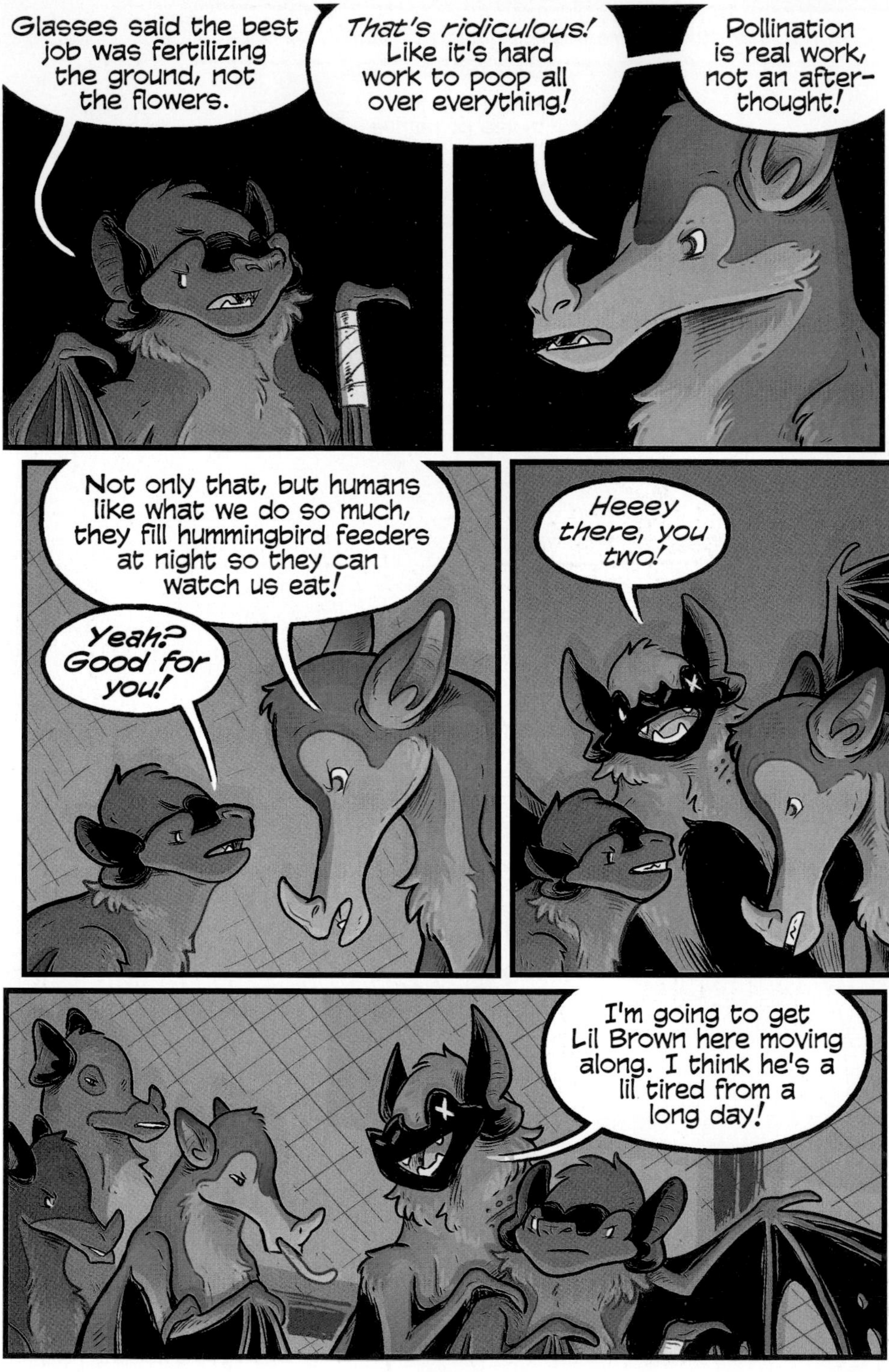
Glasses said the best job was fertilizing the ground, not the flowers.
That's ridiculous! Like it's hard work to poop all over everything!
Pollination is real work, not an after-thought!
Not only that, but humans like what we do so much, they fill hummingbird feeders at night so they can watch us eat!
Yeah? Good for you!
Heeey there, you two!
I'm going to get Lil Brown here moving along. I think he's a lil tired from a long day!

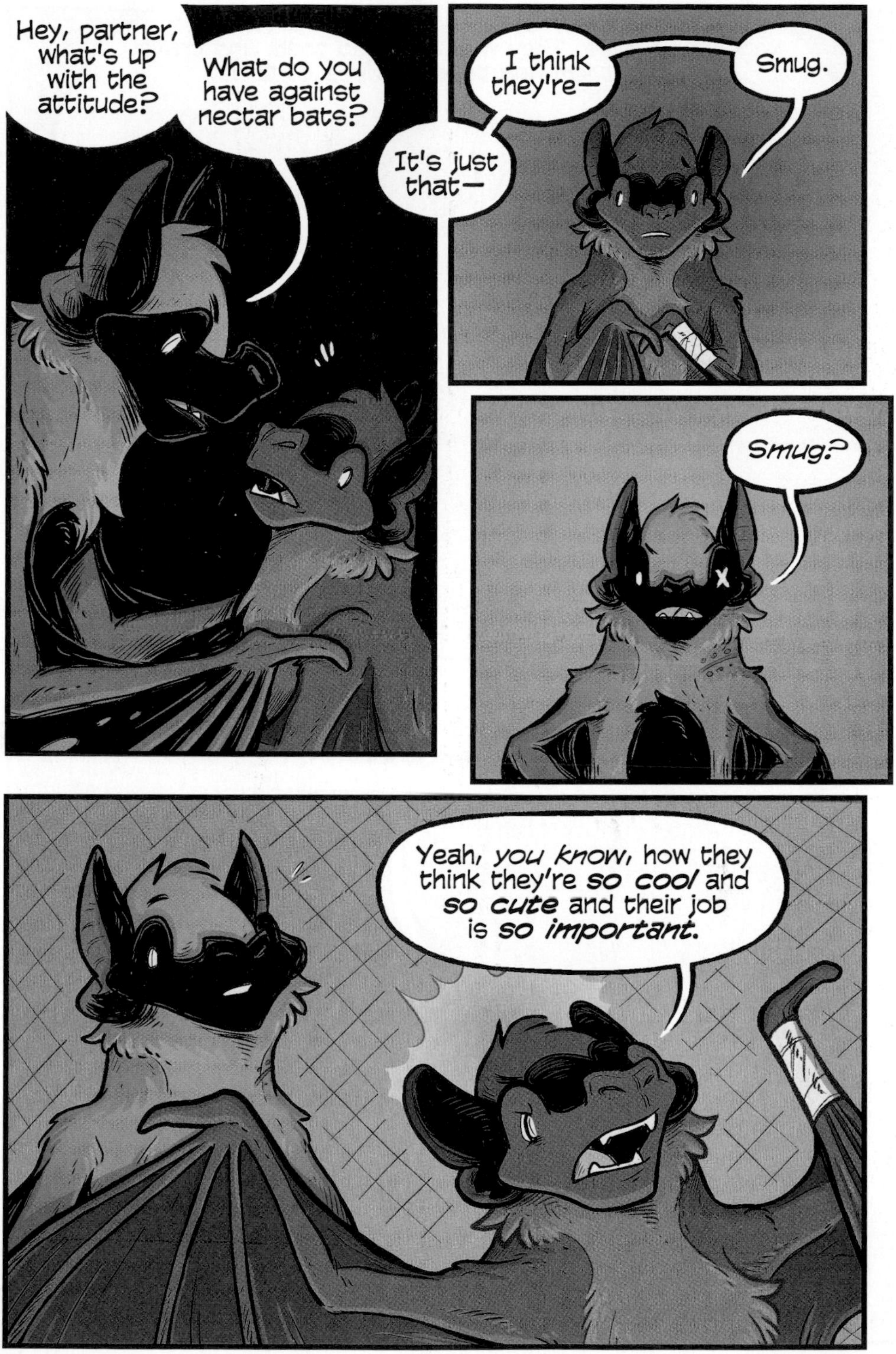
Hey, partner, what's up with the attitude?
What do you have against nectar bats?
It's just that—
I think they're—
Smug.
Smug?
Yeah, *you know*, how they think they're ***so cool*** and ***so cute*** and their job is ***so important***.

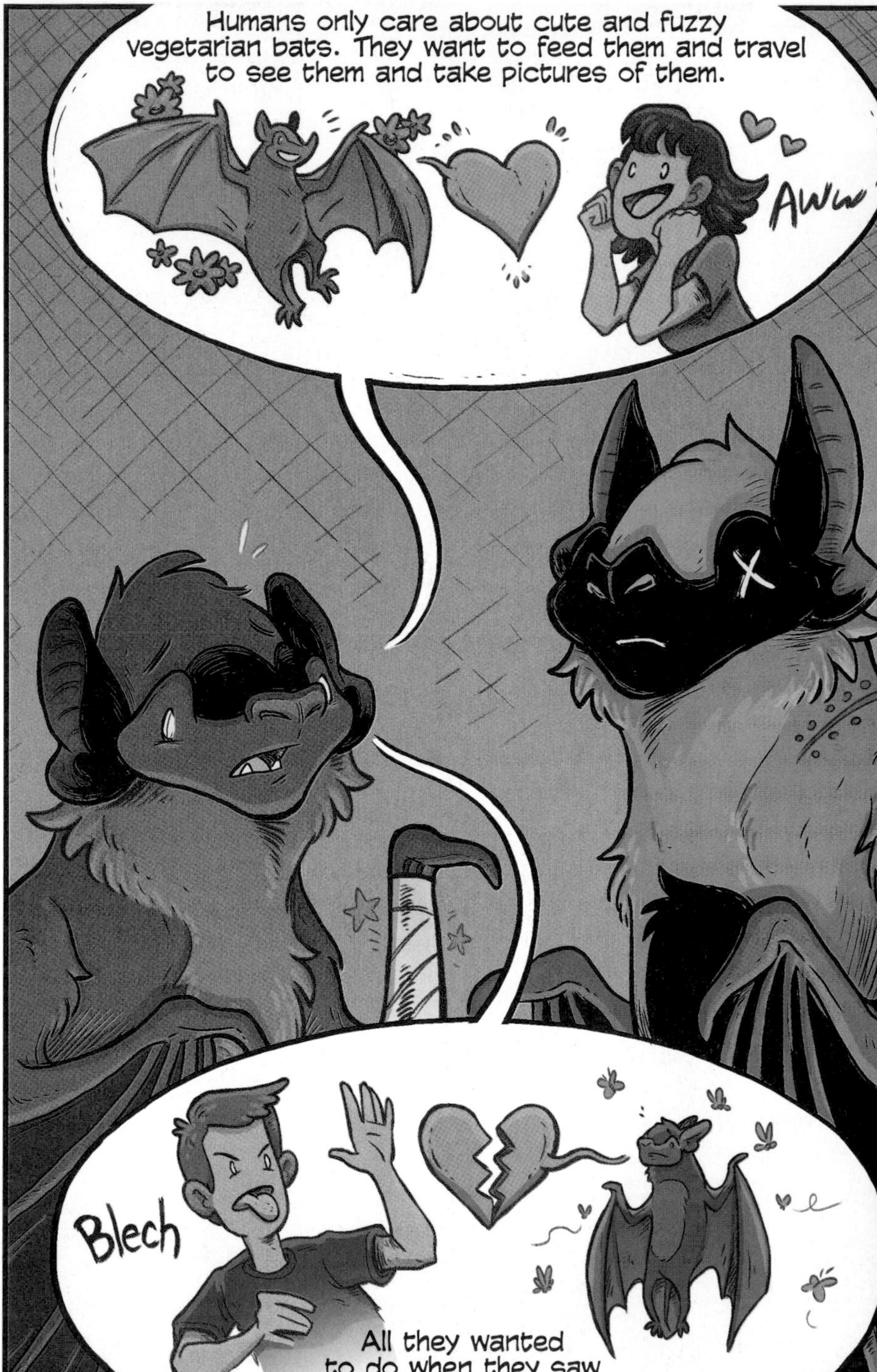
Humans only care about cute and fuzzy vegetarian bats. They want to feed them and travel to see them and take pictures of them.
AWW
Blech
All they wanted to do when they saw me was shoo me away.

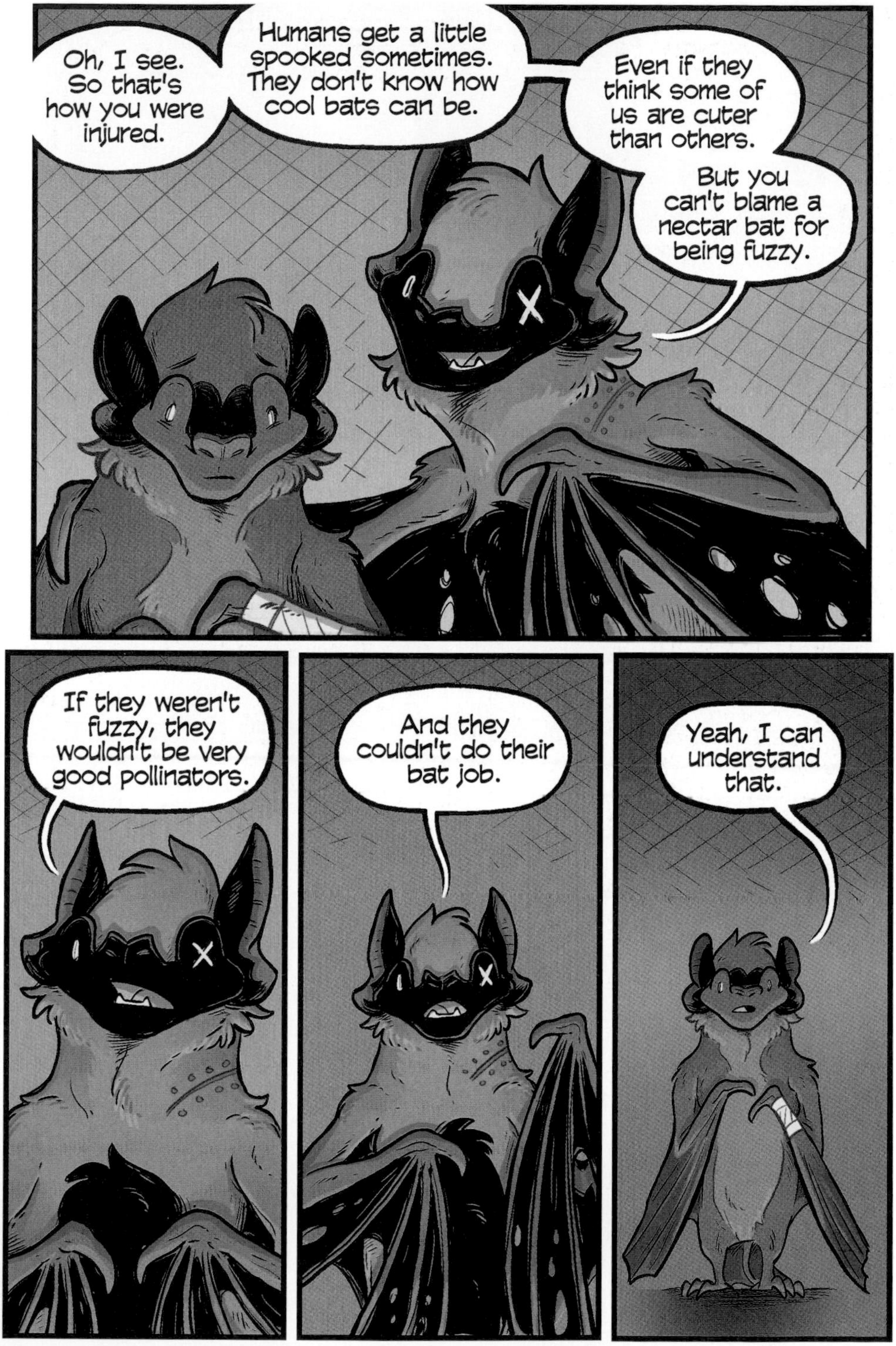
Oh, I see. So that's how you were injured.
Humans get a little spooked sometimes. They don't know how cool bats can be.
Even if they think some of us are cuter than others.
But you can't blame a nectar bat for being fuzzy.
If they weren't fuzzy, they wouldn't be very good pollinators.
And they couldn't do their bat job.
Yeah, I can understand that.

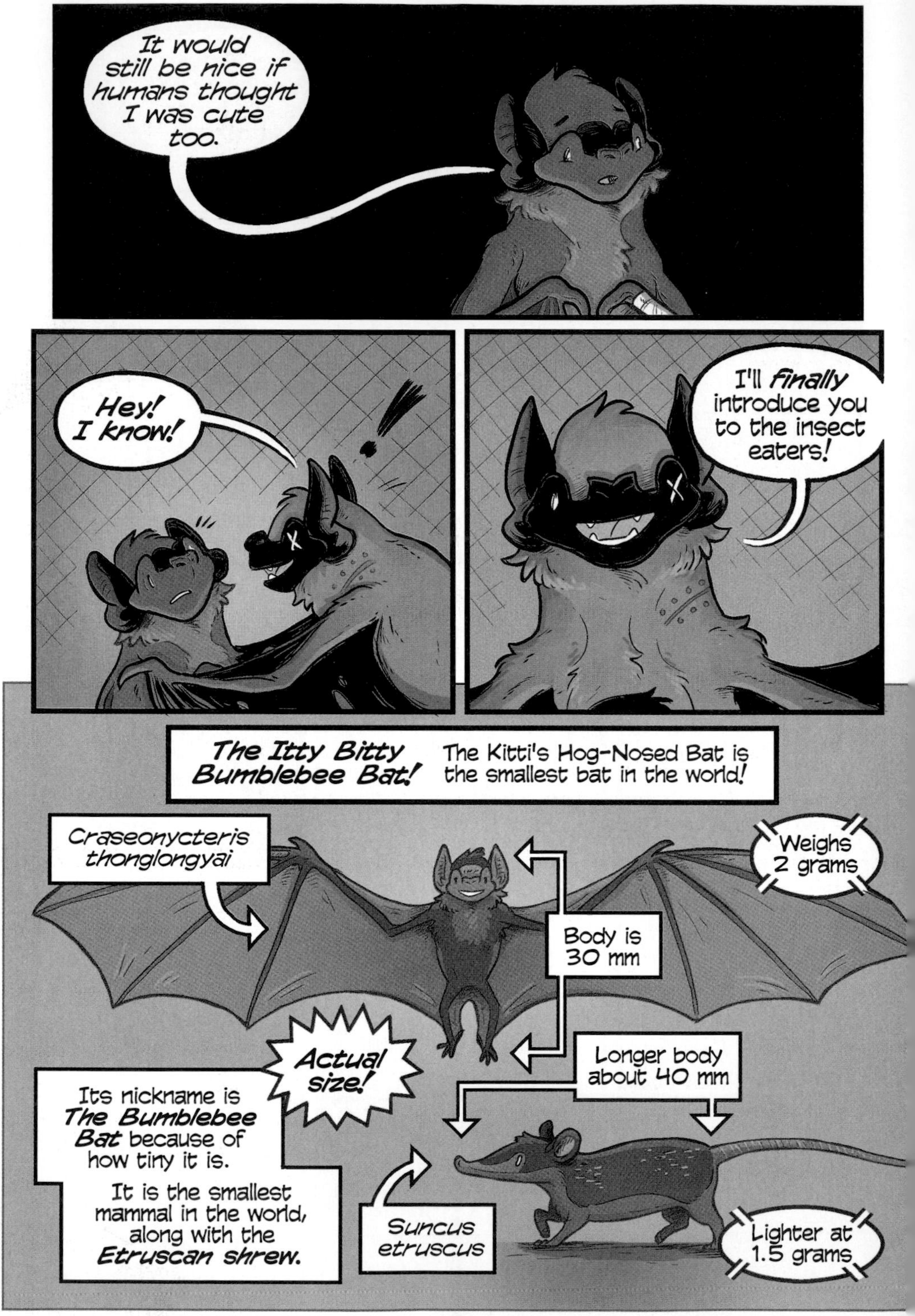
It would still be nice if humans thought I was cute too.
Hey! I know!
!
I'll finally introduce you to the insect eaters!
The Itty Bitty Bumblebee Bat!
The Kitti's Hog-Nosed Bat is the smallest bat in the world!
Craseonycteris thonglongyai
Weighs 2 grams
Body is 30 mm
Actual size!
Longer body about 40 mm
Its nickname is The Bumblebee Bat because of how tiny it is.
It is the smallest mammal in the world, along with the Etruscan shrew.
Suncus etruscus
Lighter at 1.5 grams

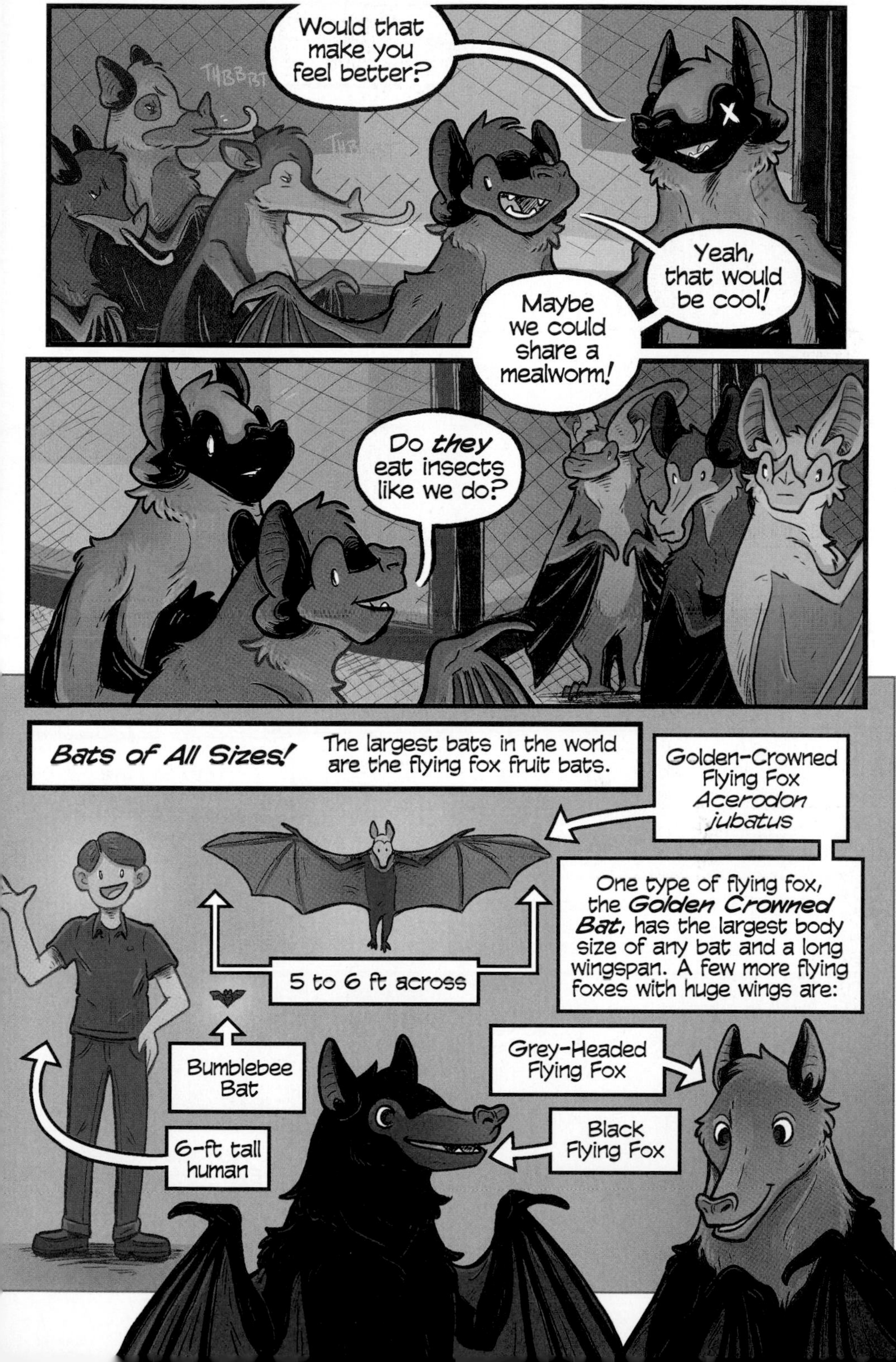

Would that make you feel better?
Yeah, that would be cool!
Maybe we could share a mealworm!
Do *they* eat insects like we do?
Bats of All Sizes!
The largest bats in the world are the flying fox fruit bats.
Golden-Crowned Flying Fox *Acerodon jubatus*
One type of flying fox, the ***Golden Crowned Bat,*** has the largest body size of any bat and a long wingspan. A few more flying foxes with huge wings are:
5 to 6 ft across
Bumblebee Bat
6-ft tall human
Grey-Headed Flying Fox
Black Flying Fox

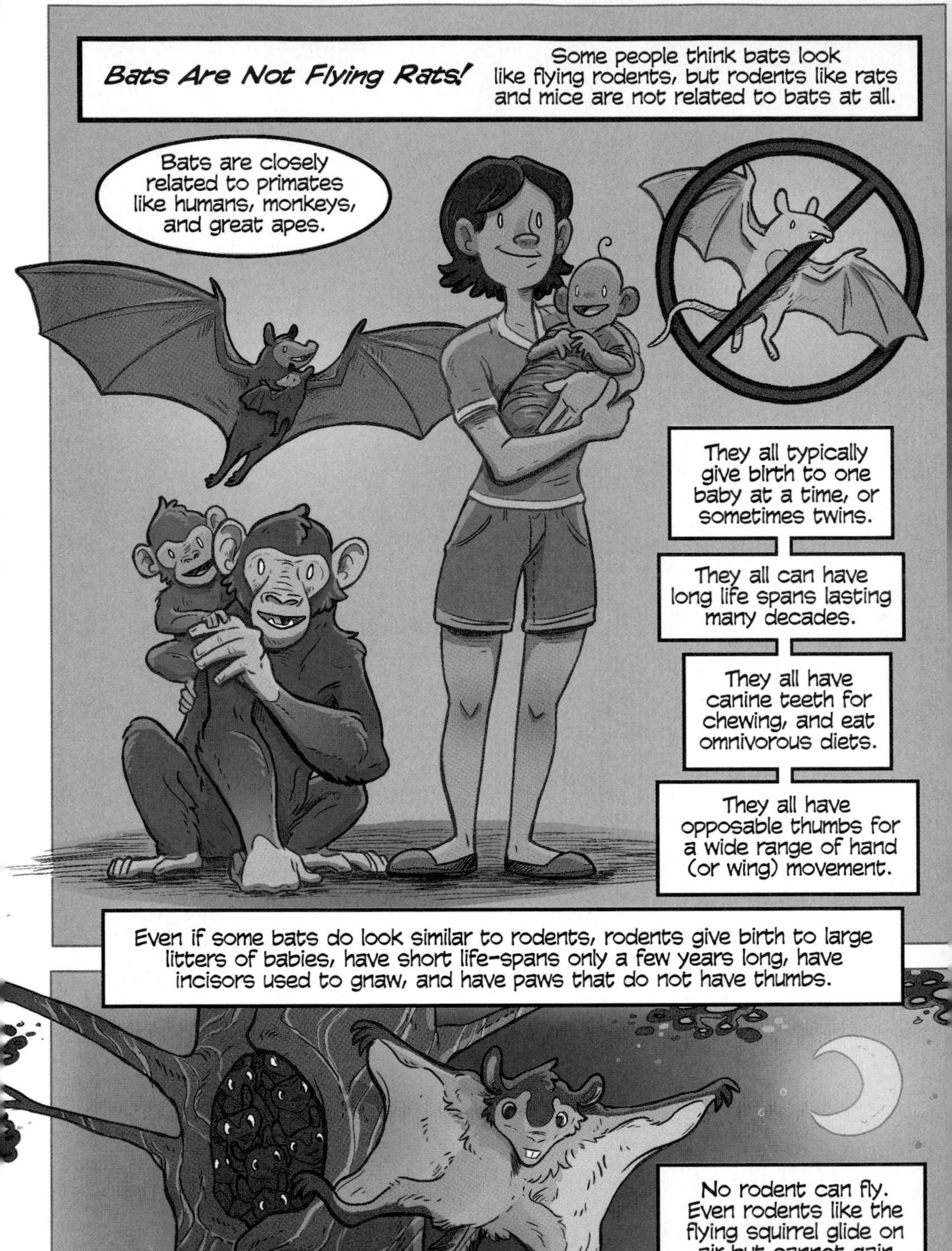
Bats Are Not Flying Rats!
Some people think bats look like flying rodents, but rodents like rats and mice are not related to bats at all.
Bats are closely related to primates like humans, monkeys, and great apes.
They all typically give birth to one baby at a time, or sometimes twins.
They all can have long life spans lasting many decades.
They all have canine teeth for chewing, and eat omnivorous diets.
They all have opposable thumbs for a wide range of hand (or wing) movement.
Even if some bats do look similar to rodents, rodents give birth to large litters of babies, have short life-spans only a few years long, have incisors used to gnaw, and have paws that do not have thumbs.
No rodent can fly. Even rodents like the flying squirrel glide on air but cannot gain altitude on their own.

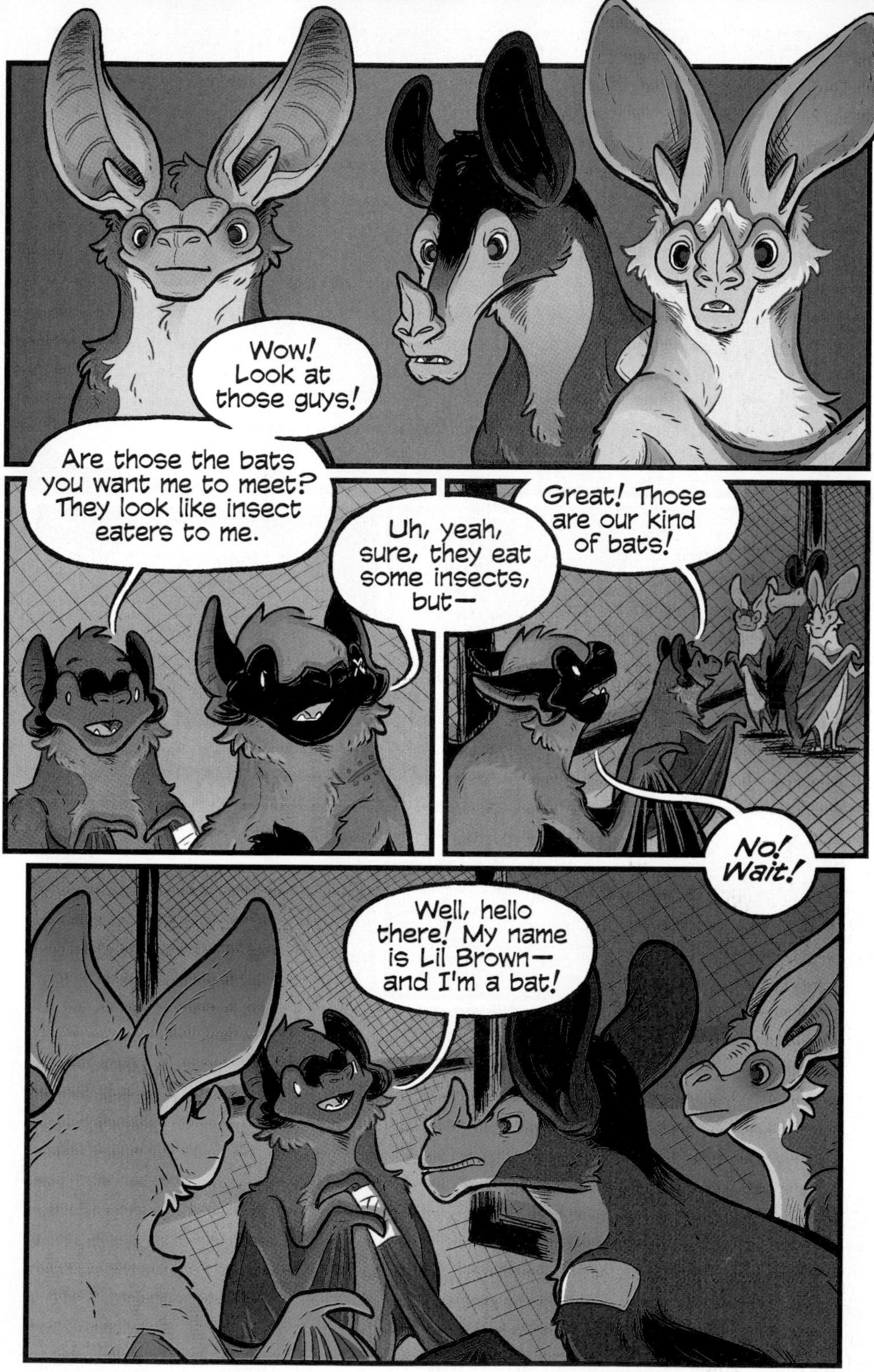
Wow! Look at those guys!
Are those the bats you want me to meet? They look like insect eaters to me.
Uh, yeah, sure, they eat some insects, but—
Great! Those are our kind of bats!
No! Wait!
Well, hello there! My name is Lil Brown— and I'm a bat!

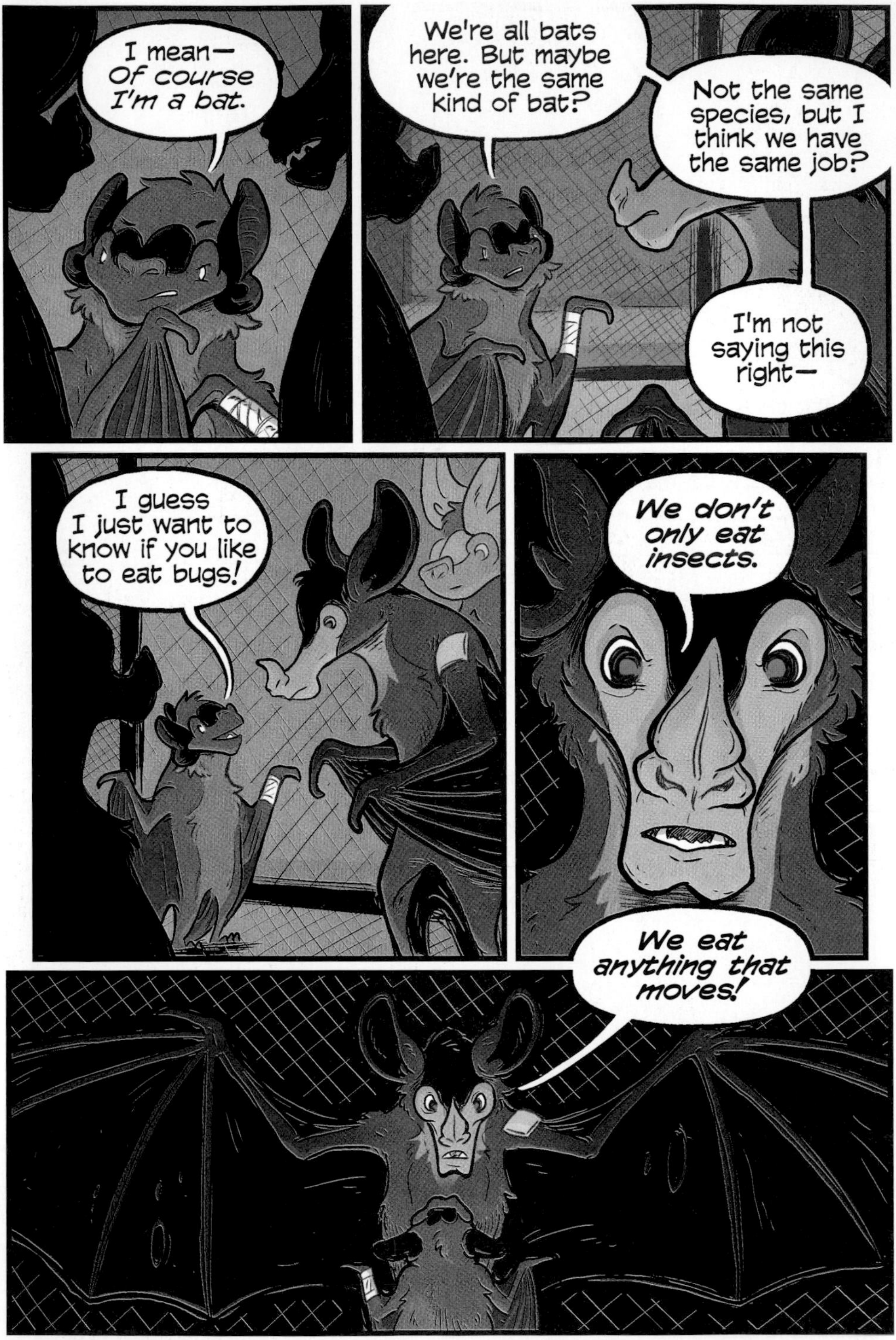
I mean— Of course I'm a bat.
We're all bats here. But maybe we're the same kind of bat?
Not the same species, but I think we have the same job?
I'm not saying this right—
I guess I just want to know if you like to eat bugs!
We don't only eat insects.
We eat anything that moves!

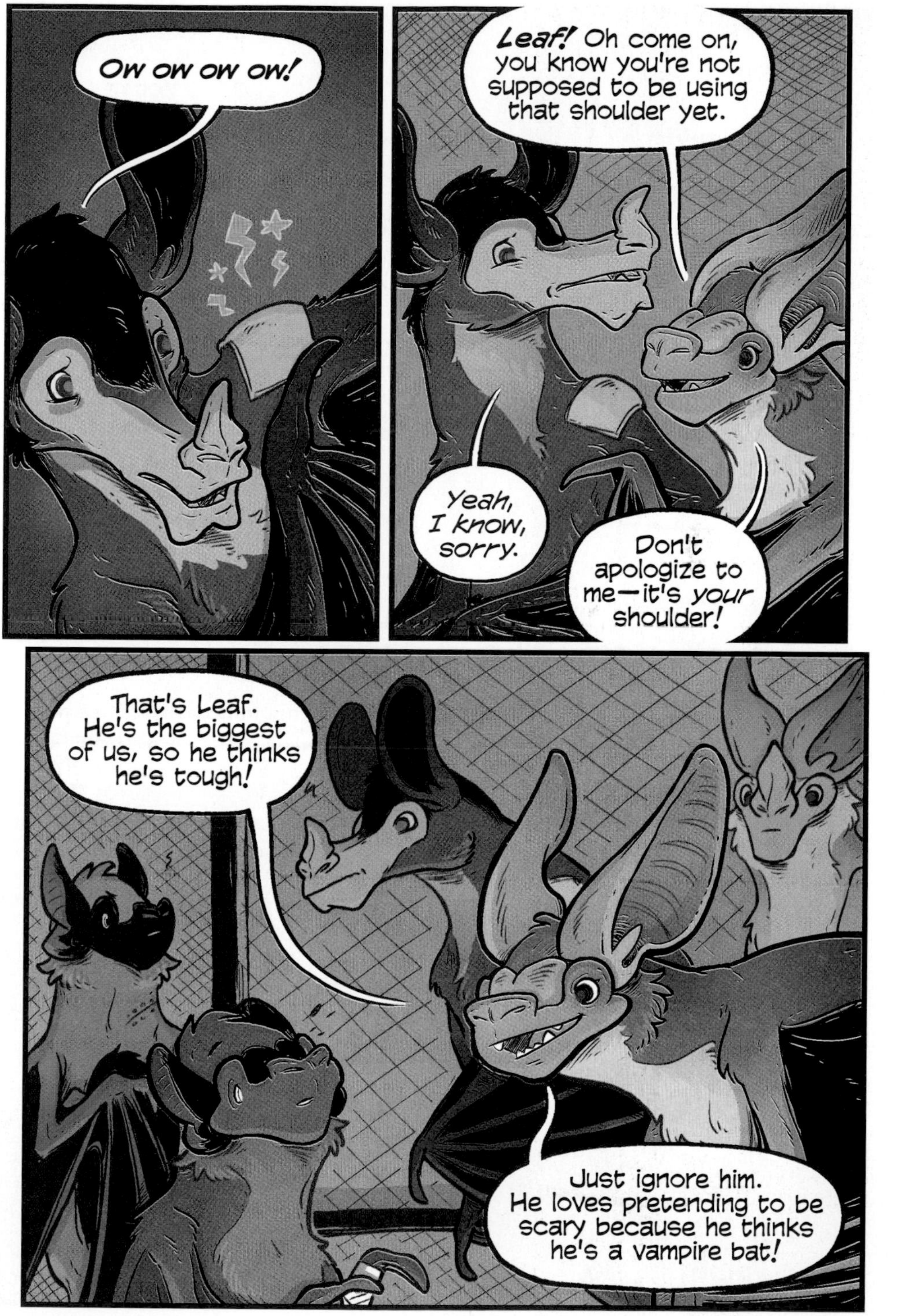
OW OW OW OW!
Leaf! Oh come on, you know you're not supposed to be using that shoulder yet.
Yeah, I know, sorry.
Don't apologize to me—it's your shoulder!
That's Leaf. He's the biggest of us, so he thinks he's tough!
Just ignore him. He loves pretending to be scary because he thinks he's a vampire bat!

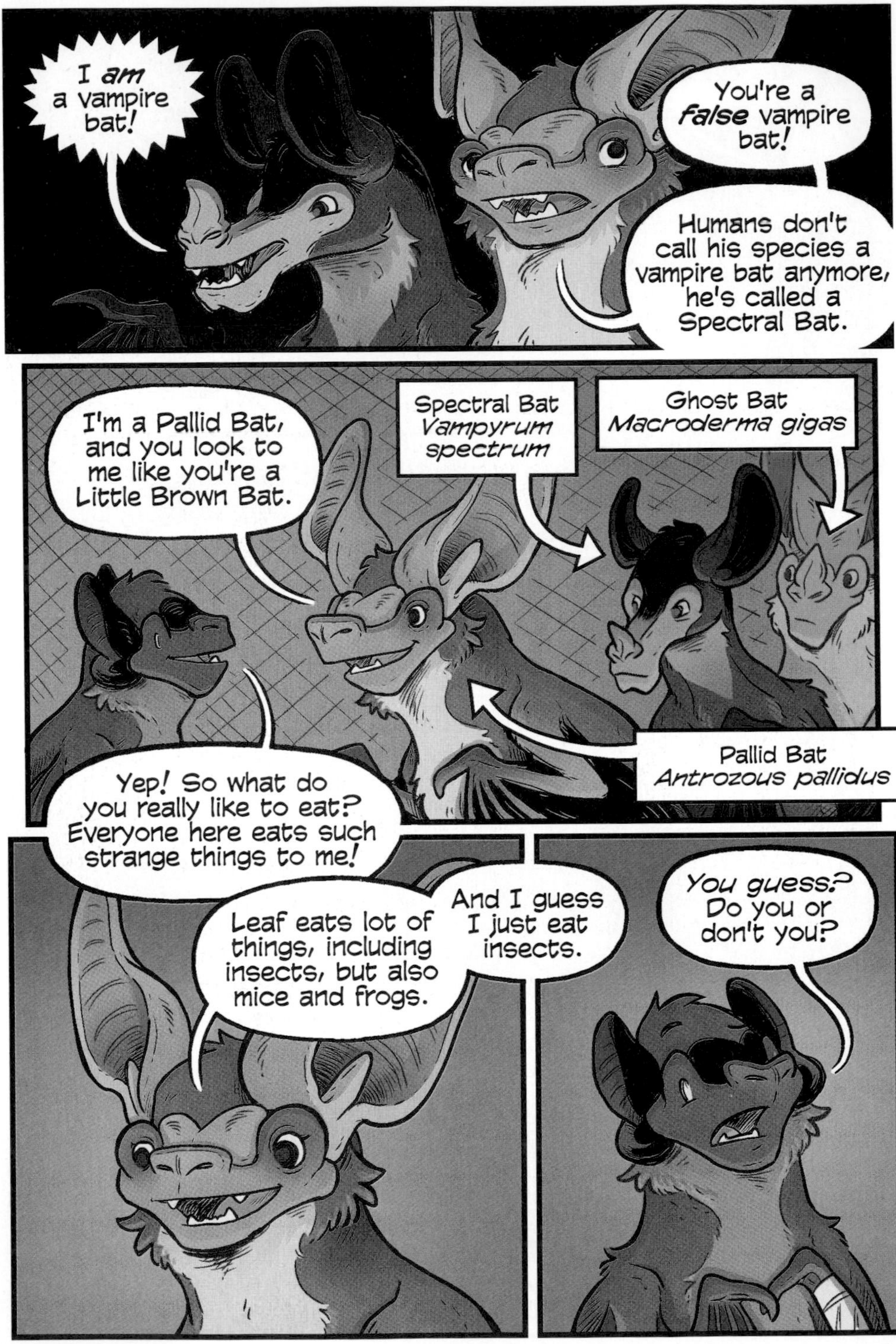
I *am* a vampire bat!
You're a *false* vampire bat!
Humans don't call his species a vampire bat anymore, he's called a Spectral Bat.
I'm a Pallid Bat, and you look to me like you're a Little Brown Bat.
Spectral Bat *Vampyrum spectrum*
Ghost Bat *Macroderma gigas*
Pallid Bat *Antrozous pallidus*
Yep! So what do you really like to eat? Everyone here eats such strange things to me!
Leaf eats lot of things, including insects, but also mice and frogs.
And I guess I just eat insects.
You guess? Do you or don't you?

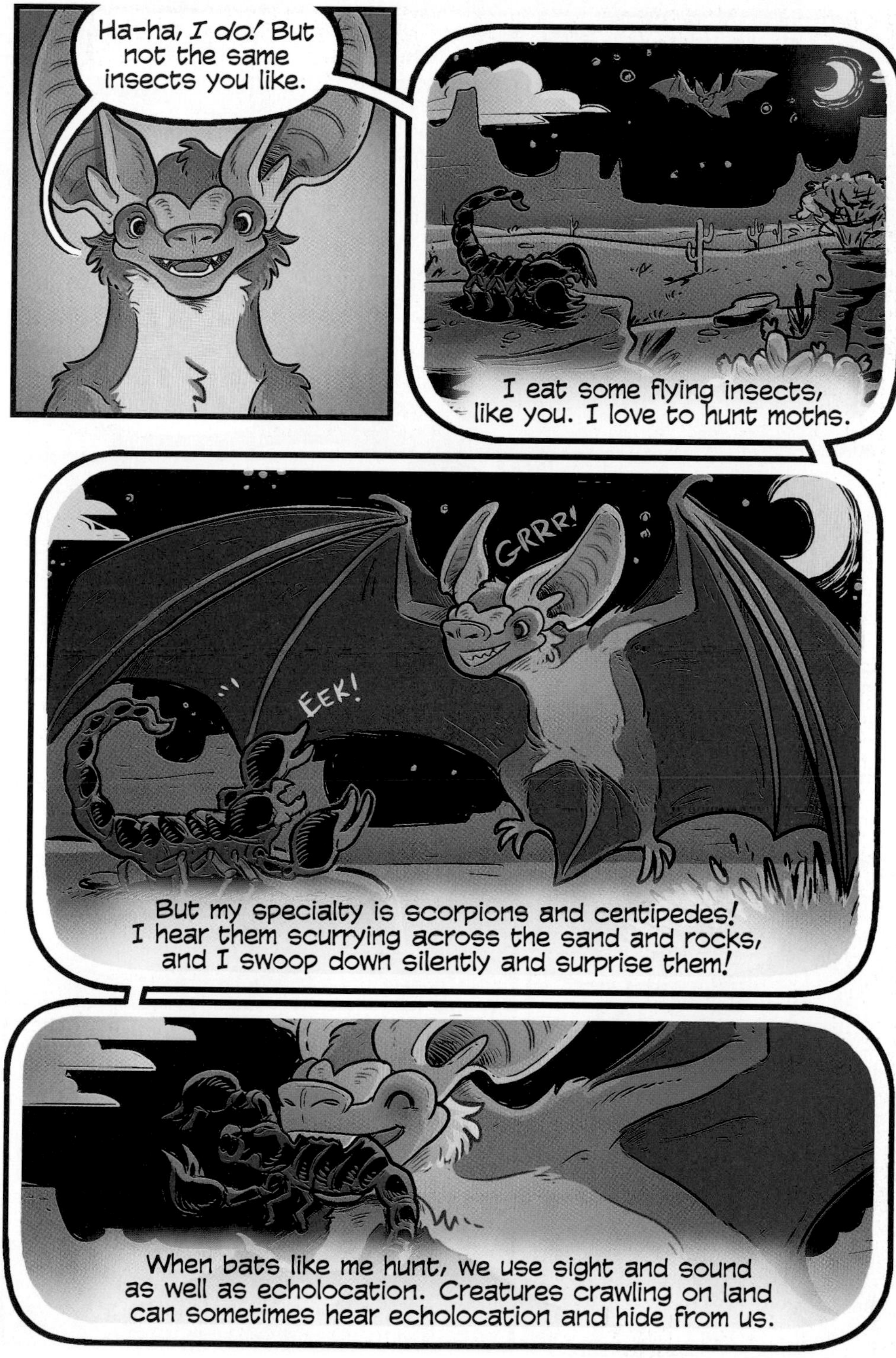
Ha-ha, *I do!* But not the same insects you like.
I eat some flying insects, like you. I love to hunt moths.
GRRR!
EEK!
But my specialty is scorpions and centipedes! I hear them scurrying across the sand and rocks, and I swoop down silently and surprise them!
When bats like me hunt, we use sight and sound as well as echolocation. Creatures crawling on land can sometimes hear echolocation and hide from us.

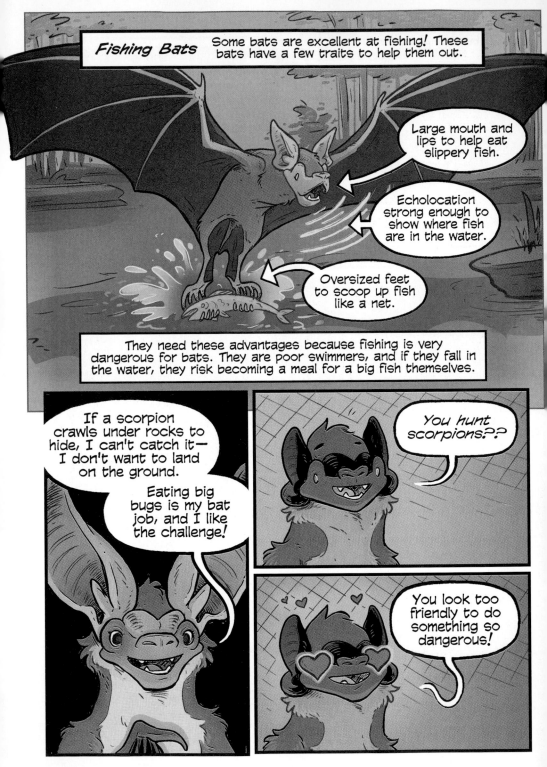

Fishing Bats Some bats are excellent at fishing! These bats have a few traits to help them out.

Large mouth and lips to help eat slippery fish.

Echolocation strong enough to show where fish are in the water.

Oversized feet to scoop up fish like a net.

They need these advantages because fishing is very dangerous for bats. They are poor swimmers, and if they fall in the water, they risk becoming a meal for a big fish themselves.

If a scorpion crawls under rocks to hide, I can't catch it— I don't want to land on the ground.

Eating big bugs is my bat job, and I like the challenge!

You hunt scorpions??

You look too friendly to do something so dangerous!

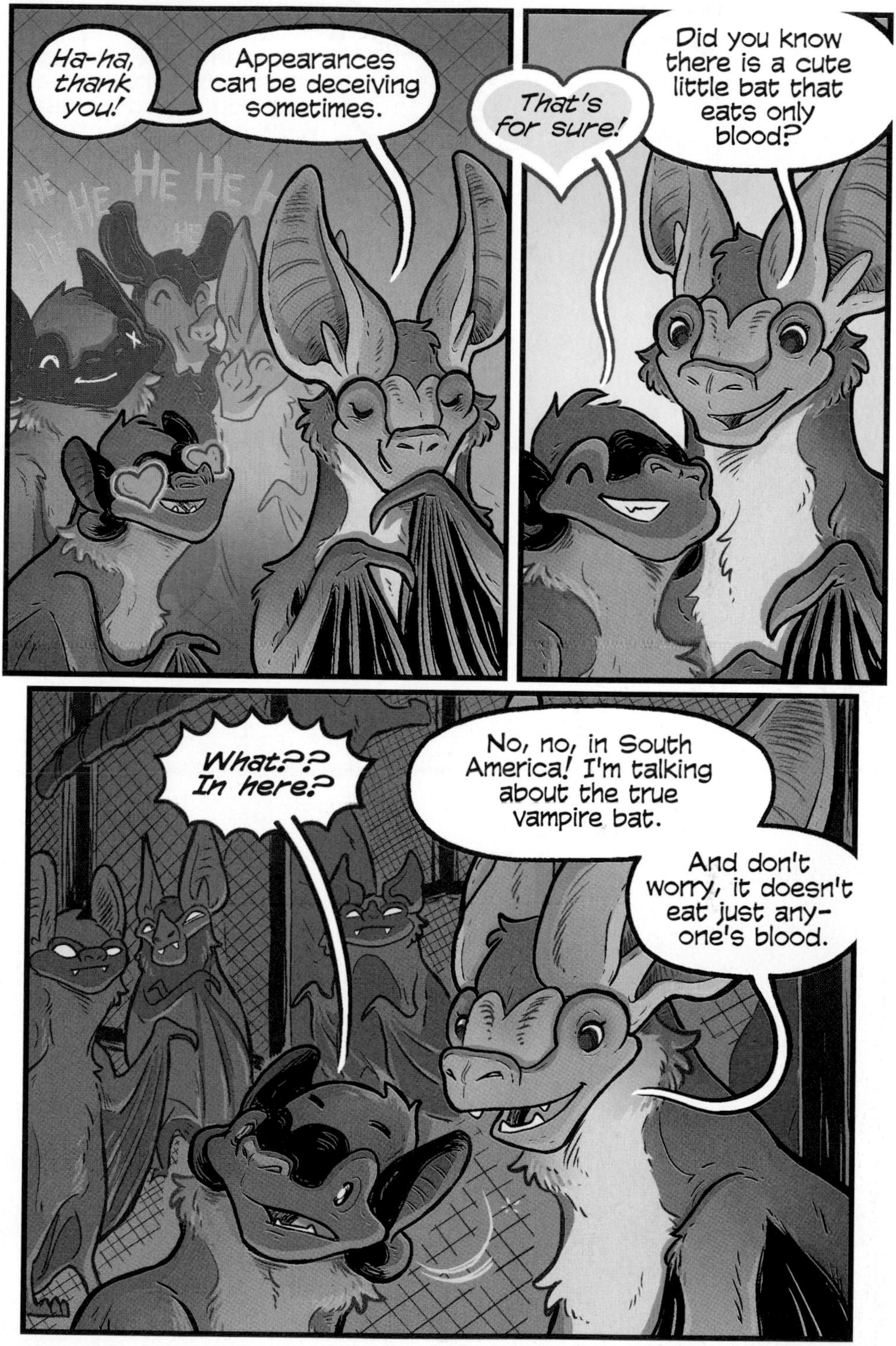
Ha-ha, thank you!
Appearances can be deceiving sometimes.
HE HE HE HE HE
That's for sure!
Did you know there is a cute little bat that eats only blood?
What?? In here?
No, no, in South America! I'm talking about the true vampire bat.
And don't worry, it doesn't eat just any-one's blood.

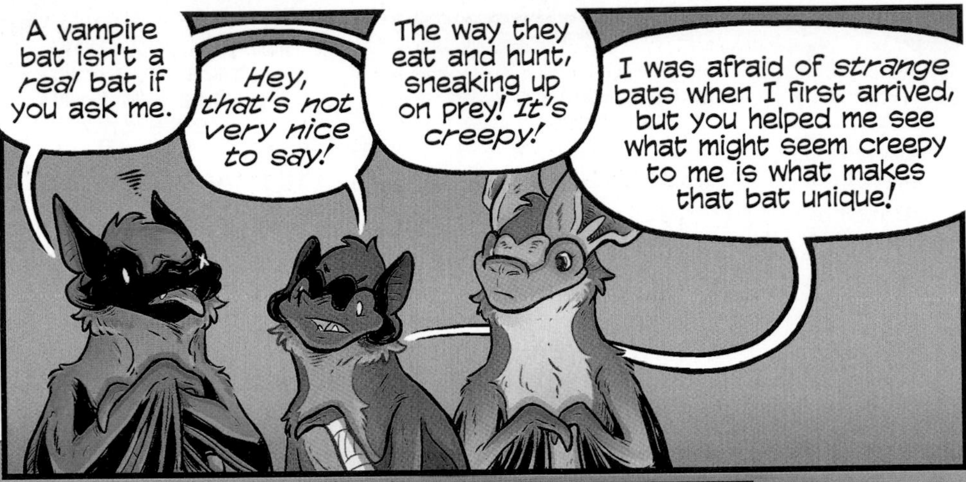
A vampire bat isn't a *real* bat if you ask me.
Hey, that's not very nice to say!
The way they eat and hunt, sneaking up on prey! *It's creepy!*
I was afraid of *strange* bats when I first arrived, but you helped me see what might seem creepy to me is what makes that bat unique!

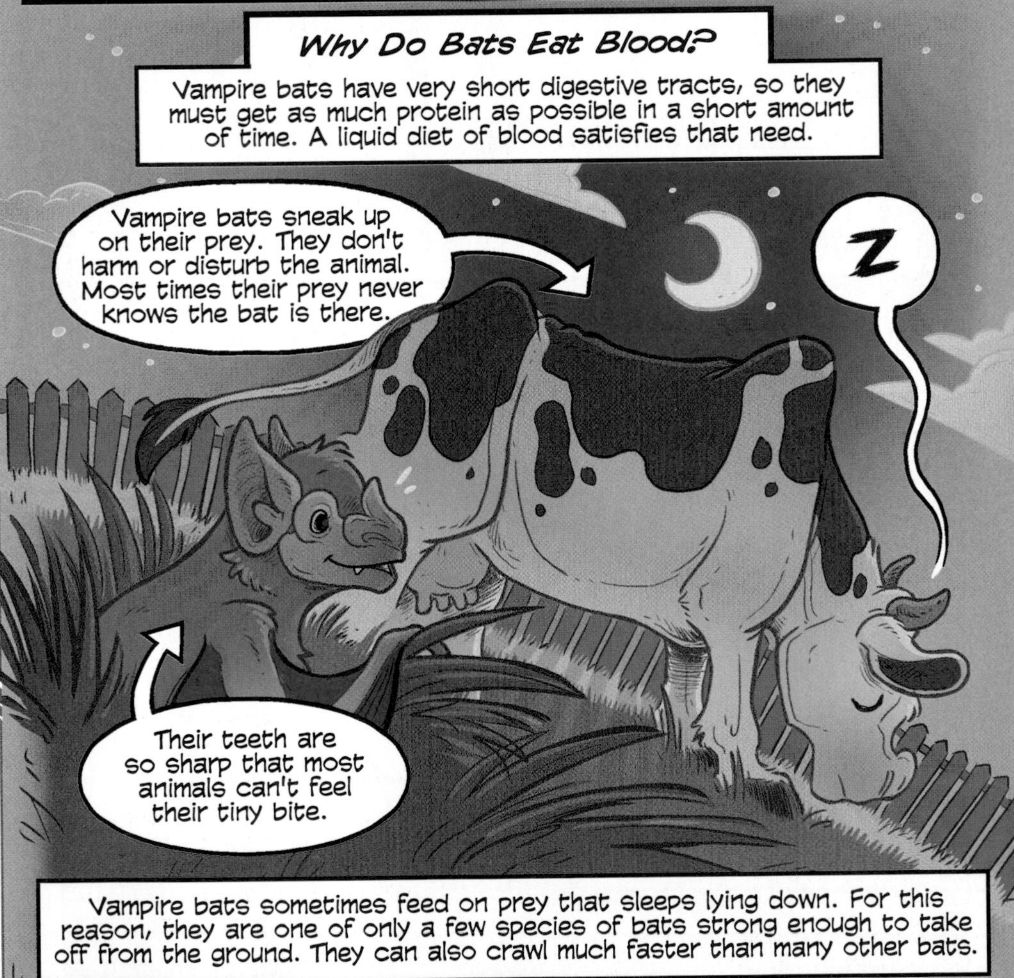
Why Do Bats Eat Blood?
Vampire bats have very short digestive tracts, so they must get as much protein as possible in a short amount of time. A liquid diet of blood satisfies that need.
Vampire bats sneak up on their prey. They don't harm or disturb the animal. Most times their prey never knows the bat is there.
Z
Their teeth are so sharp that most animals can't feel their tiny bite.
Vampire bats sometimes feed on prey that sleeps lying down. For this reason, they are one of only a few species of bats strong enough to take off from the ground. They can also crawl much faster than many other bats.

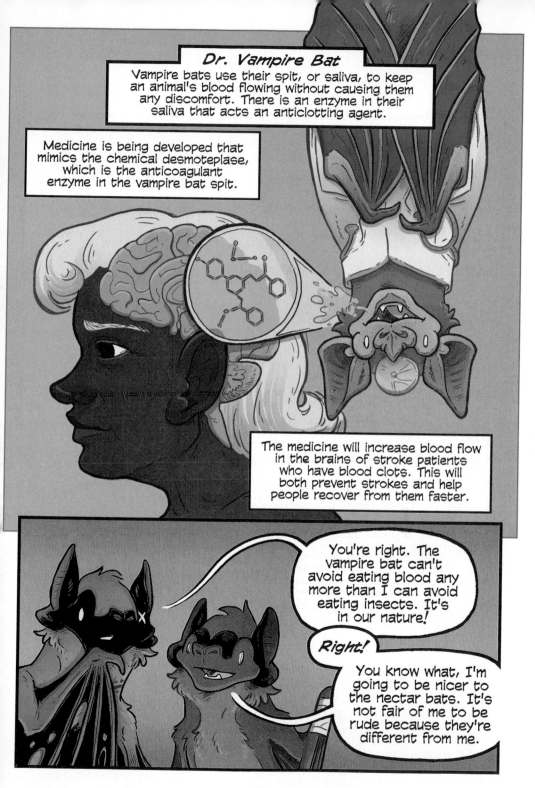

Dr. Vampire Bat

Vampire bats use their spit, or saliva, to keep an animal's blood flowing without causing them any discomfort. There is an enzyme in their saliva that acts an anticlotting agent.

Medicine is being developed that mimics the chemical desmoteplase, which is the anticoagulant enzyme in the vampire bat spit.

The medicine will increase blood flow in the brains of stroke patients who have blood clots. This will both prevent strokes and help people recover from them faster.

You're right. The vampire bat can't avoid eating blood any more than I can avoid eating insects. It's in our nature!

Right!

You know what, I'm going to be nicer to the nectar bats. It's not fair of me to be rude because they're different from me.

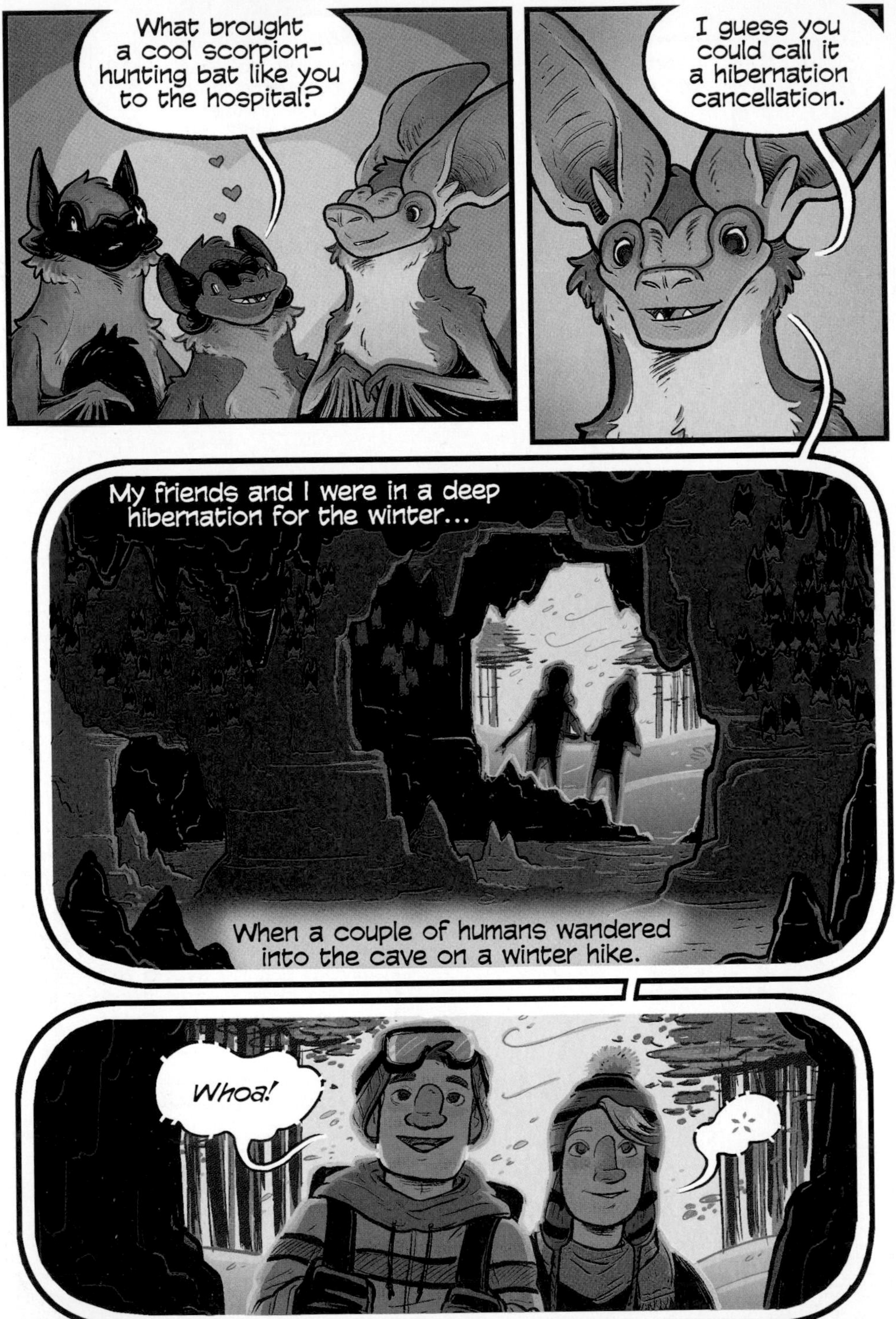
What brought a cool scorpion-hunting bat like you to the hospital?
I guess you could call it a hibernation cancellation.
My friends and I were in a deep hibernation for the winter...
When a couple of humans wandered into the cave on a winter hike.
Whoa!

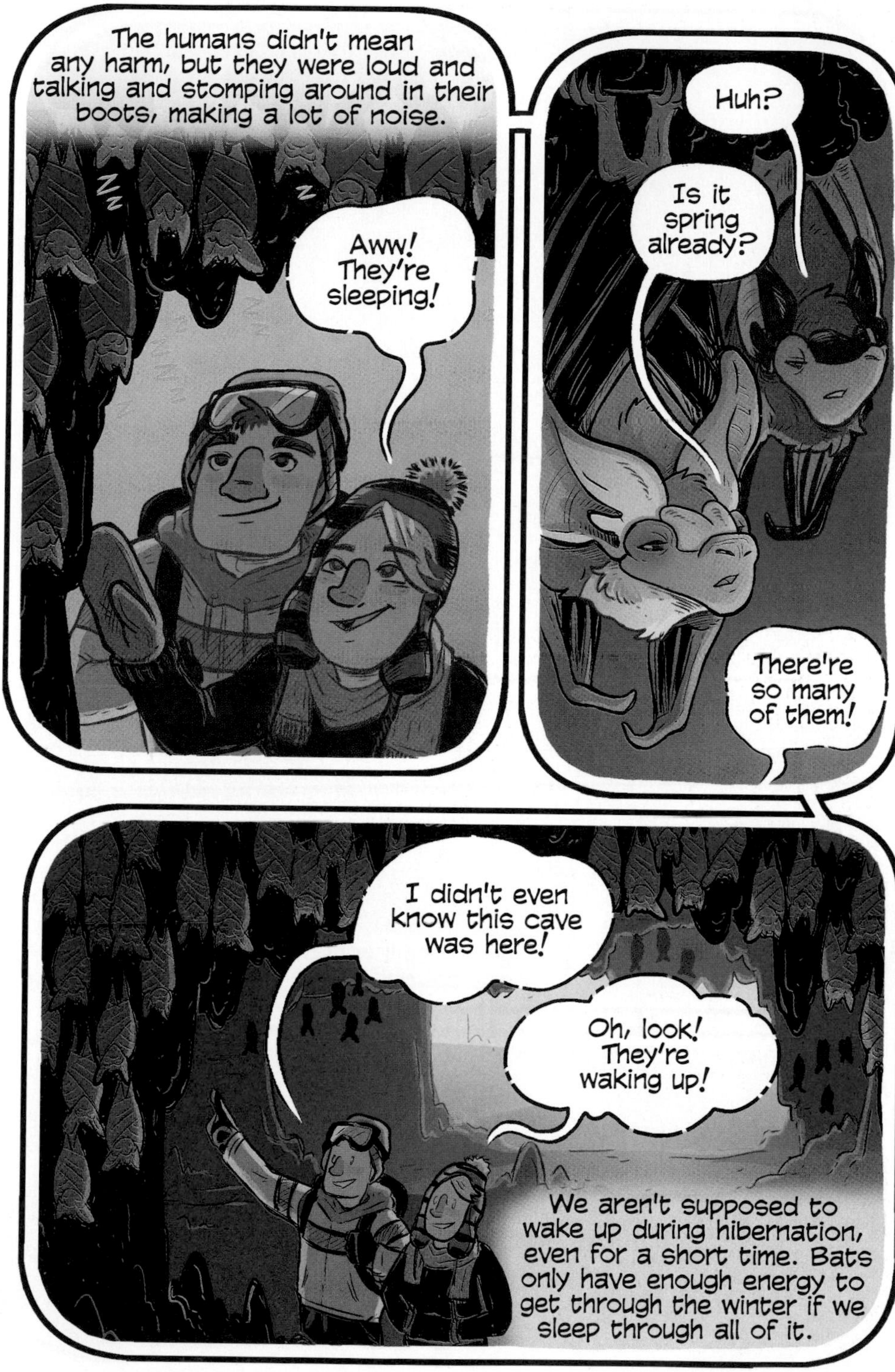

The humans didn't mean any harm, but they were loud and talking and stomping around in their boots, making a lot of noise.
ZZZ
Z
Aww! They're sleeping!
Huh?
Is it spring already?
There're so many of them!
I didn't even know this cave was here!
Oh, look! They're waking up!
We aren't supposed to wake up during hibernation, even for a short time. Bats only have enough energy to get through the winter if we sleep through all of it.

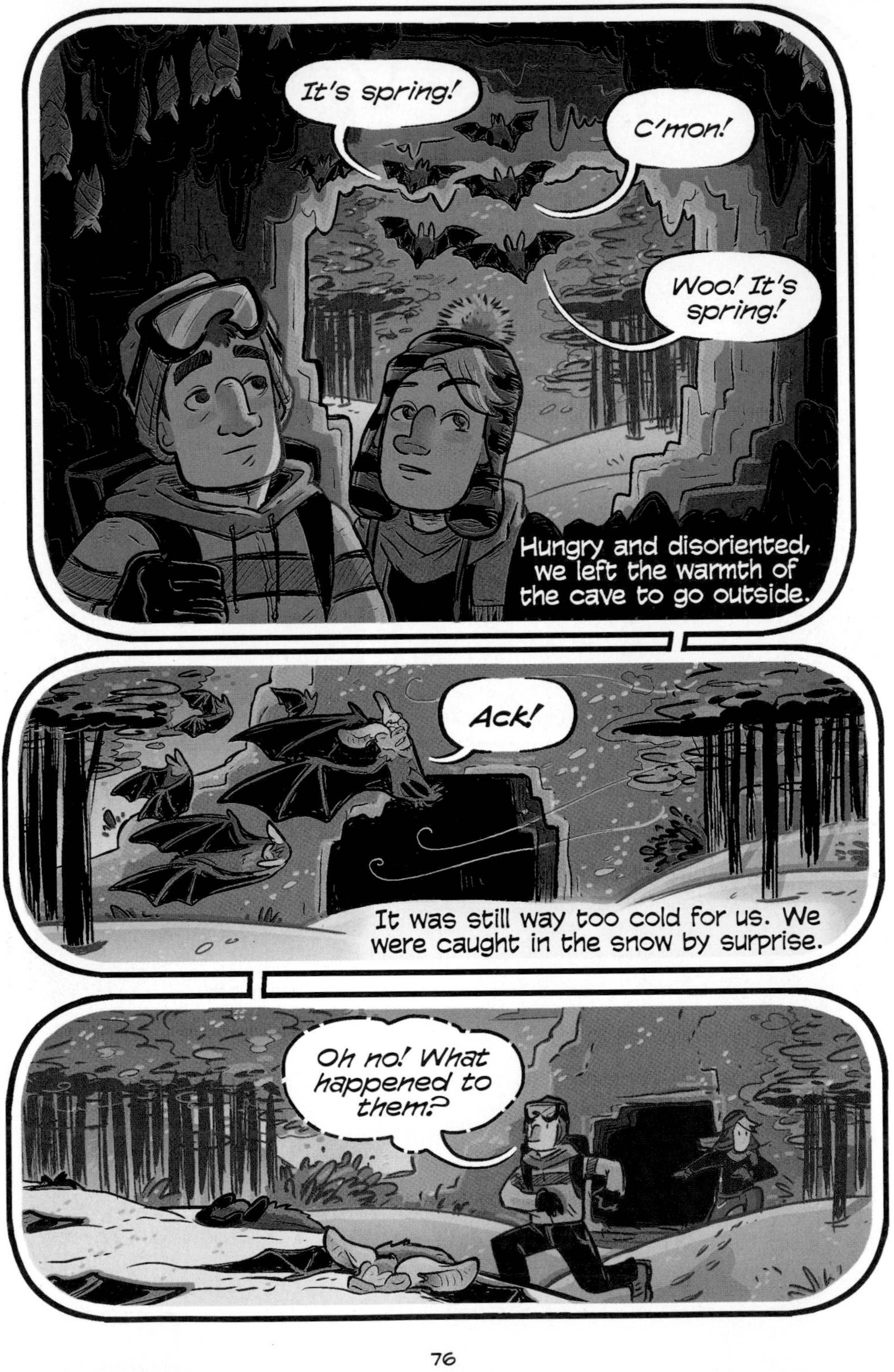
It's spring!
C'mon!
Woo! It's spring!
Hungry and disoriented, we left the warmth of the cave to go outside.
Ack!
It was still way too cold for us. We were caught in the snow by surprise.
Oh no! What happened to them?

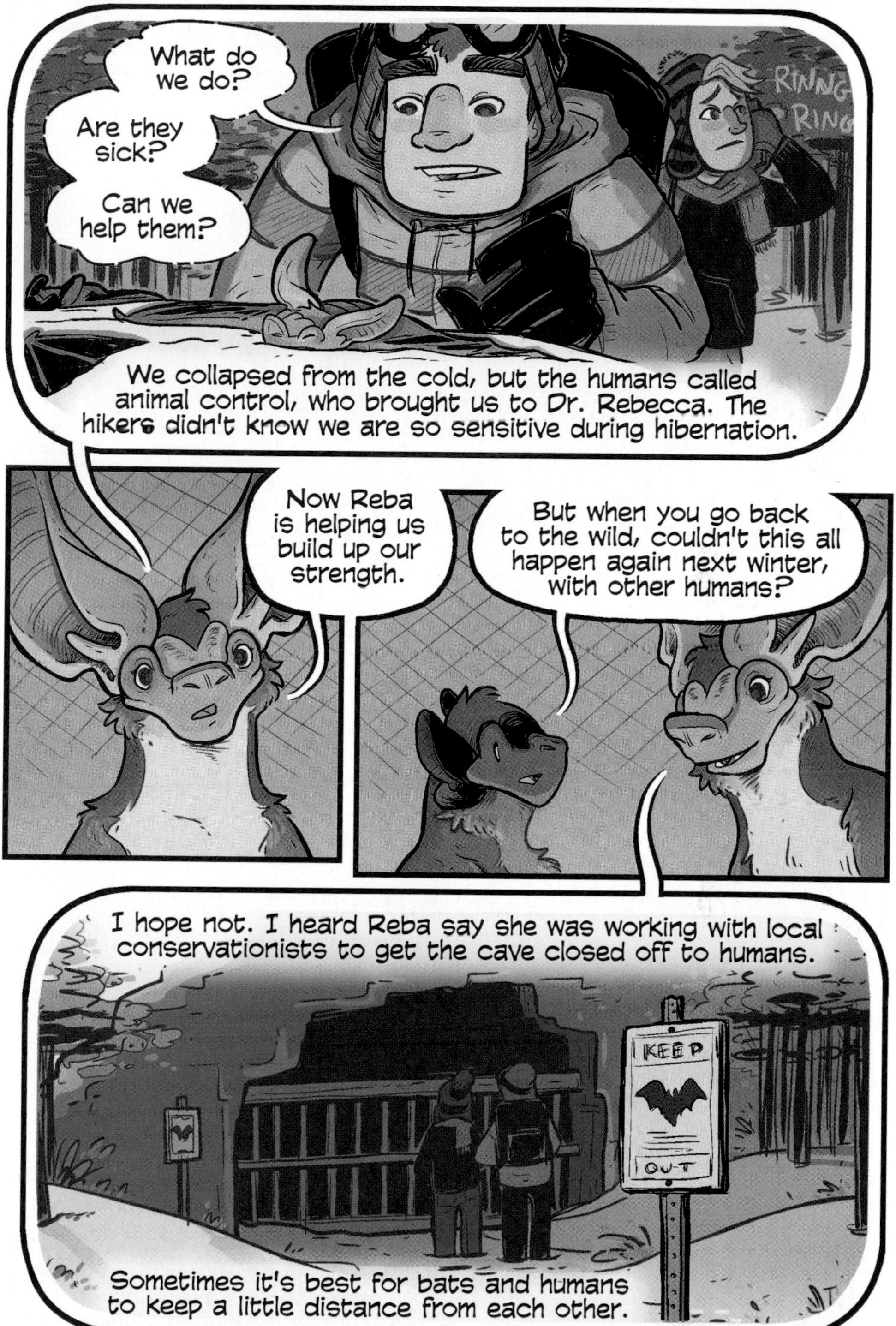
What do we do?
Are they sick?
Can we help them?
RING RING
We collapsed from the cold, but the humans called animal control, who brought us to Dr. Rebecca. The hikers didn't know we are so sensitive during hibernation.
Now Reba is helping us build up our strength.
But when you go back to the wild, couldn't this all happen again next winter, with other humans?
I hope not. I heard Reba say she was working with local conservationists to get the cave closed off to humans.
KEEP
OUT
Sometimes it's best for bats and humans to keep a little distance from each other.

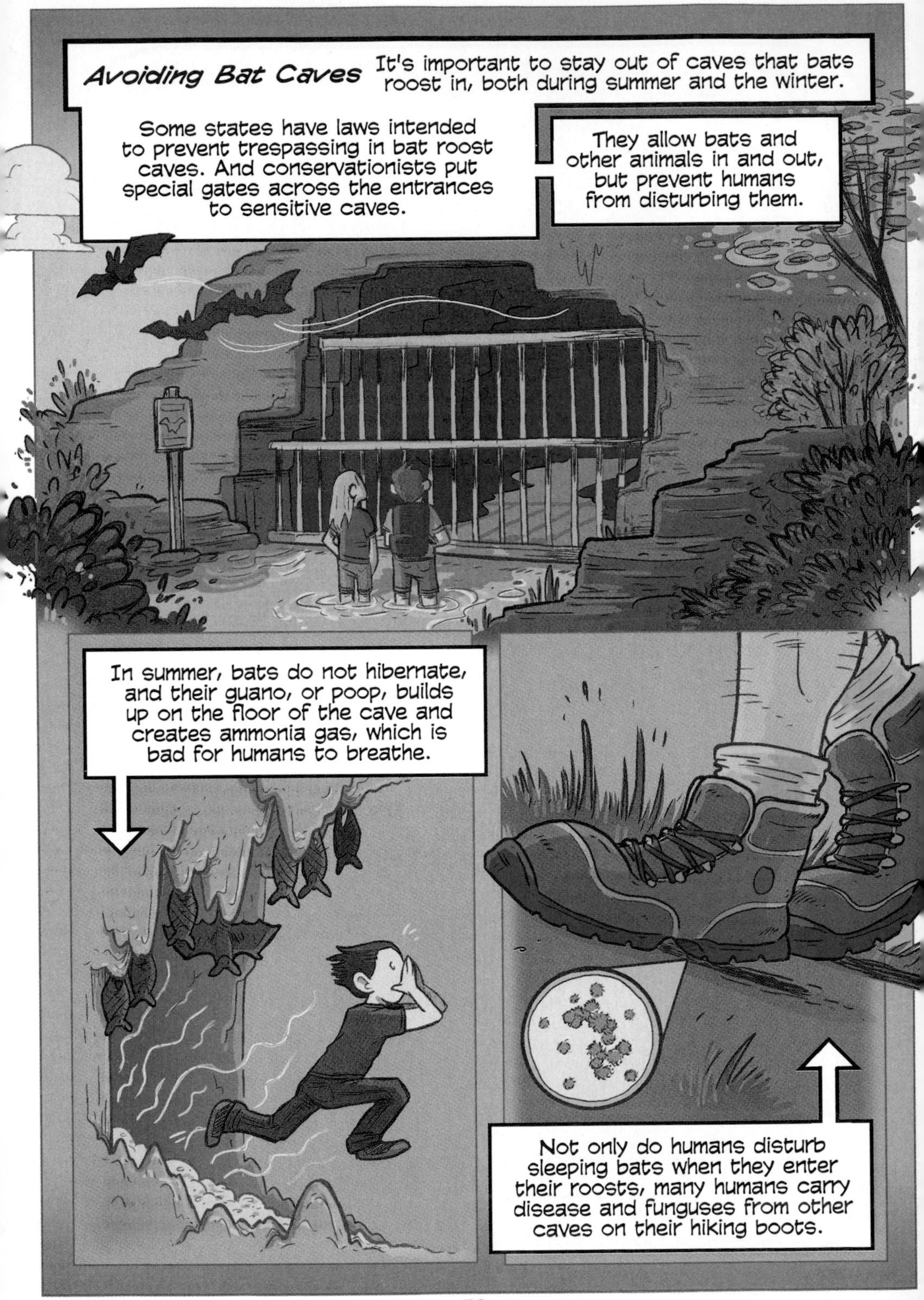
Avoiding Bat Caves
It's important to stay out of caves that bats roost in, both during summer and the winter.
Some states have laws intended to prevent trespassing in bat roost caves. And conservationists put special gates across the entrances to sensitive caves.
They allow bats and other animals in and out, but prevent humans from disturbing them.
In summer, bats do not hibernate, and their guano, or poop, builds up on the floor of the cave and creates ammonia gas, which is bad for humans to breathe.
Not only do humans disturb sleeping bats when they enter their roosts, many humans carry disease and funguses from other caves on their hiking boots.

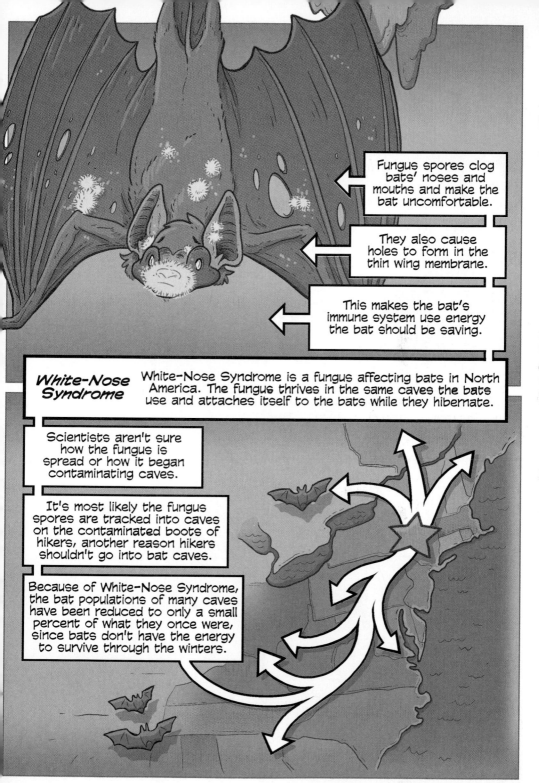

Fungus spores clog bats' noses and mouths and make the bat uncomfortable.

They also cause holes to form in the thin wing membrane.

This makes the bat's immune system use energy the bat should be saving.

White-Nose Syndrome

White-Nose Syndrome is a fungus affecting bats in North America. The fungus thrives in the same caves the bats use and attaches itself to the bats while they hibernate.

Scientists aren't sure how the fungus is spread or how it began contaminating caves.

It's most likely the fungus spores are tracked into caves on the contaminated boots of hikers, another reason hikers shouldn't go into bat caves.

Because of White-Nose Syndrome, the bat populations of many caves have been reduced to only a small percent of what they once were, since bats don't have the energy to survive through the winters.

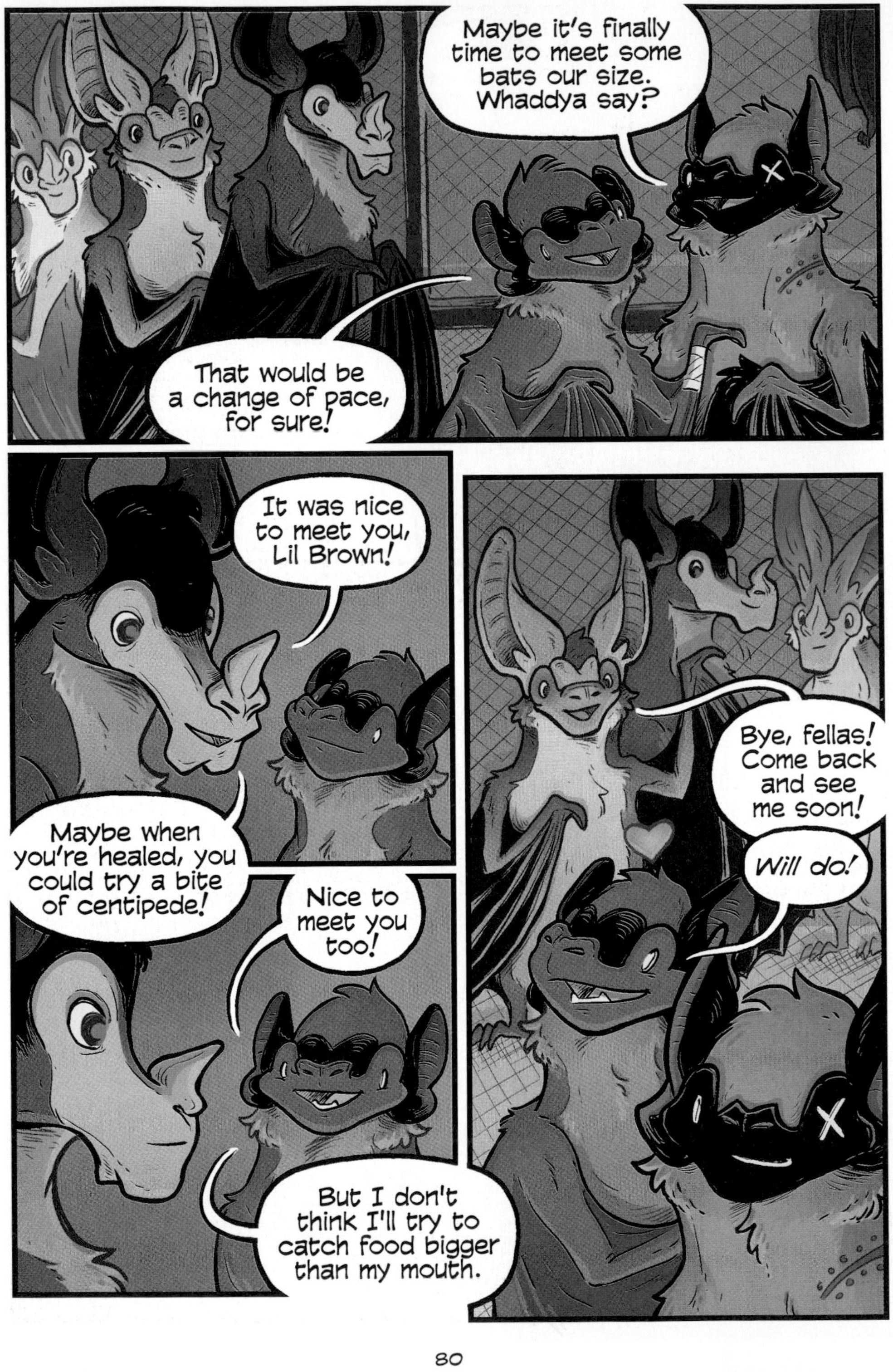
Maybe it's finally time to meet some bats our size. Whaddya say?
That would be a change of pace, for sure!
It was nice to meet you, Lil Brown!
Maybe when you're healed, you could try a bite of centipede!
Nice to meet you too!
But I don't think I'll try to catch food bigger than my mouth.
Bye, fellas! Come back and see me soon!
Will do!

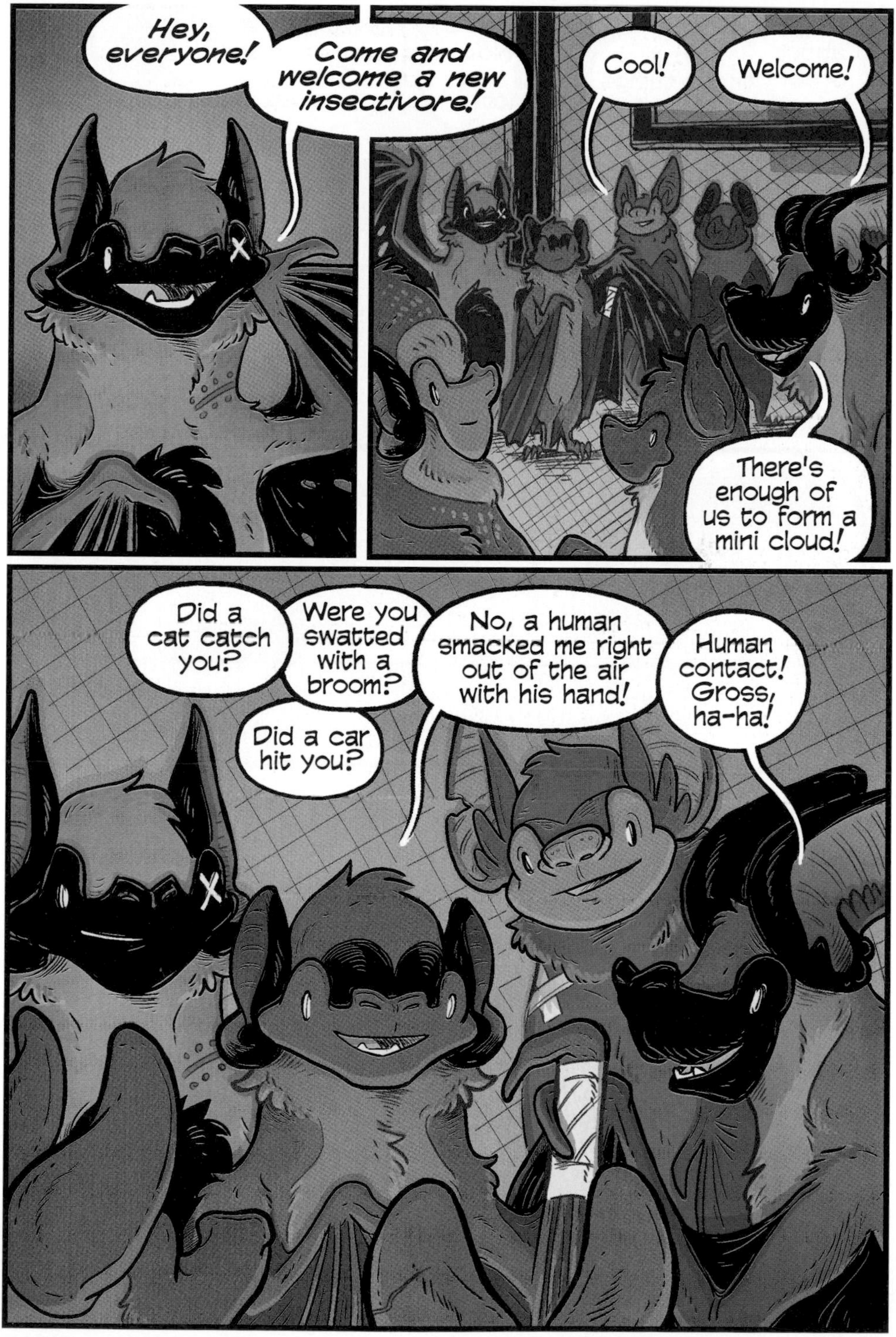
Hey, everyone!
Come and welcome a new insectivore!
Cool!
Welcome!
There's enough of us to form a mini cloud!
Did a cat catch you?
Were you swatted with a broom?
Did a car hit you?
No, a human smacked me right out of the air with his hand!
Human contact! Gross, ha-ha!

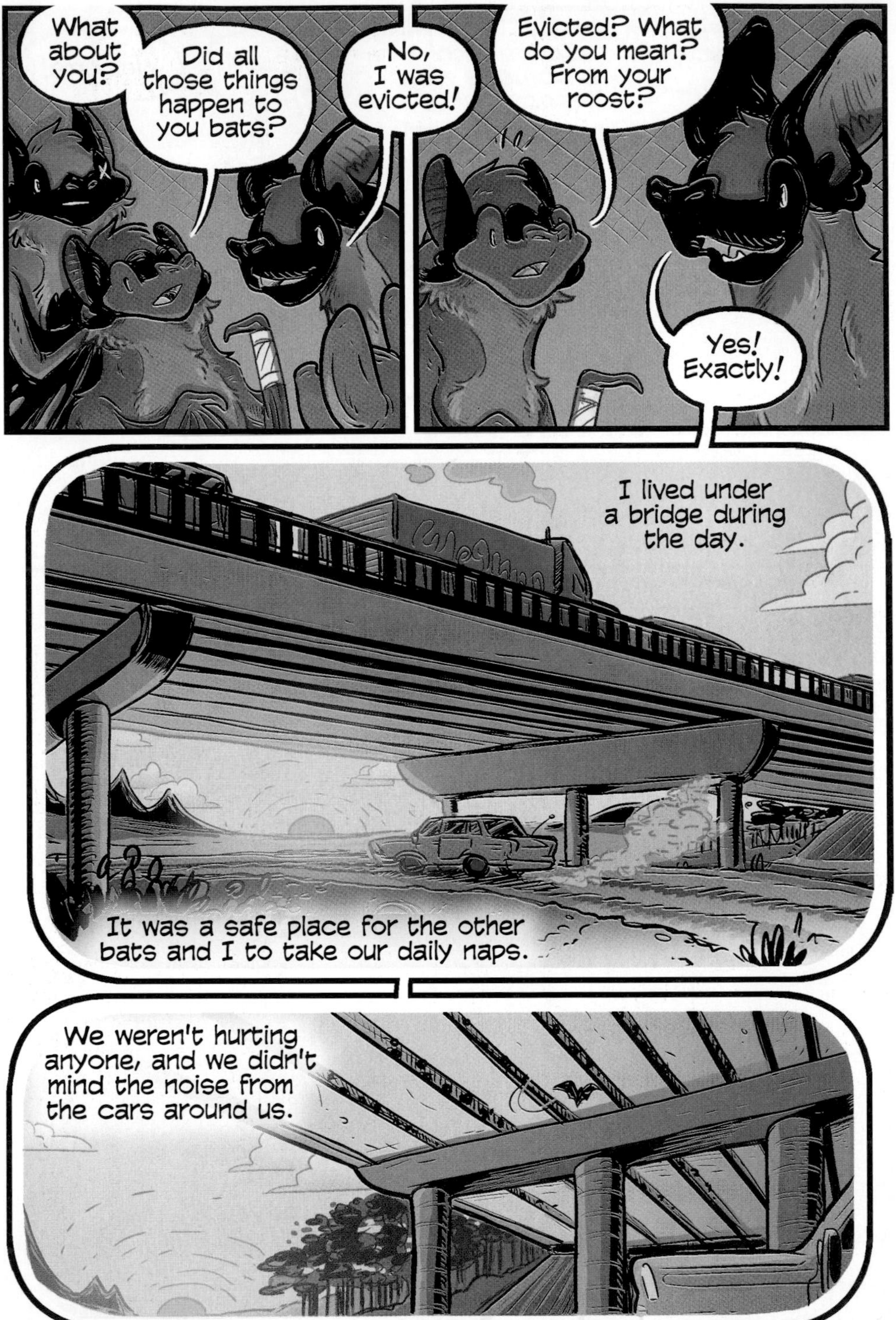
What about you?
Did all those things happen to you bats?
No, I was evicted!
Evicted? What do you mean? From your roost?
Yes! Exactly!
I lived under a bridge during the day.
It was a safe place for the other bats and I to take our daily naps.
We weren't hurting anyone, and we didn't mind the noise from the cars around us.

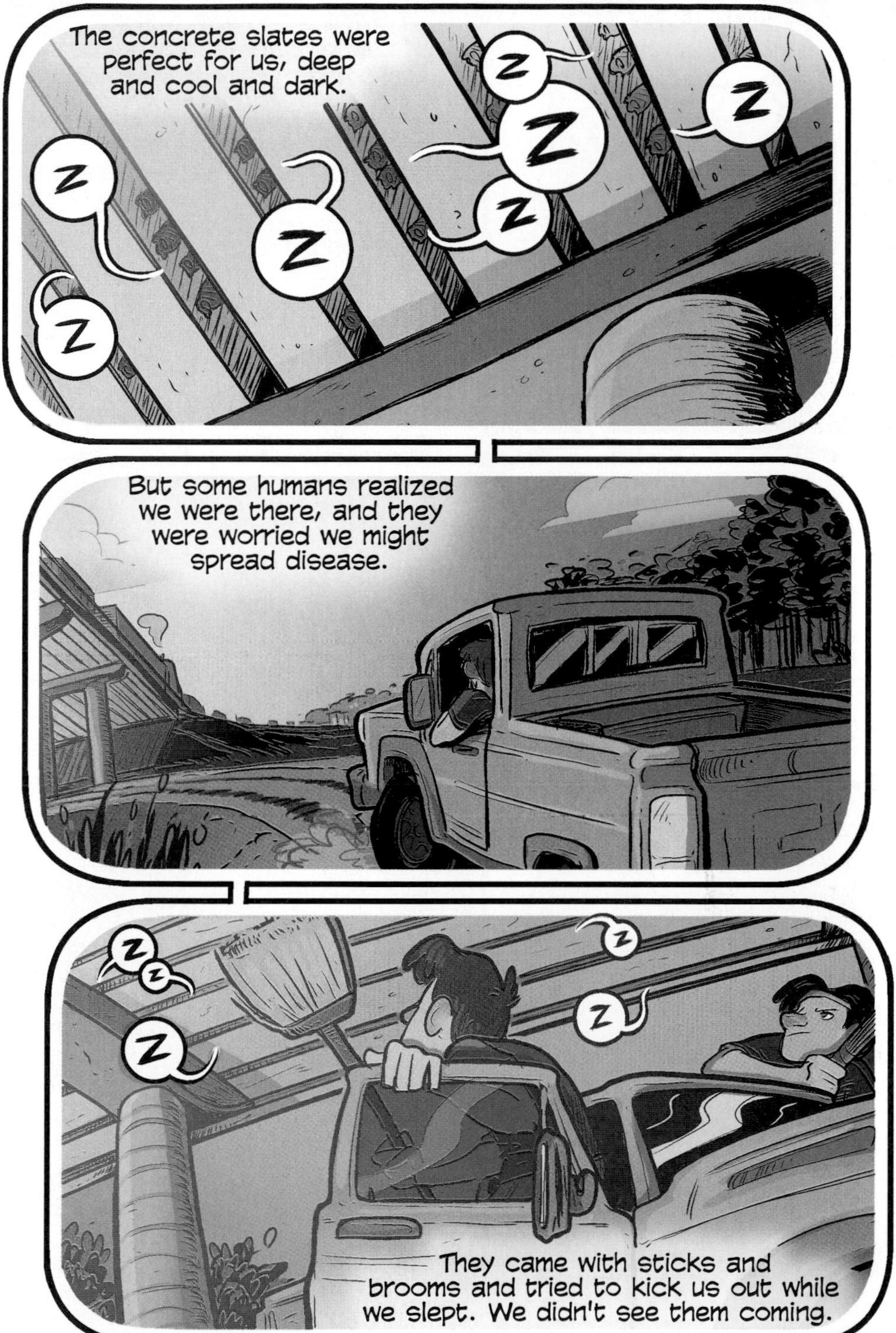
The concrete slates were perfect for us, deep and cool and dark.
Z
Z
Z
Z
Z
Z
Z
But some humans realized we were there, and they were worried we might spread disease.
Z
Z
Z
Z
Z
They came with sticks and brooms and tried to kick us out while we slept. We didn't see them coming.

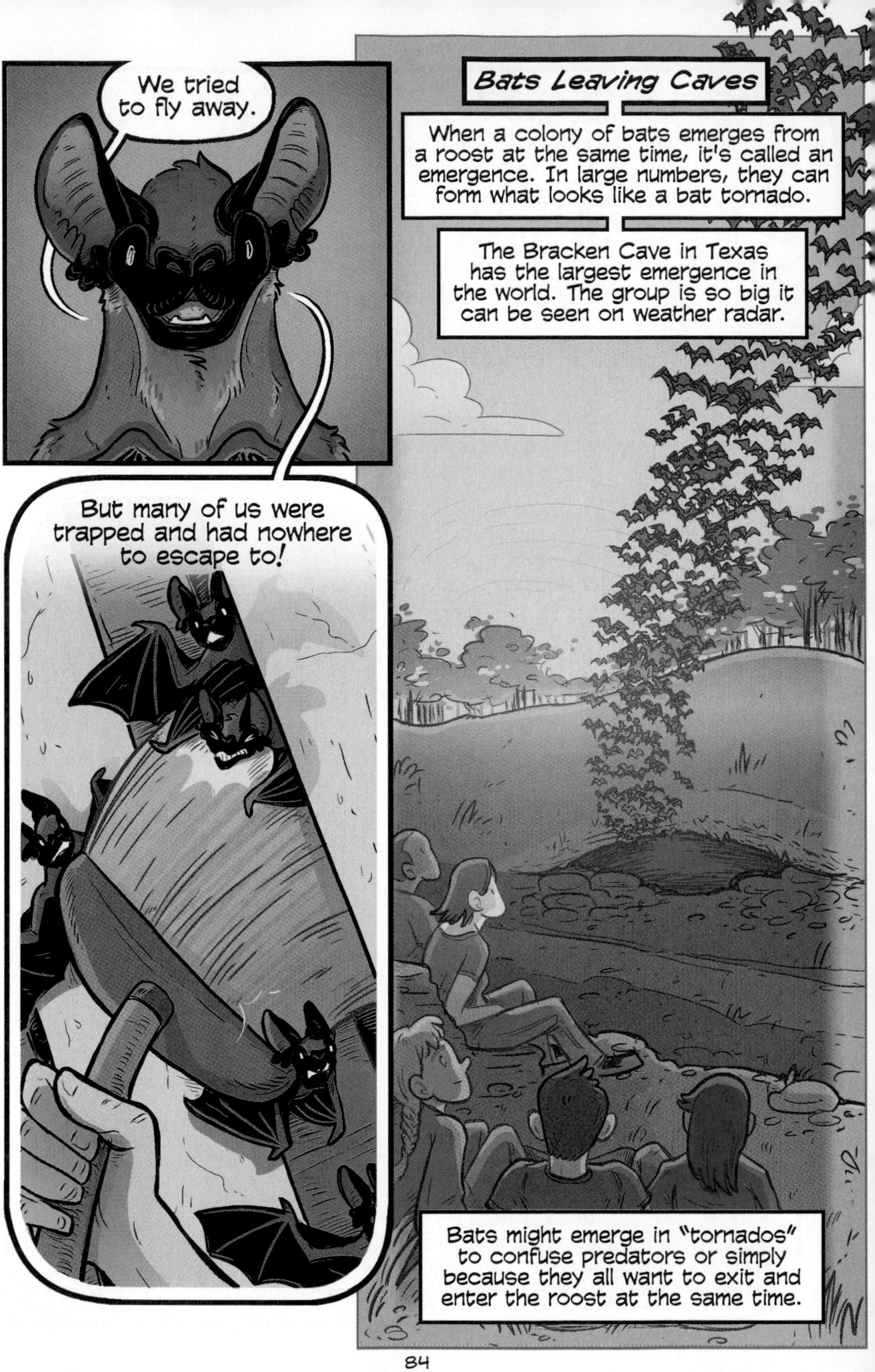
We tried to fly away.
But many of us were trapped and had nowhere to escape to!
Bats Leaving Caves
When a colony of bats emerges from a roost at the same time, it's called an emergence. In large numbers, they can form what looks like a bat tornado.
The Bracken Cave in Texas has the largest emergence in the world. The group is so big it can be seen on weather radar.
Bats might emerge in "tornados" to confuse predators or simply because they all want to exit and enter the roost at the same time.

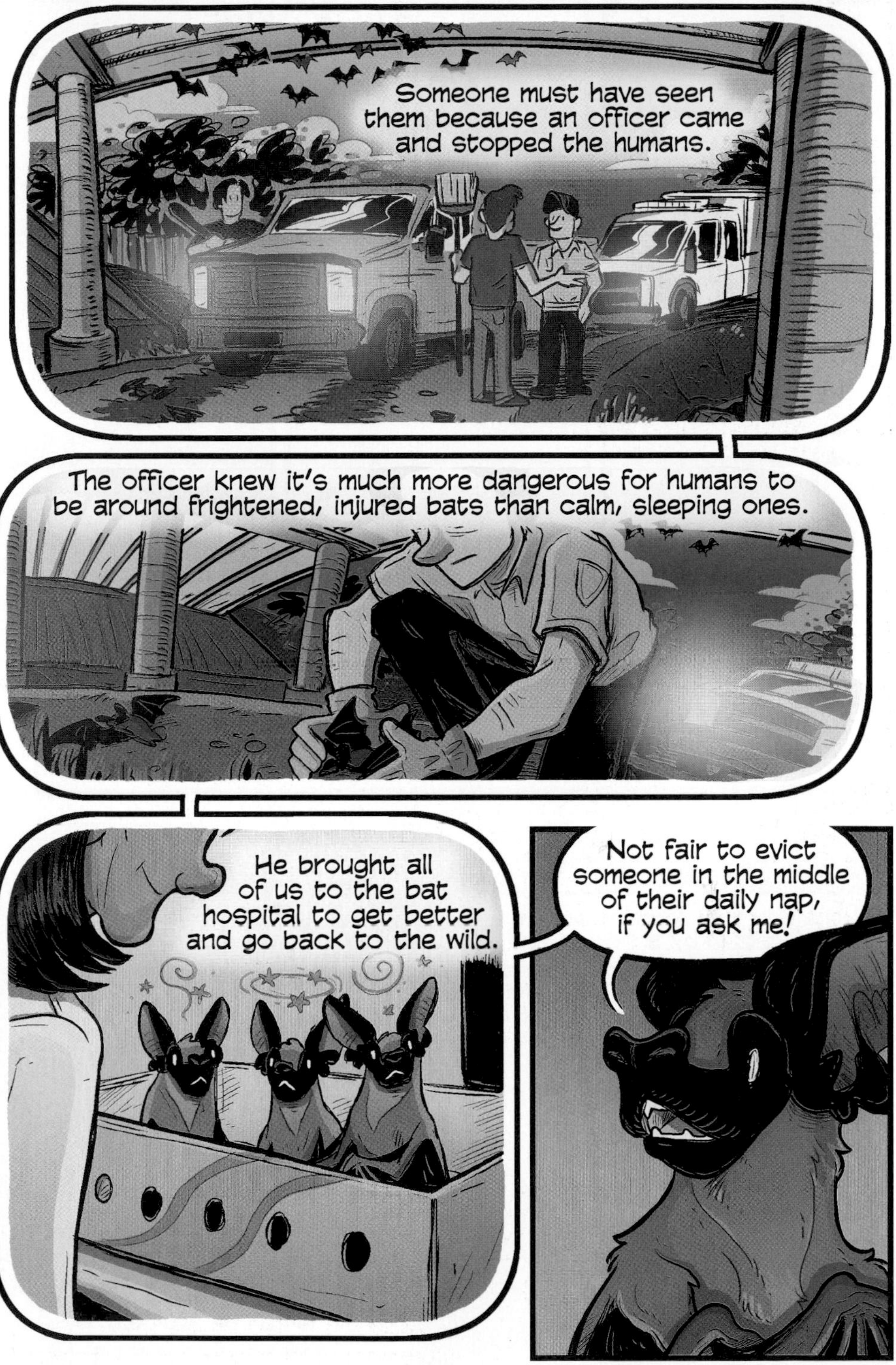
Someone must have seen them because an officer came and stopped the humans.
The officer knew it's much more dangerous for humans to be around frightened, injured bats than calm, sleeping ones.
He brought all of us to the bat hospital to get better and go back to the wild.
Not fair to evict someone in the middle of their daily nap, if you ask me!

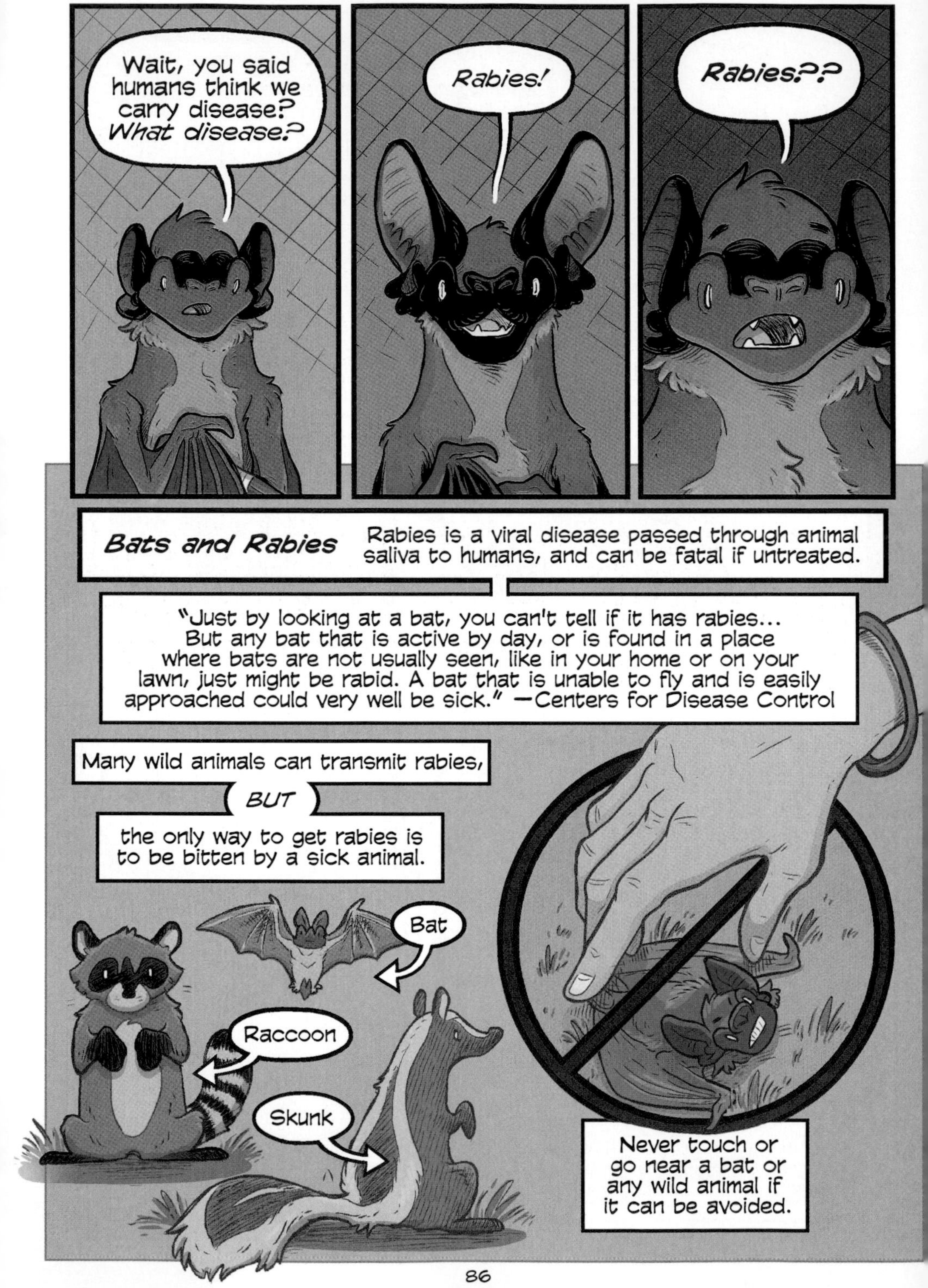
Wait, you said humans think we carry disease? *What disease?*
Rabies!
Rabies??
Bats and Rabies
Rabies is a viral disease passed through animal saliva to humans, and can be fatal if untreated.
"Just by looking at a bat, you can't tell if it has rabies... But any bat that is active by day, or is found in a place where bats are not usually seen, like in your home or on your lawn, just might be rabid. A bat that is unable to fly and is easily approached could very well be sick." —Centers for Disease Control
Many wild animals can transmit rabies,
BUT
the only way to get rabies is to be bitten by a sick animal.
Bat
Raccoon
Skunk
Never touch or go near a bat or any wild animal if it can be avoided.

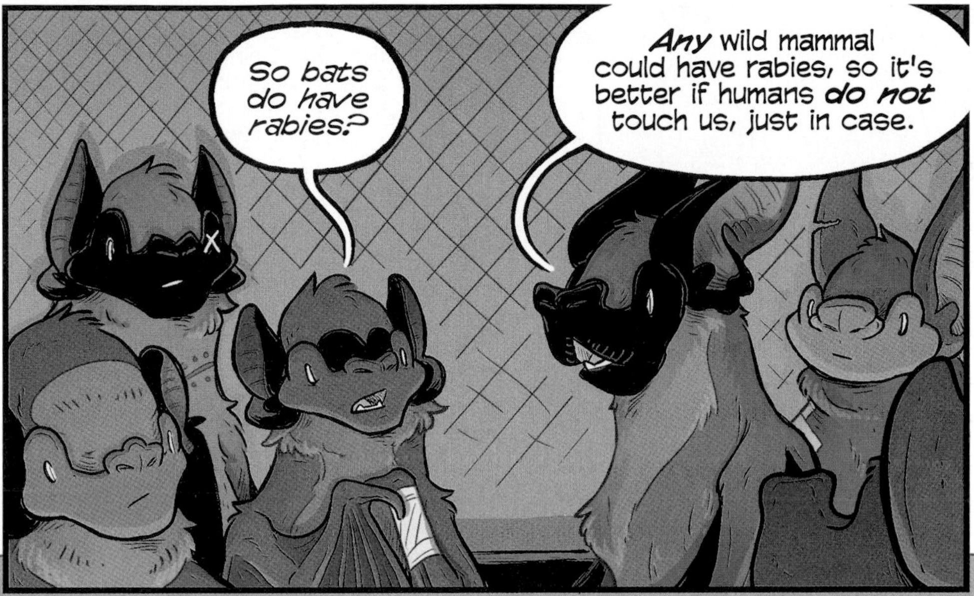
So bats do have rabies?
Any wild mammal could have rabies, so it's better if humans ***do not*** touch us, just in case.

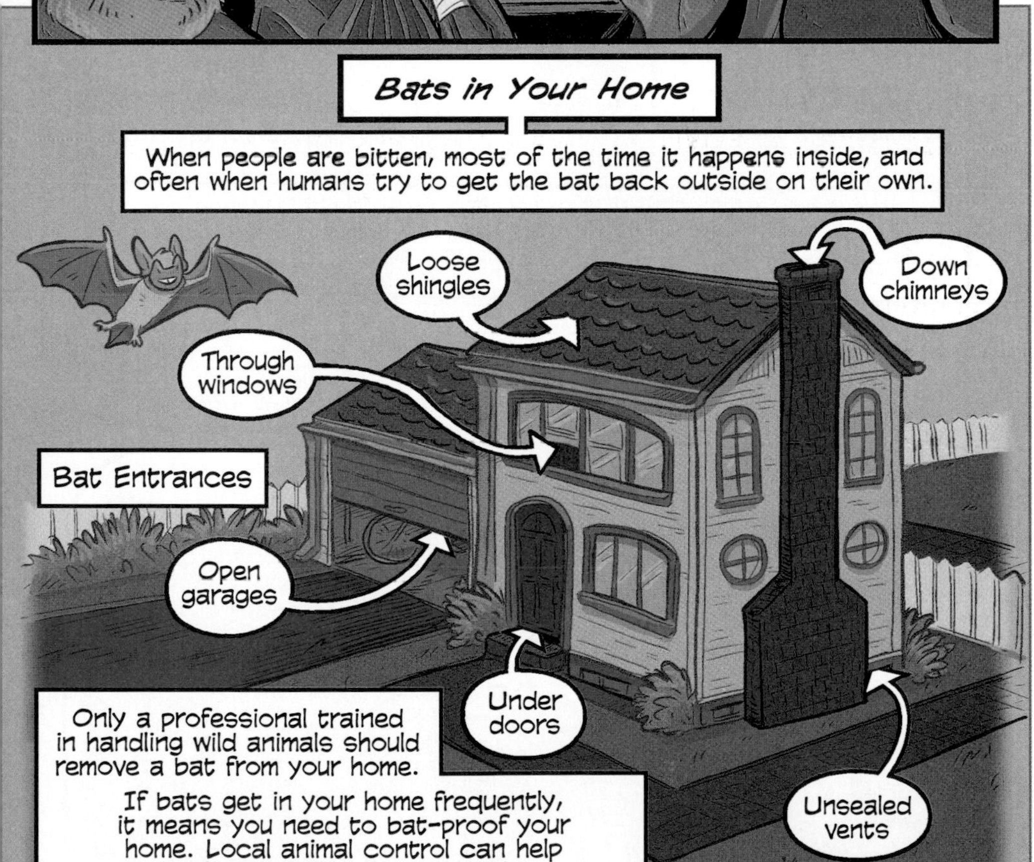
Bats in Your Home
When people are bitten, most of the time it happens inside, and often when humans try to get the bat back outside on their own.
Loose shingles
Down chimneys
Through windows
Bat Entrances
Open garages
Under doors
Unsealed vents
Only a professional trained in handling wild animals should remove a bat from your home.
If bats get in your home frequently, it means you need to bat-proof your home. Local animal control can help with prevention and removal.

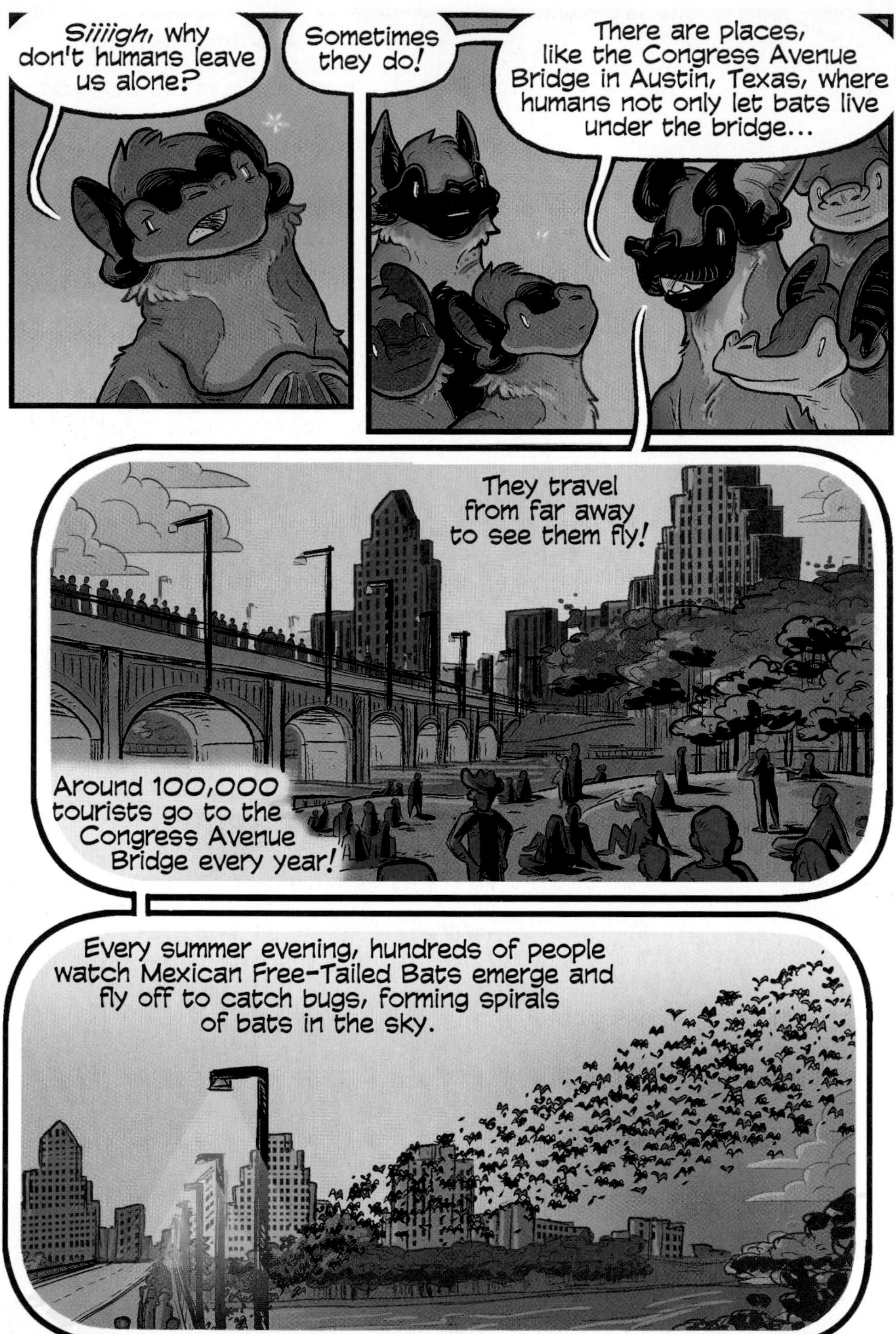
Siiiigh, why don't humans leave us alone?
Sometimes they do!
There are places, like the Congress Avenue Bridge in Austin, Texas, where humans not only let bats live under the bridge...
They travel from far away to see them fly!
Around 100,000 tourists go to the Congress Avenue Bridge every year!
Every summer evening, hundreds of people watch Mexican Free-Tailed Bats emerge and fly off to catch bugs, forming spirals of bats in the sky.

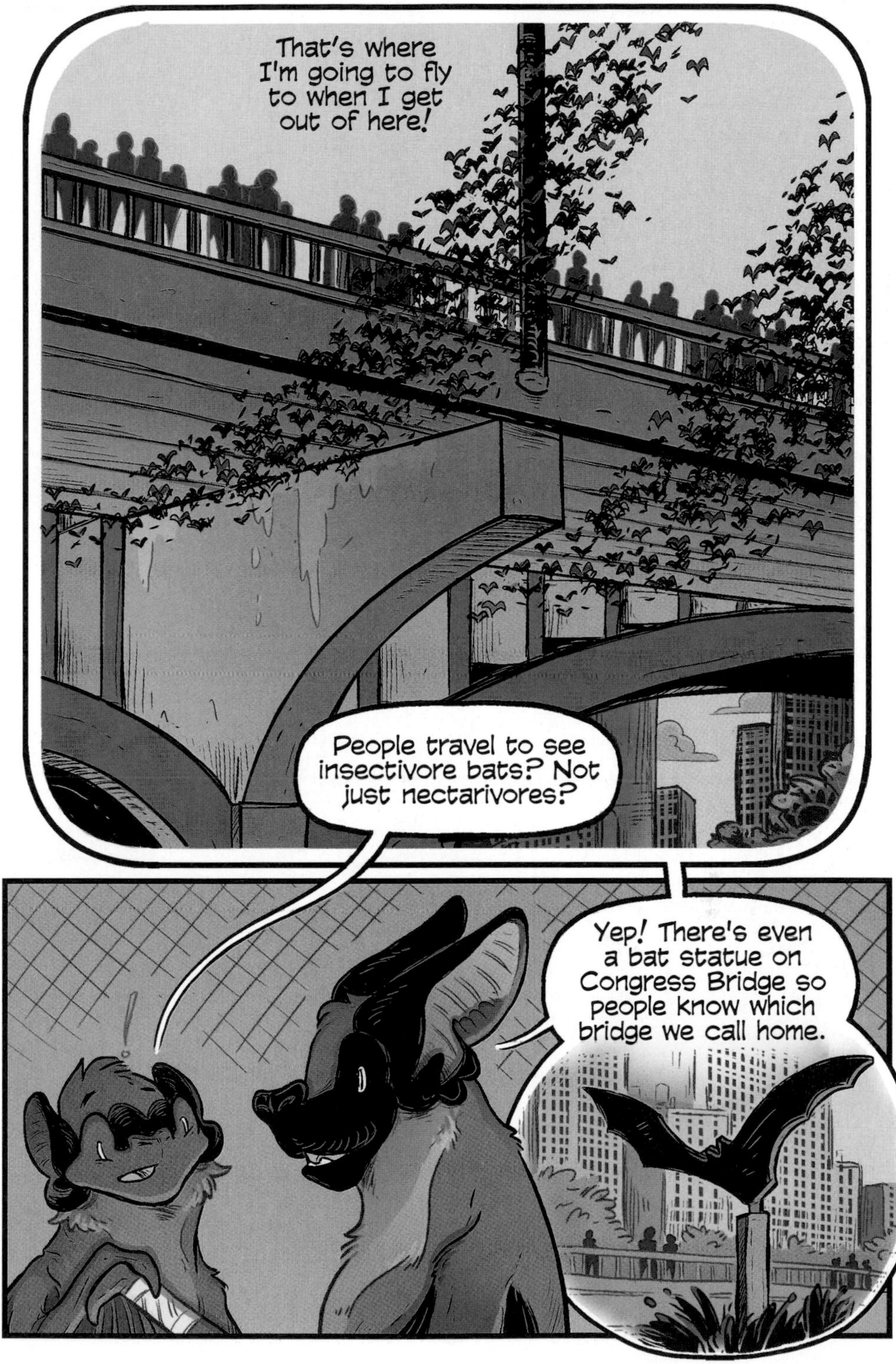
That's where I'm going to fly to when I get out of here!
People travel to see insectivore bats? Not just nectarivores?
!
Yep! There's even a bat statue on Congress Bridge so people know which bridge we call home.

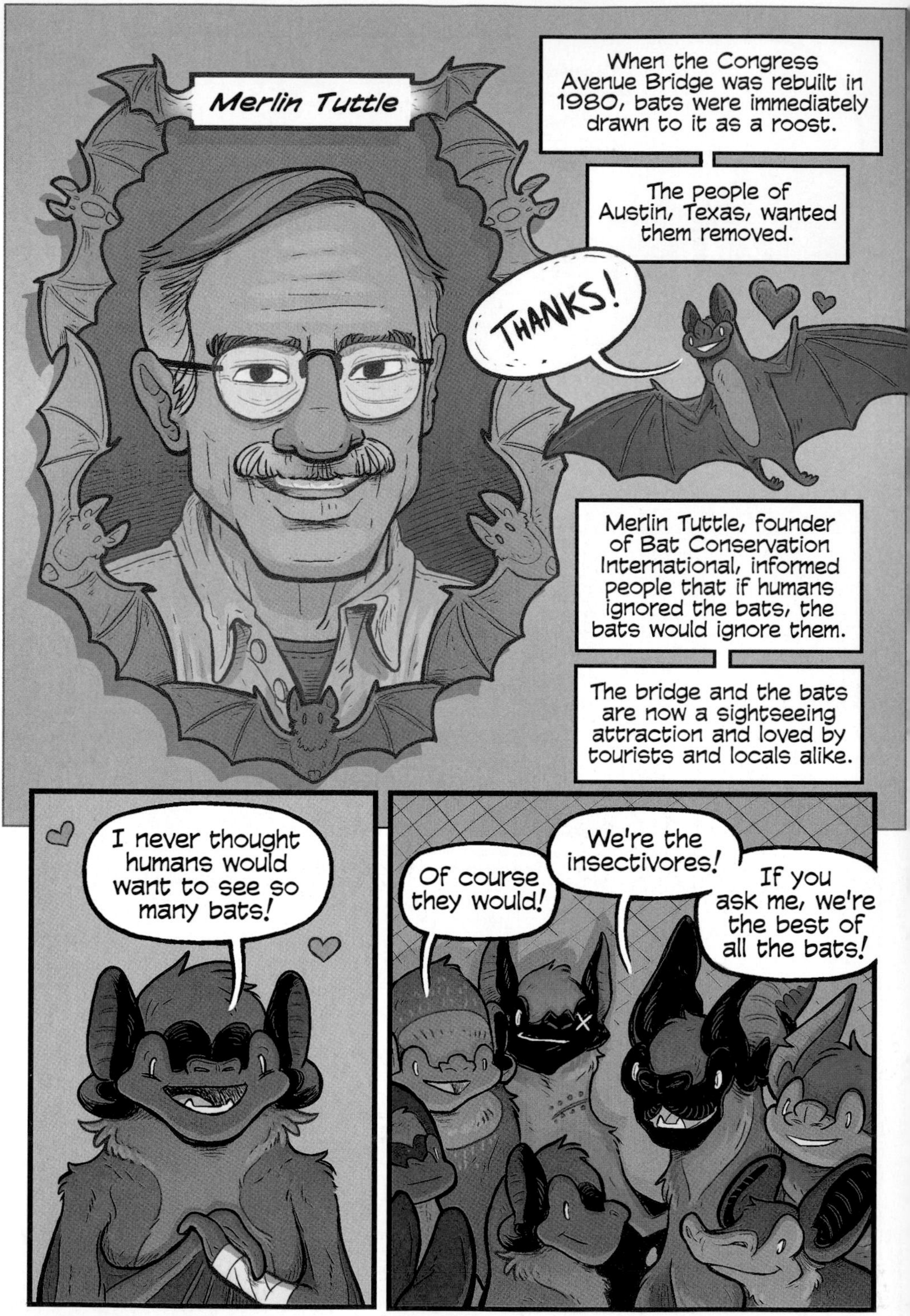
Merlin Tuttle
When the Congress Avenue Bridge was rebuilt in 1980, bats were immediately drawn to it as a roost.
The people of Austin, Texas, wanted them removed.
THANKS!
Merlin Tuttle, founder of Bat Conservation International, informed people that if humans ignored the bats, the bats would ignore them.
The bridge and the bats are now a sightseeing attraction and loved by tourists and locals alike.
I never thought humans would want to see so many bats!
Of course they would!
We're the insectivores!
If you ask me, we're the best of all the bats!

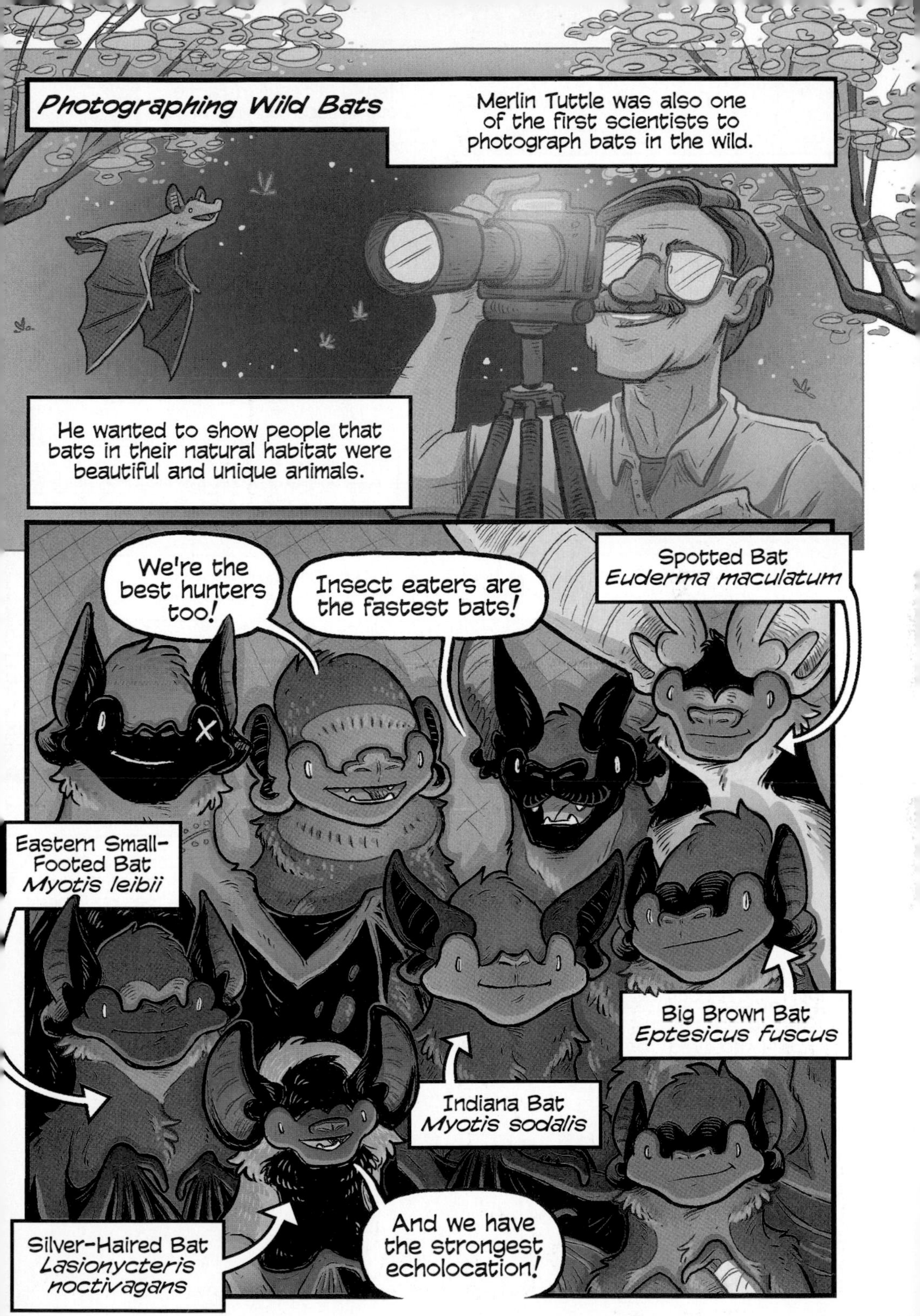
Photographing Wild Bats
Merlin Tuttle was also one of the first scientists to photograph bats in the wild.
He wanted to show people that bats in their natural habitat were beautiful and unique animals.
We're the best hunters too!
Insect eaters are the fastest bats!
Spotted Bat *Euderma maculatum*
Eastern Small-Footed Bat *Myotis leibii*
Big Brown Bat *Eptesicus fuscus*
Indiana Bat *Myotis sodalis*
Silver-Haired Bat *Lasionycteris noctivagans*
And we have the strongest echolocation!

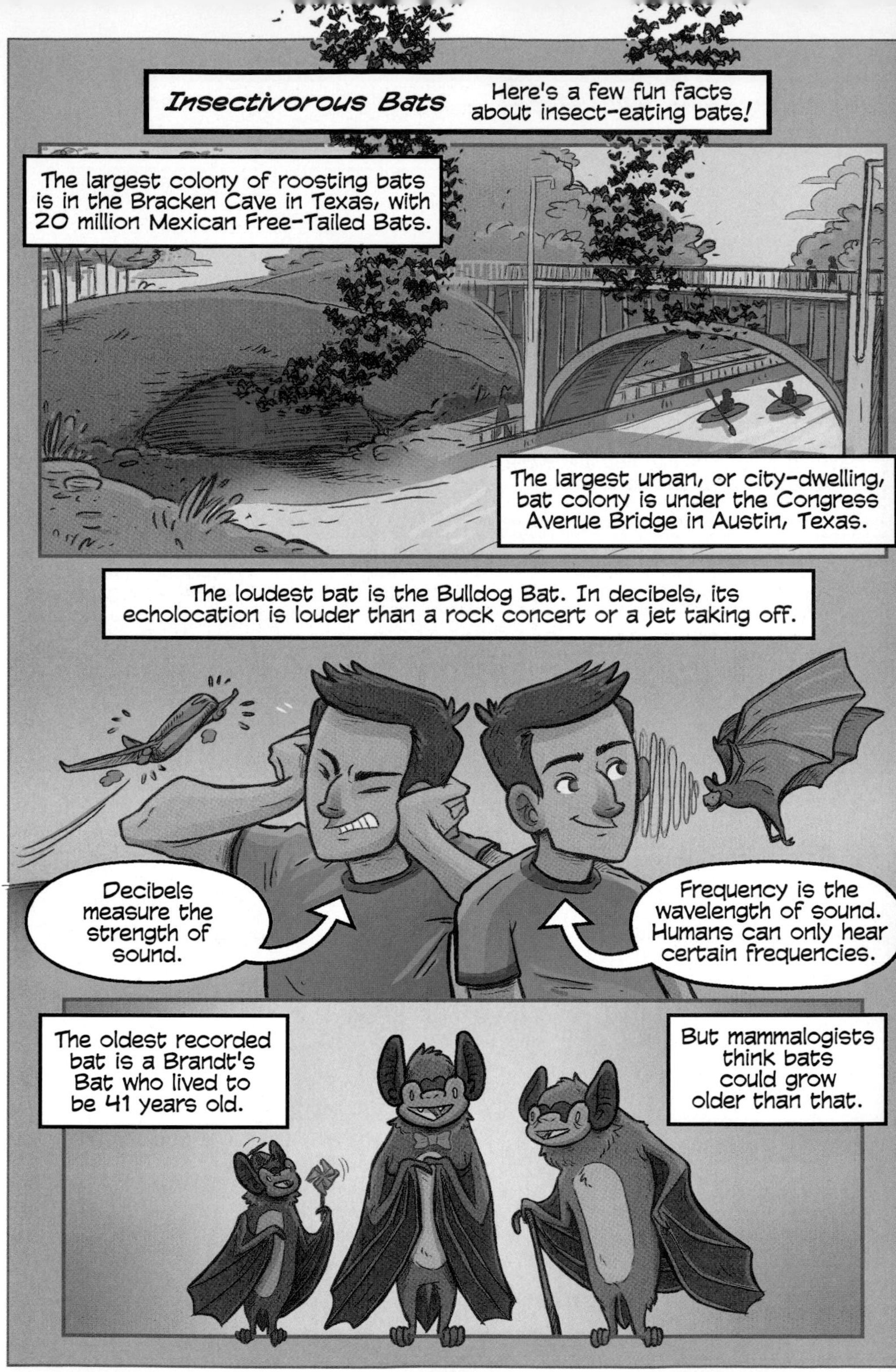
Insectivorous Bats
Here's a few fun facts about insect-eating bats!
The largest colony of roosting bats is in the Bracken Cave in Texas, with 20 million Mexican Free-Tailed Bats.
The largest urban, or city-dwelling, bat colony is under the Congress Avenue Bridge in Austin, Texas.
The loudest bat is the Bulldog Bat. In decibels, its echolocation is louder than a rock concert or a jet taking off.
Decibels measure the strength of sound.
Frequency is the wavelength of sound. Humans can only hear certain frequencies.
The oldest recorded bat is a Brandt's Bat who lived to be 41 years old.
But mammalogists think bats could grow older than that.

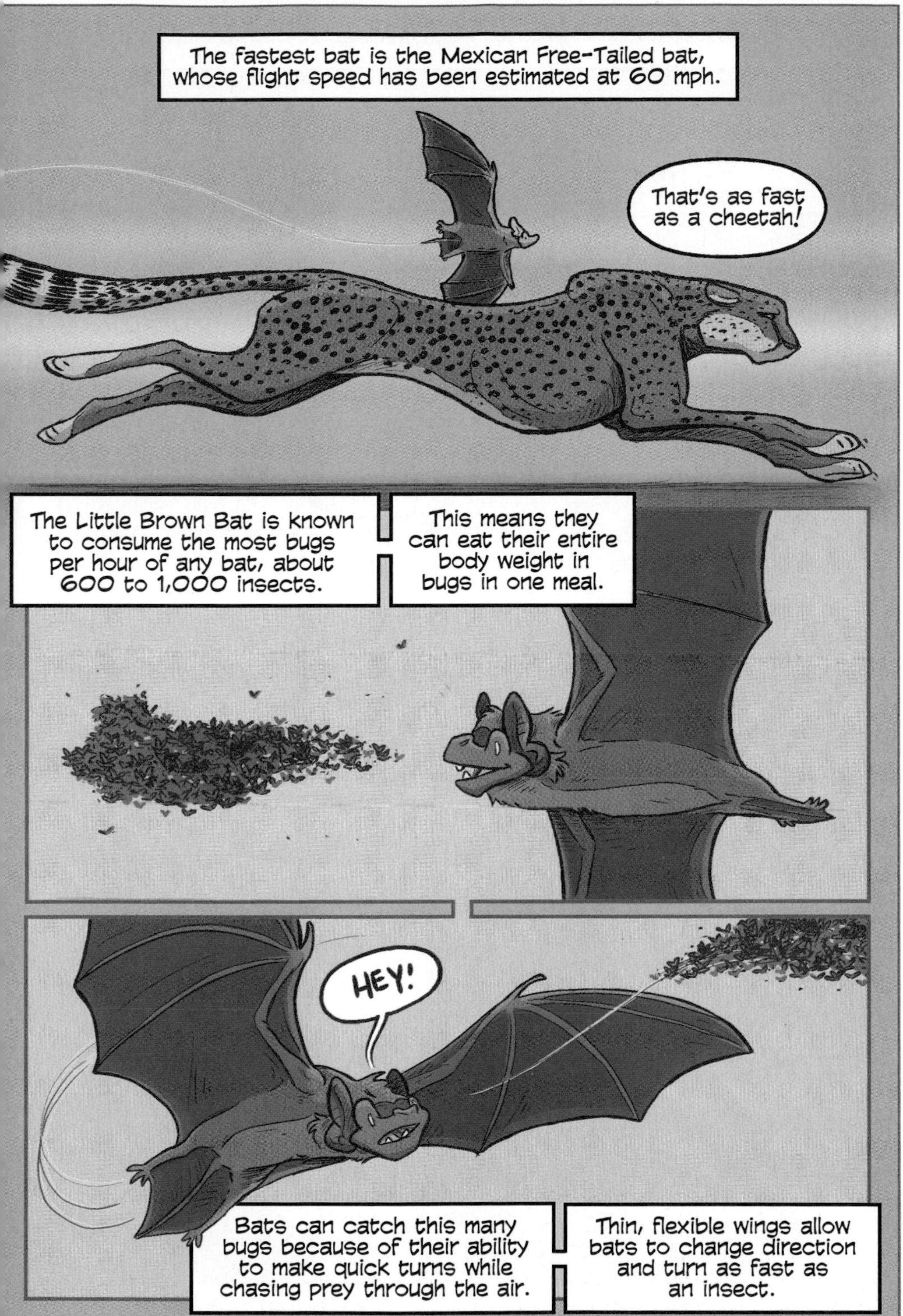

The fastest bat is the Mexican Free-Tailed bat, whose flight speed has been estimated at 60 mph.
That's as fast as a cheetah!
The Little Brown Bat is known to consume the most bugs per hour of any bat, about 600 to 1,000 insects.
This means they can eat their entire body weight in bugs in one meal.
HEY!
Bats can catch this many bugs because of their ability to make quick turns while chasing prey through the air.
Thin, flexible wings allow bats to change direction and turn as fast as an insect.

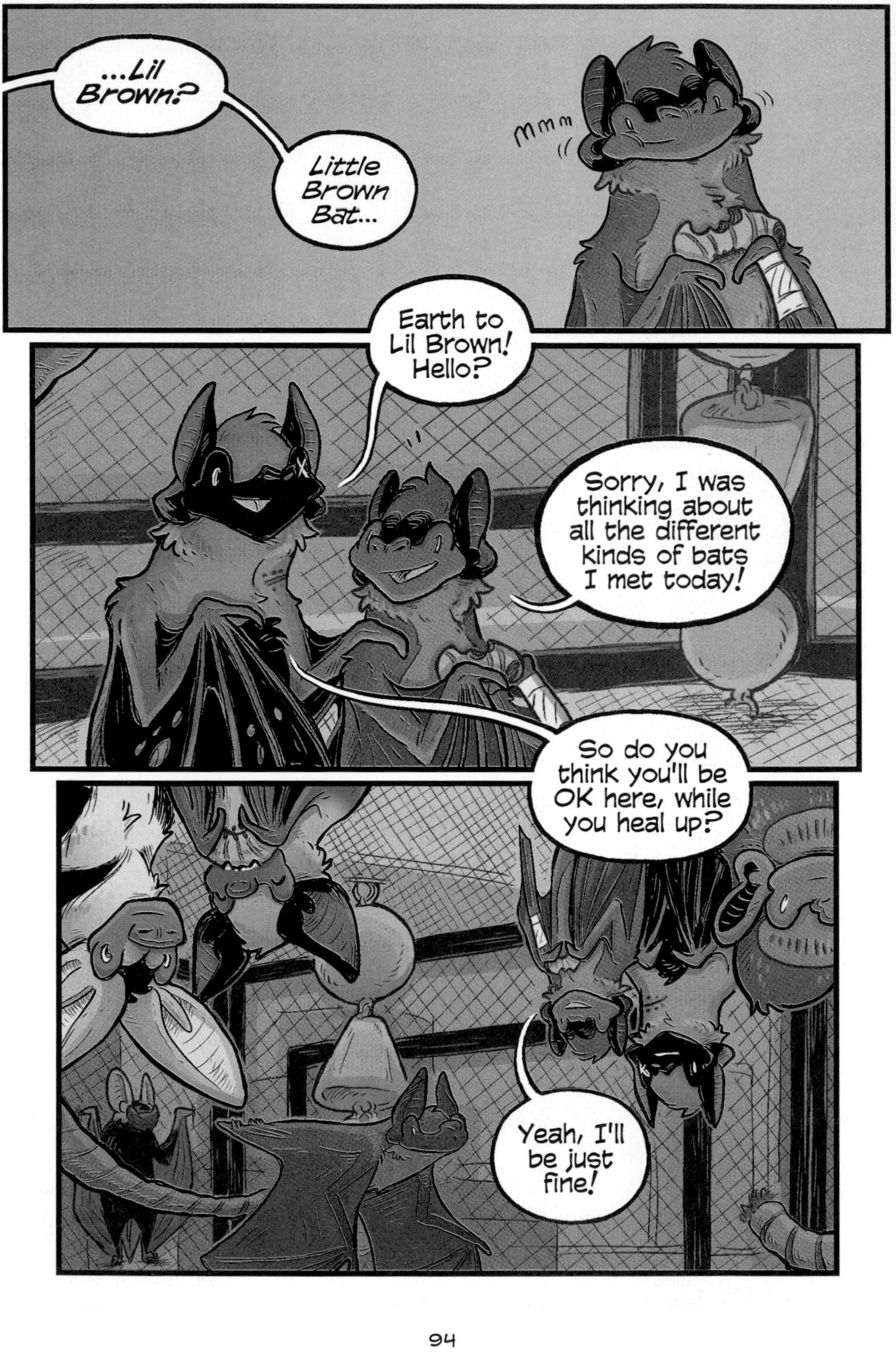
...Lil Brown?
Little Brown Bat...
Mmm
Earth to Lil Brown! Hello?
Sorry, I was thinking about all the different kinds of bats I met today!
So do you think you'll be OK here, while you heal up?
Yeah, I'll be just fine!

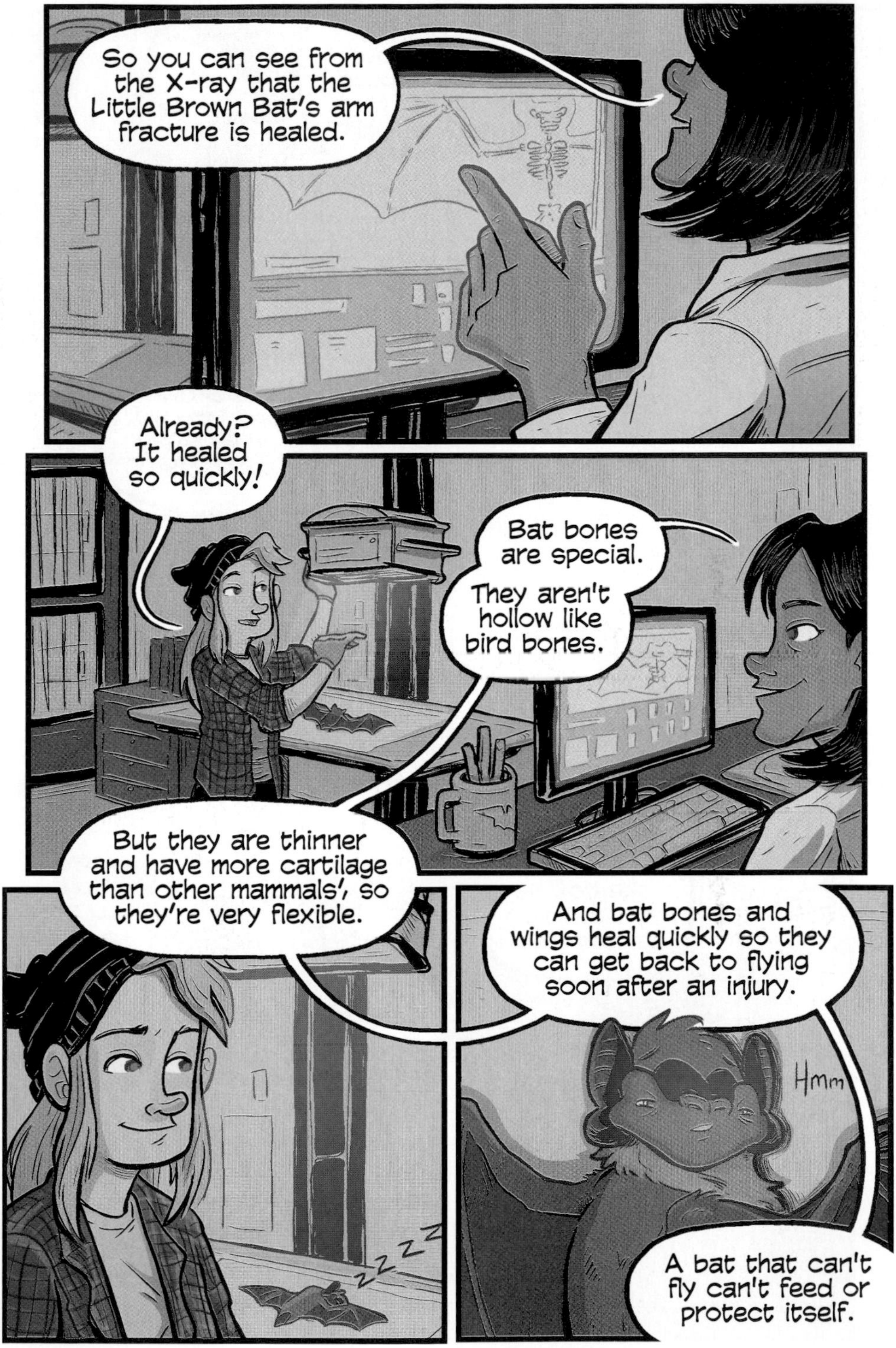
So you can see from the X-ray that the Little Brown Bat's arm fracture is healed.
Already? It healed so quickly!
Bat bones are special.
They aren't hollow like bird bones.
But they are thinner and have more cartilage than other mammals', so they're very flexible.
And bat bones and wings heal quickly so they can get back to flying soon after an injury.
Hmm
ZZZZ
A bat that can't fly can't feed or protect itself.

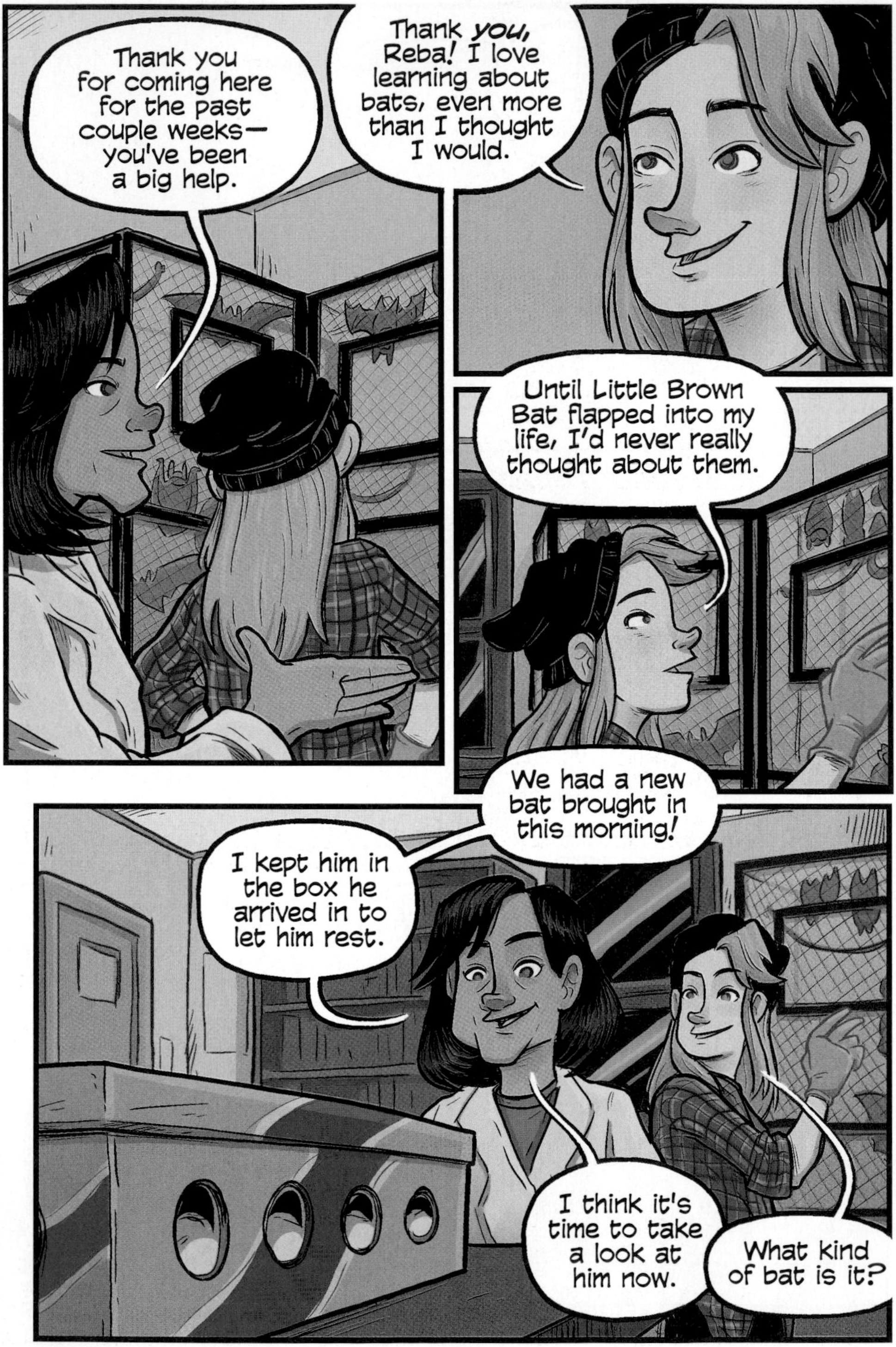
Thank you for coming here for the past couple weeks— you've been a big help.
Thank *you*, Reba! I love learning about bats, even more than I thought I would.
Until Little Brown Bat flapped into my life, I'd never really thought about them.
We had a new bat brought in this morning!
I kept him in the box he arrived in to let him rest.
I think it's time to take a look at him now.
What kind of bat is it?

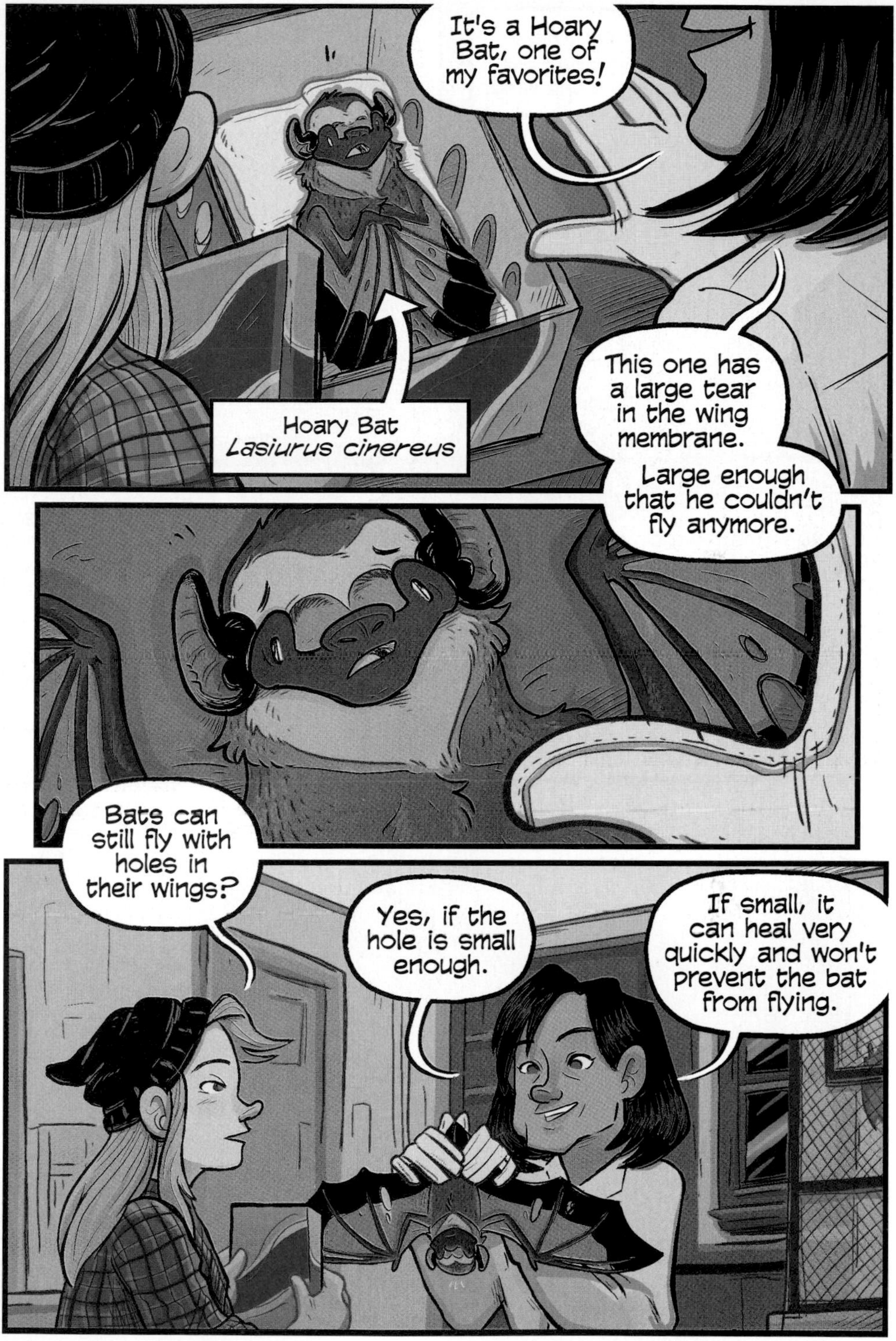
It's a Hoary Bat, one of my favorites!
Hoary Bat
Lasiurus cinereus
This one has a large tear in the wing membrane.
Large enough that he couldn't fly anymore.
Bats can still fly with holes in their wings?
Yes, if the hole is small enough.
If small, it can heal very quickly and won't prevent the bat from flying.

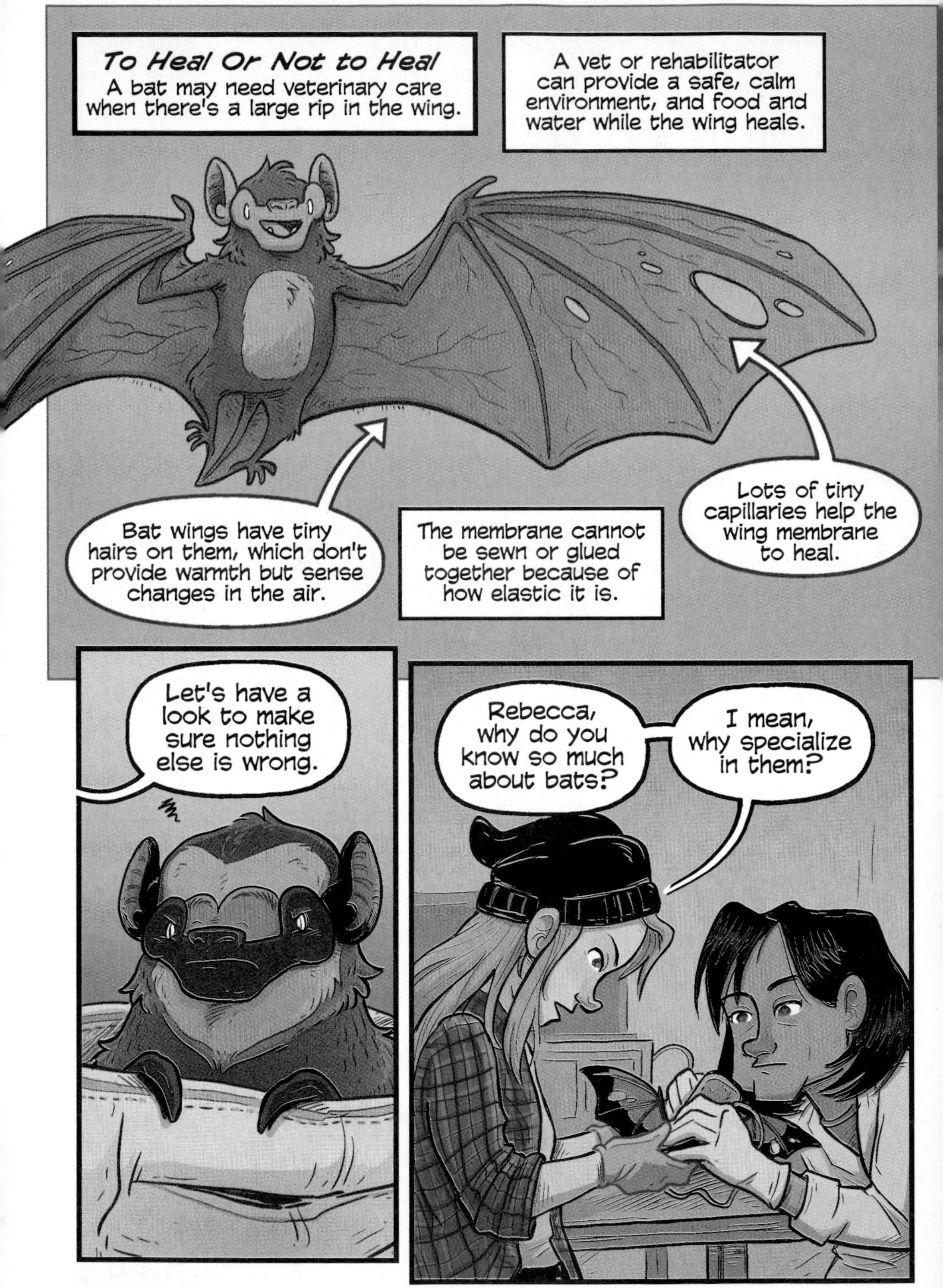
To Heal Or Not to Heal
A bat may need veterinary care when there's a large rip in the wing.
A vet or rehabilitator can provide a safe, calm environment, and food and water while the wing heals.
Bat wings have tiny hairs on them, which don't provide warmth but sense changes in the air.
The membrane cannot be sewn or glued together because of how elastic it is.
Lots of tiny capillaries help the wing membrane to heal.
Let's have a look to make sure nothing else is wrong.
Rebecca, why do you know so much about bats?
I mean, why specialize in them?

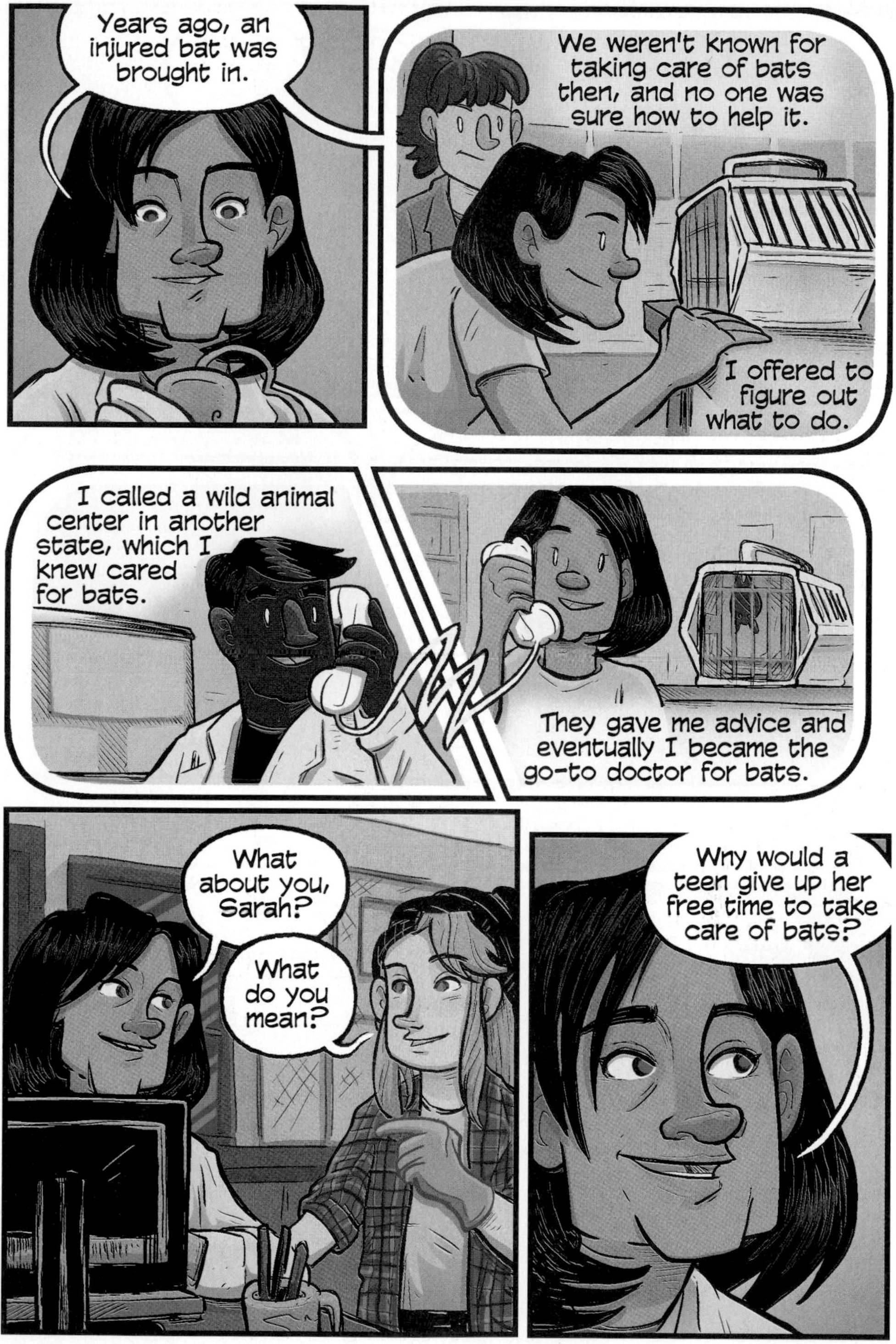
Years ago, an injured bat was brought in.
We weren't known for taking care of bats then, and no one was sure how to help it.
I offered to figure out what to do.
I called a wild animal center in another state, which I knew cared for bats.
They gave me advice and eventually I became the go-to doctor for bats.
What about you, Sarah?
What do you mean?
Why would a teen give up her free time to take care of bats?

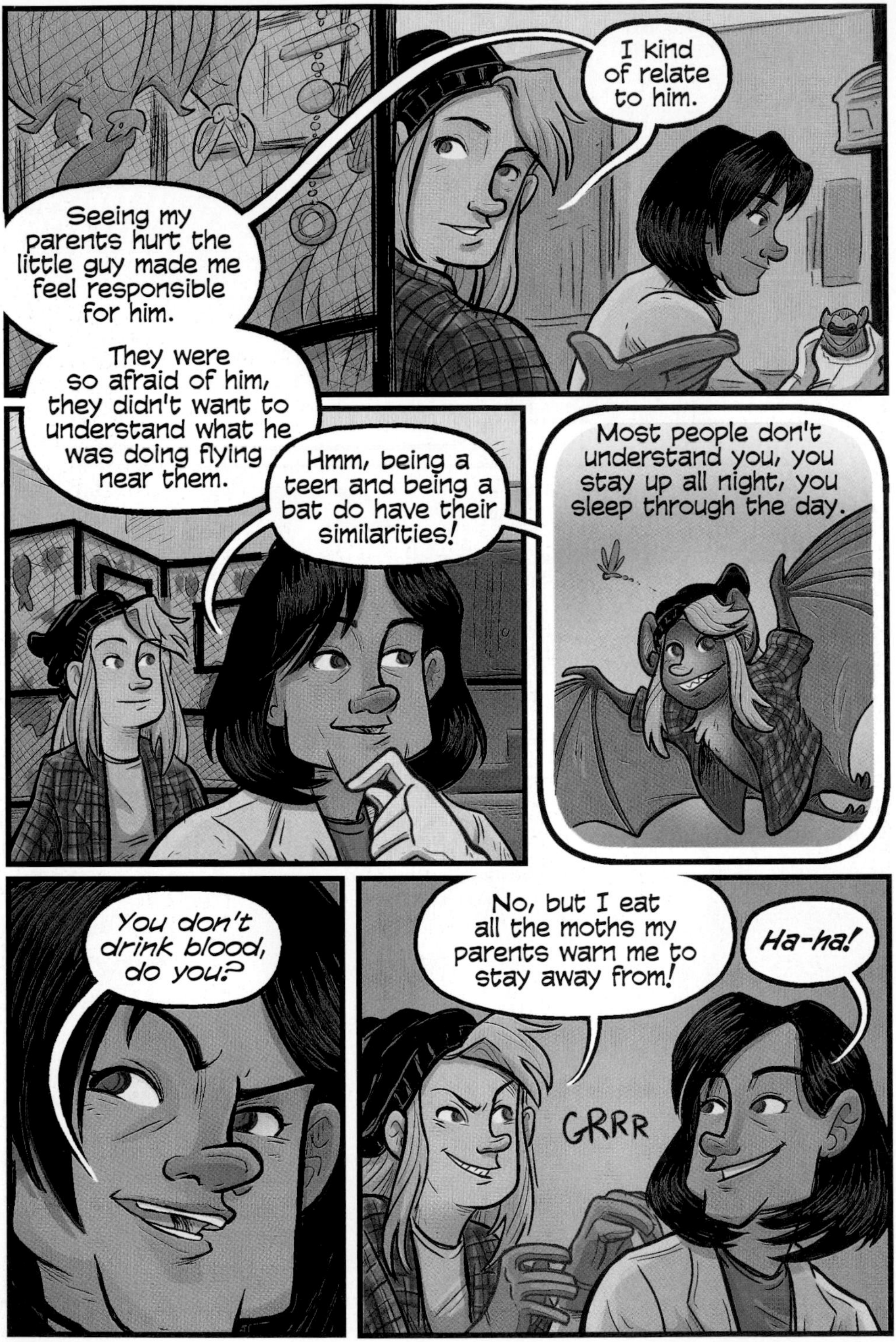
I kind of relate to him.
Seeing my parents hurt the little guy made me feel responsible for him.
They were so afraid of him, they didn't want to understand what he was doing flying near them.
Hmm, being a teen and being a bat do have their similarities!
Most people don't understand you, you stay up all night, you sleep through the day.
You don't drink blood, do you?
No, but I eat all the moths my parents warn me to stay away from!
Ha-ha!
GRRR

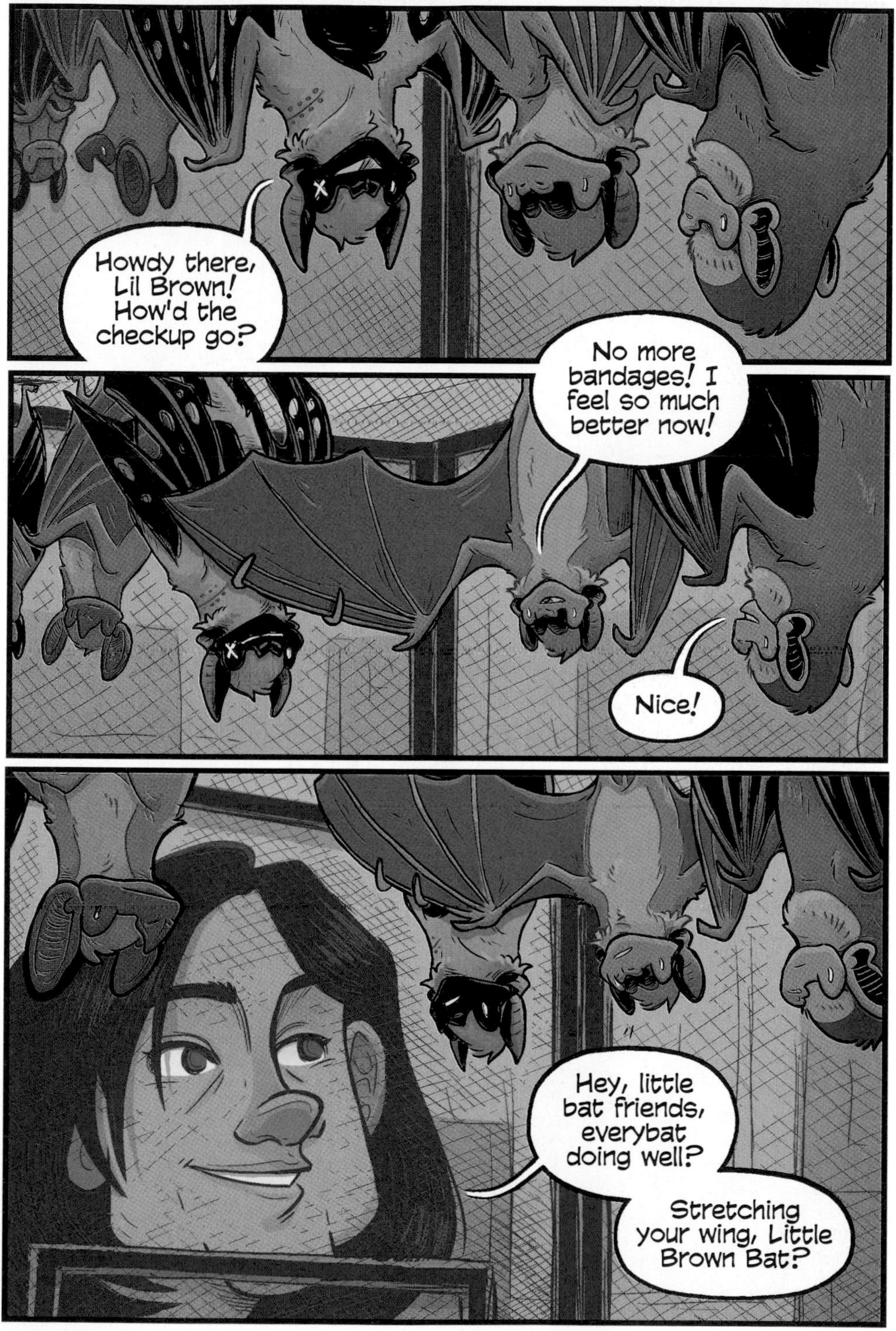
Howdy there, Lil Brown! How'd the checkup go?
No more bandages! I feel so much better now!
Nice!
Hey, little bat friends, everybat doing well?
Stretching your wing, Little Brown Bat?

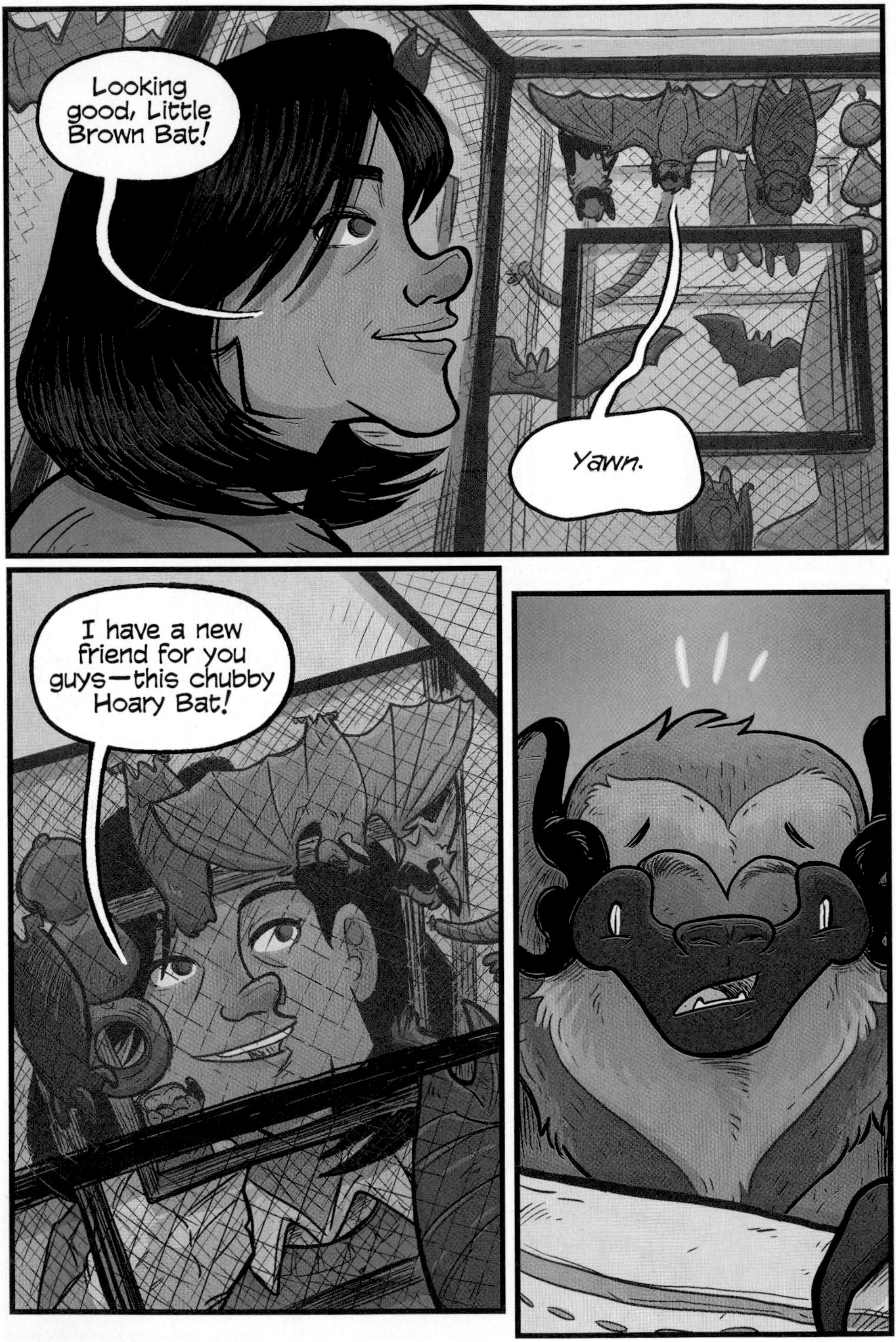
Looking good, Little Brown Bat!
Yawn.
I have a new friend for you guys—this chubby Hoary Bat!

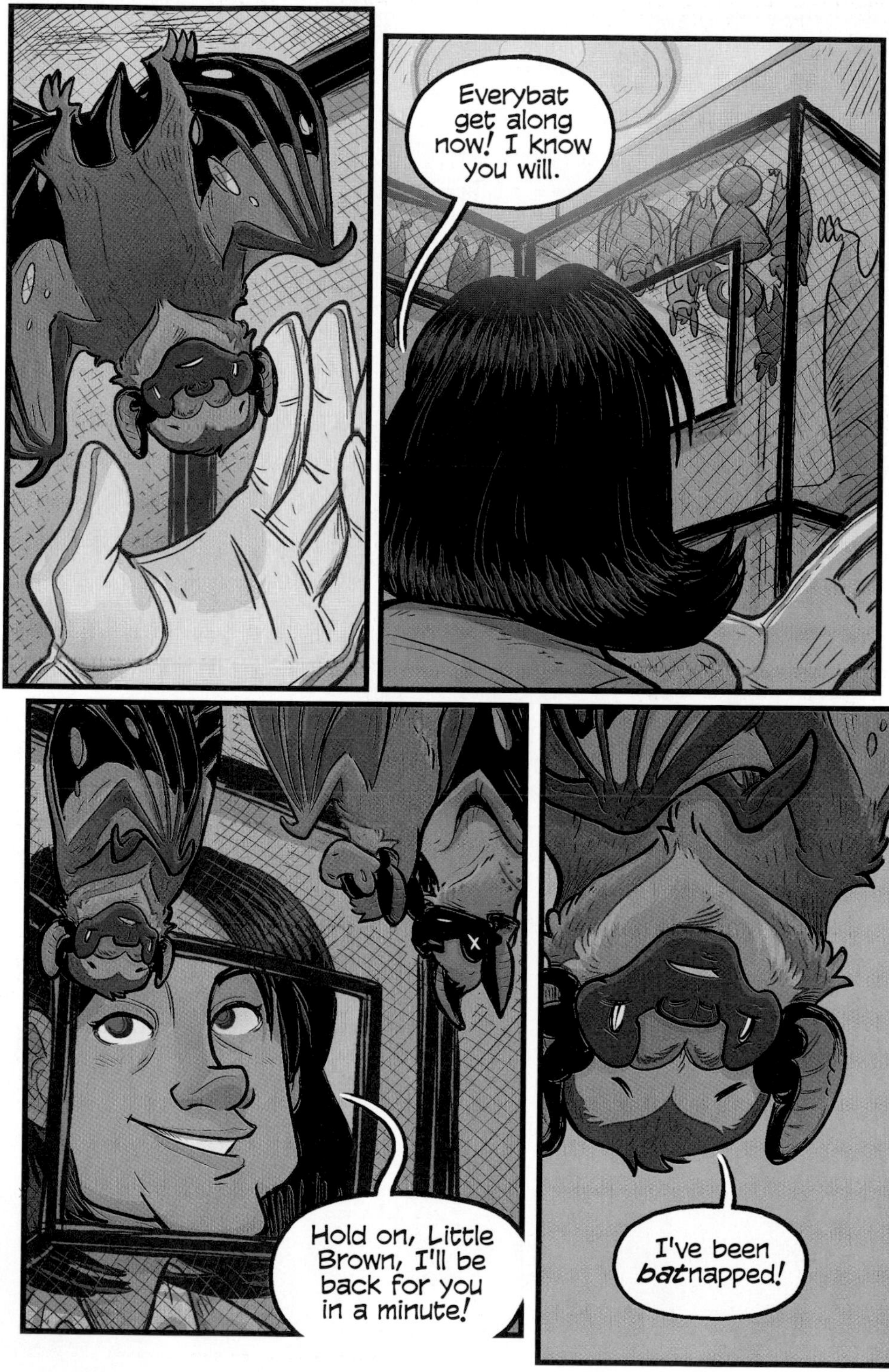
Everybat get along now! I know you will.
Hold on, Little Brown, I'll be back for you in a minute!
I've been ***bat***napped!

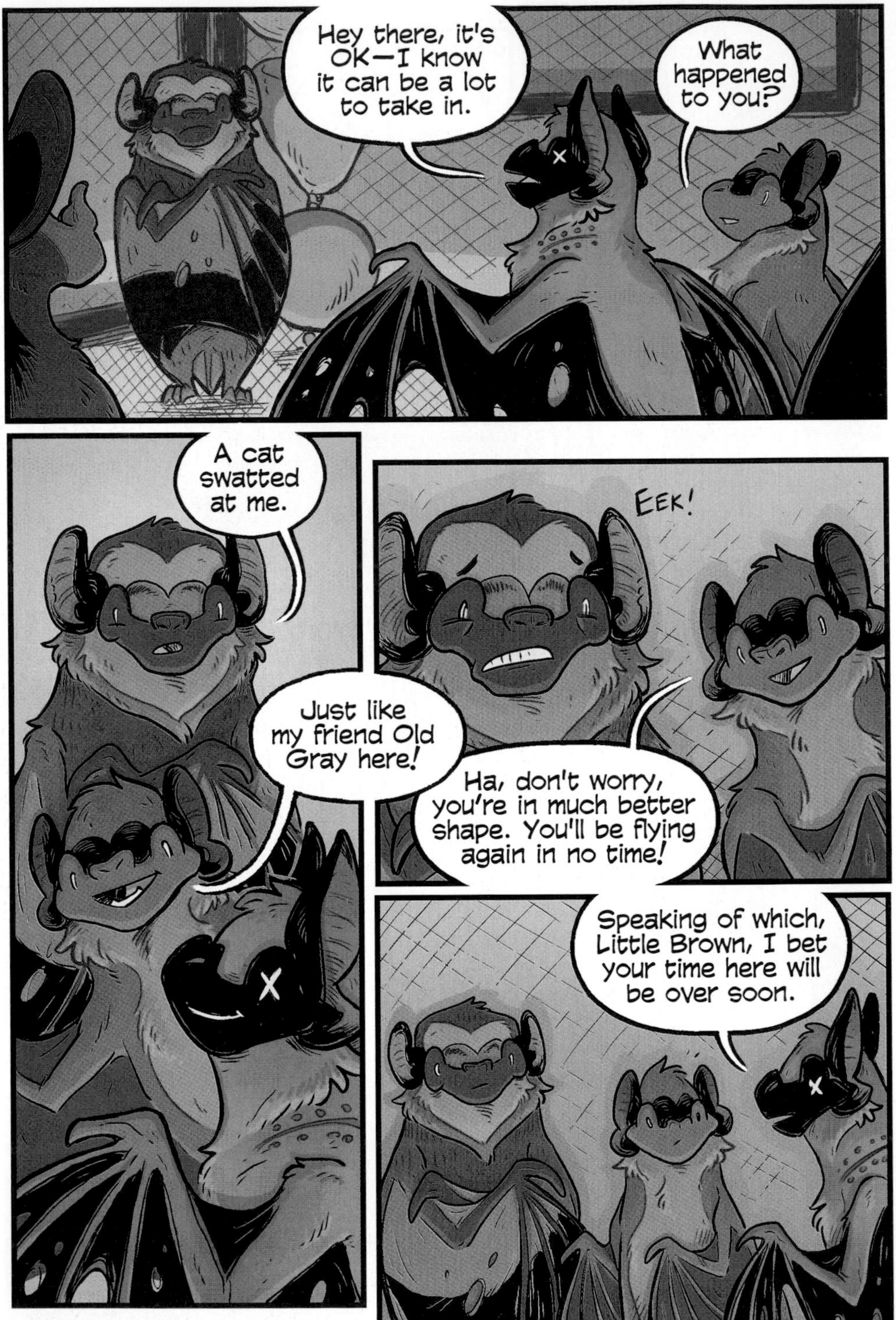
Hey there, it's OK—I know it can be a lot to take in.
What happened to you?
A cat swatted at me.
Just like my friend Old Gray here!
EEK!
Ha, don't worry, you're in much better shape. You'll be flying again in no time!
Speaking of which, Little Brown, I bet your time here will be over soon.

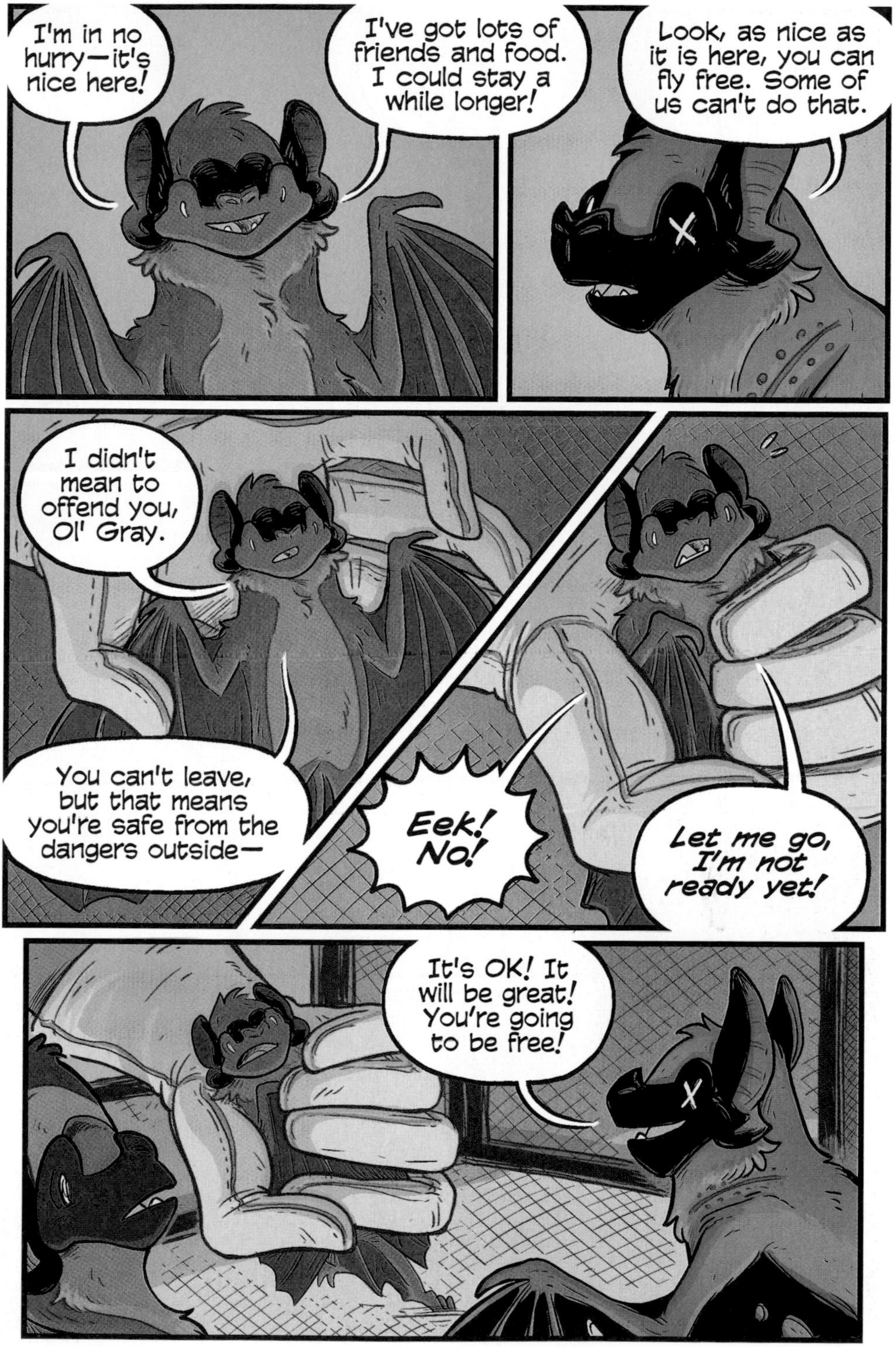
I'm in no hurry—it's nice here!
I've got lots of friends and food. I could stay a while longer!
Look, as nice as it is here, you can fly free. Some of us can't do that.
I didn't mean to offend you, Ol' Gray.
You can't leave, but that means you're safe from the dangers outside—
Eek! No!
Let me go, I'm not ready yet!
It's OK! It will be great! You're going to be free!

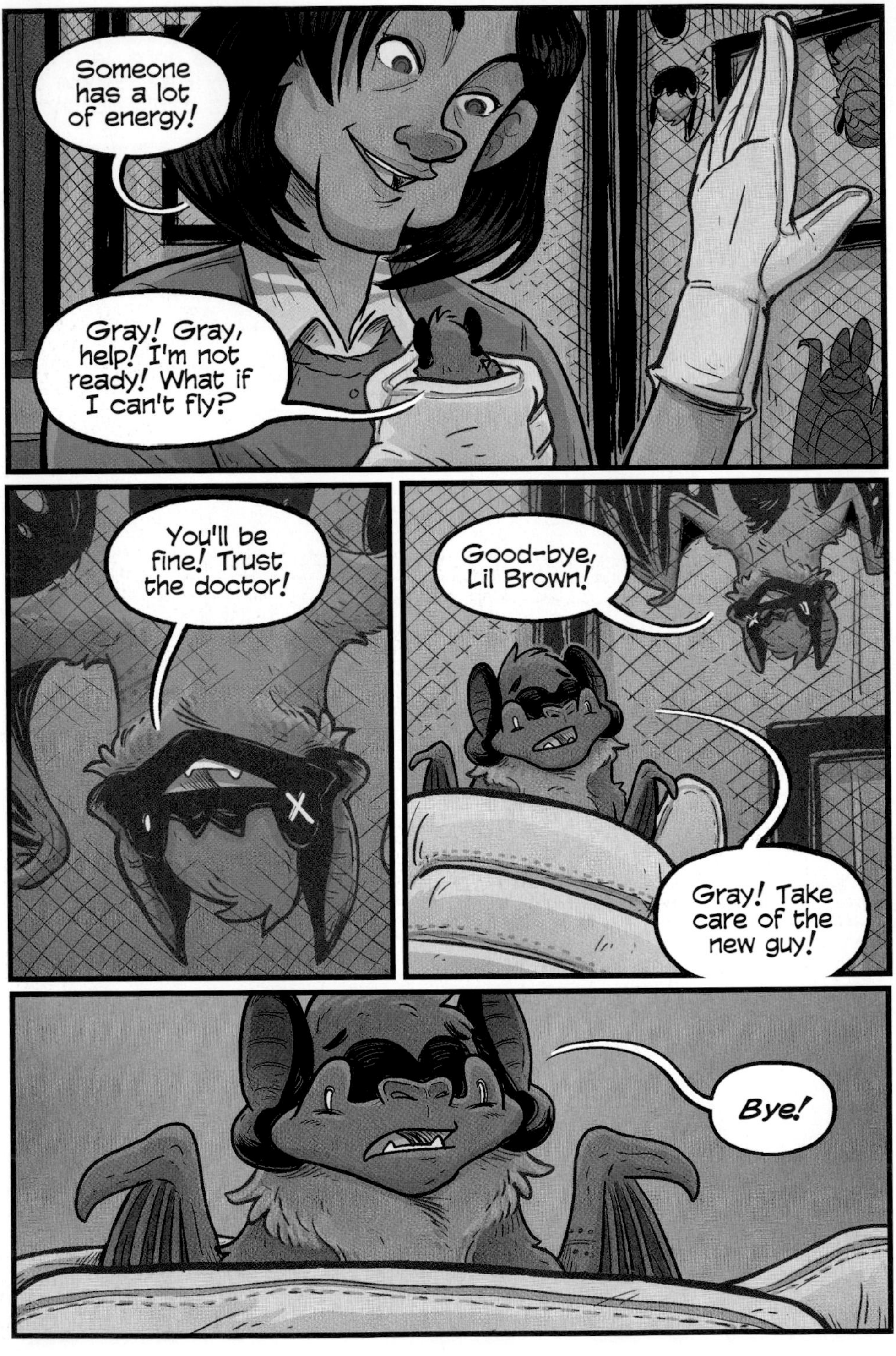
Someone has a lot of energy!
Gray! Gray, help! I'm not ready! What if I can't fly?
You'll be fine! Trust the doctor!
Good-bye, Lil Brown!
Gray! Take care of the new guy!
Bye!

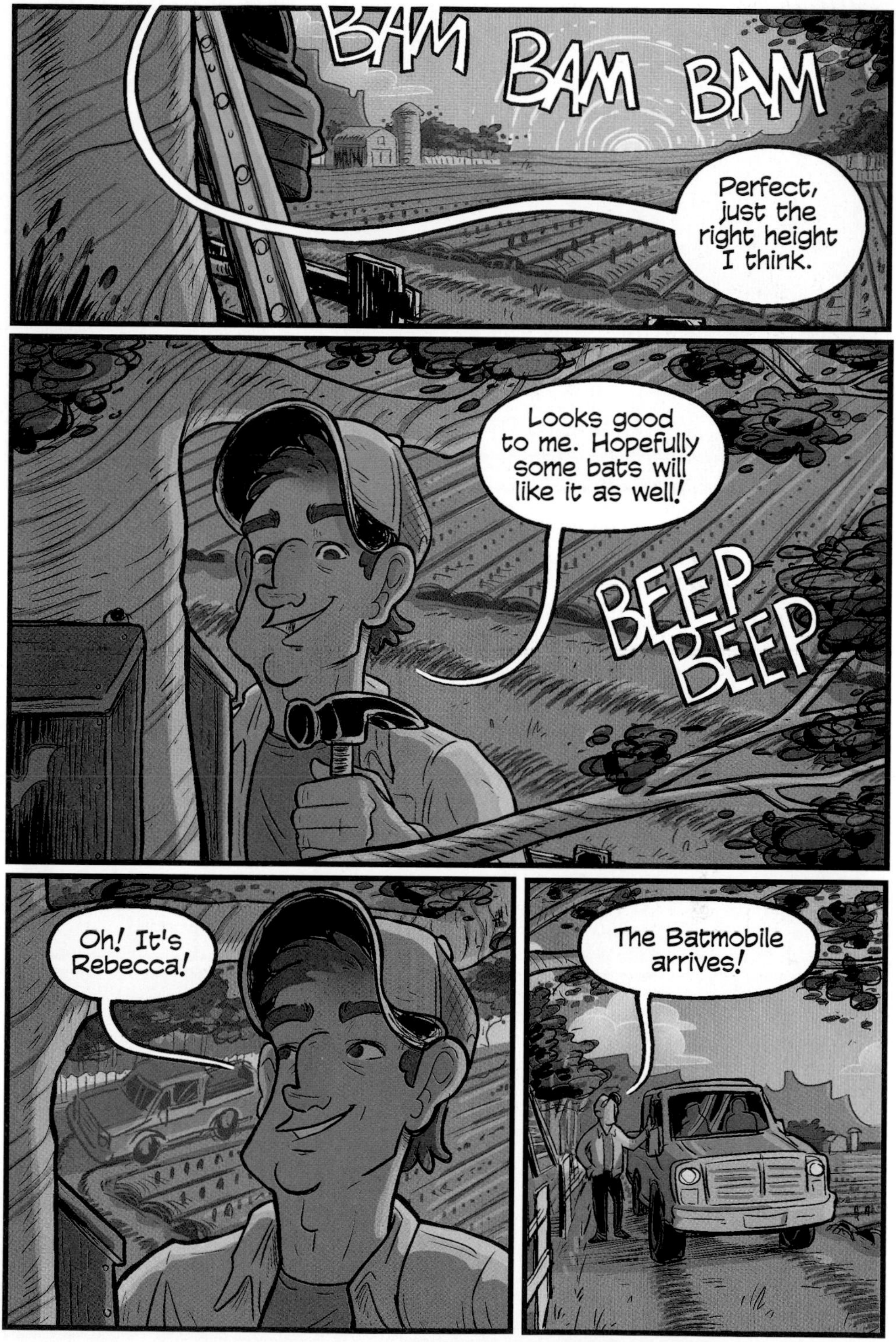
BAM BAM BAM
Perfect, just the right height I think.
Looks good to me. Hopefully some bats will like it as well!
BEEP BEEP
Oh! It's Rebecca!
The Batmobile arrives!

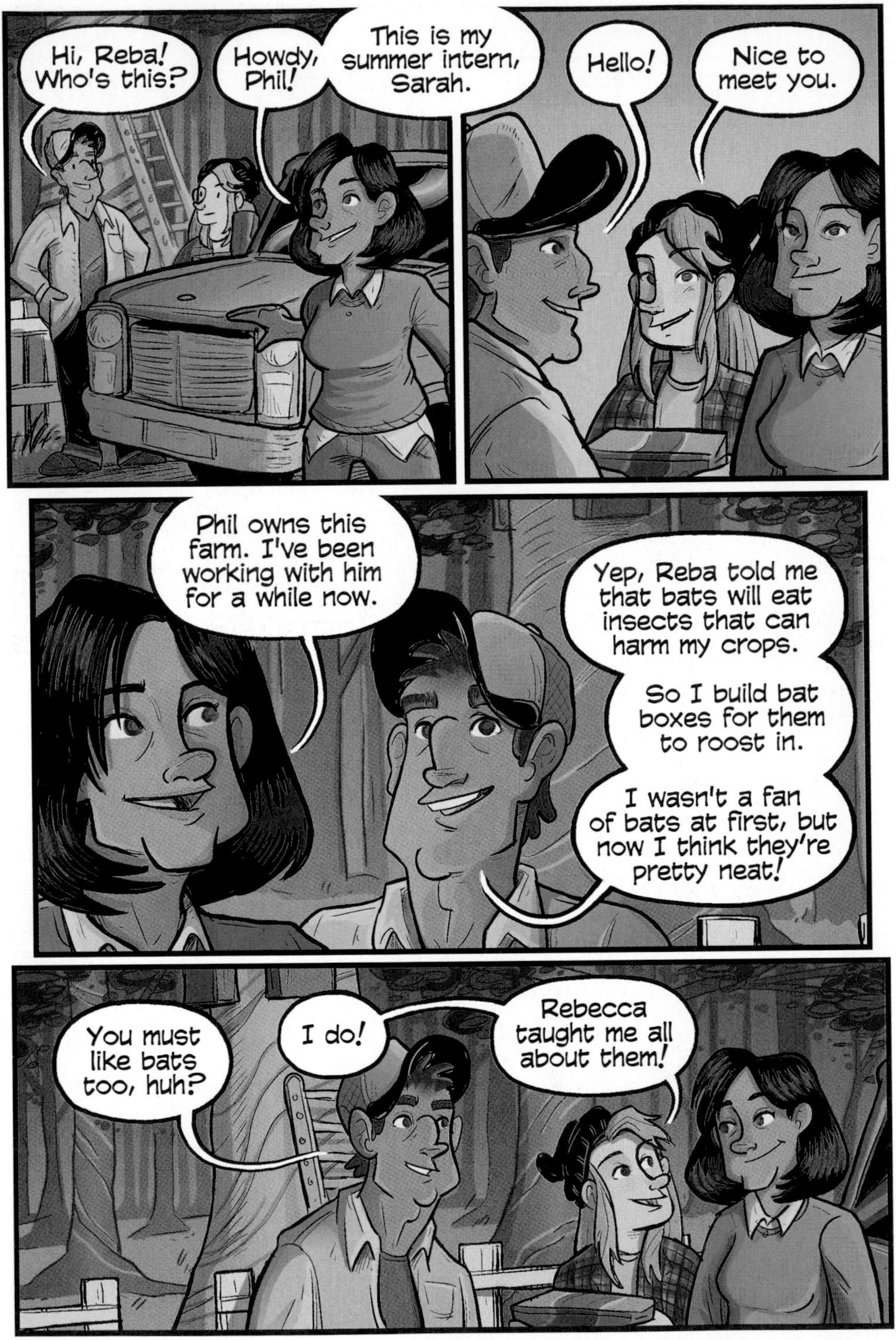
Hi, Reba! Who's this?
Howdy, Phil!
This is my summer intern, Sarah.
Hello!
Nice to meet you.
Phil owns this farm. I've been working with him for a while now.
Yep, Reba told me that bats will eat insects that can harm my crops.
So I build bat boxes for them to roost in.
I wasn't a fan of bats at first, but now I think they're pretty neat!
You must like bats too, huh?
I do!
Rebecca taught me all about them!

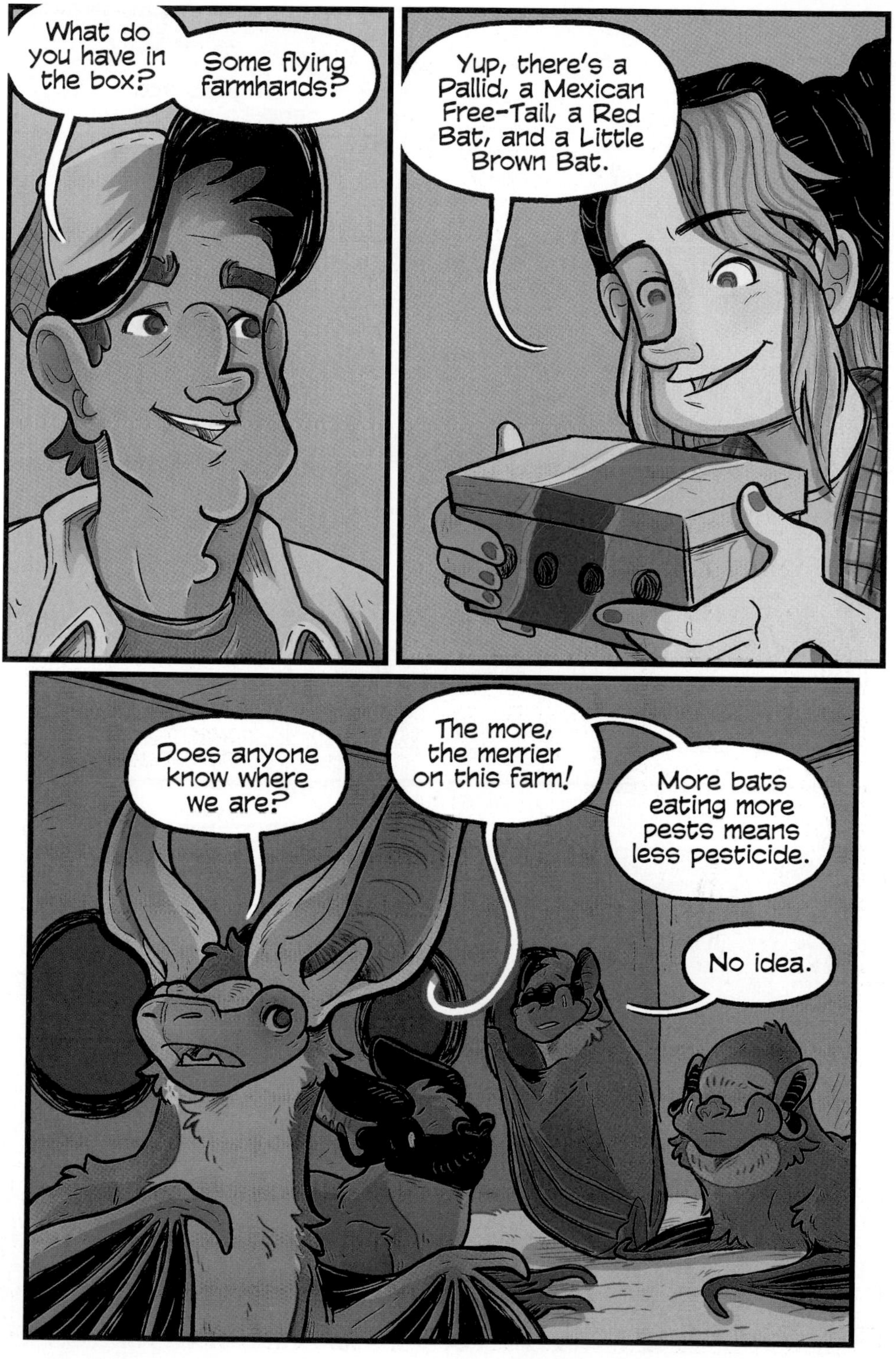
What do you have in the box?
Some flying farmhands?
Yup, there's a Pallid, a Mexican Free-Tail, a Red Bat, and a Little Brown Bat.
Does anyone know where we are?
The more, the merrier on this farm!
More bats eating more pests means less pesticide.
No idea.

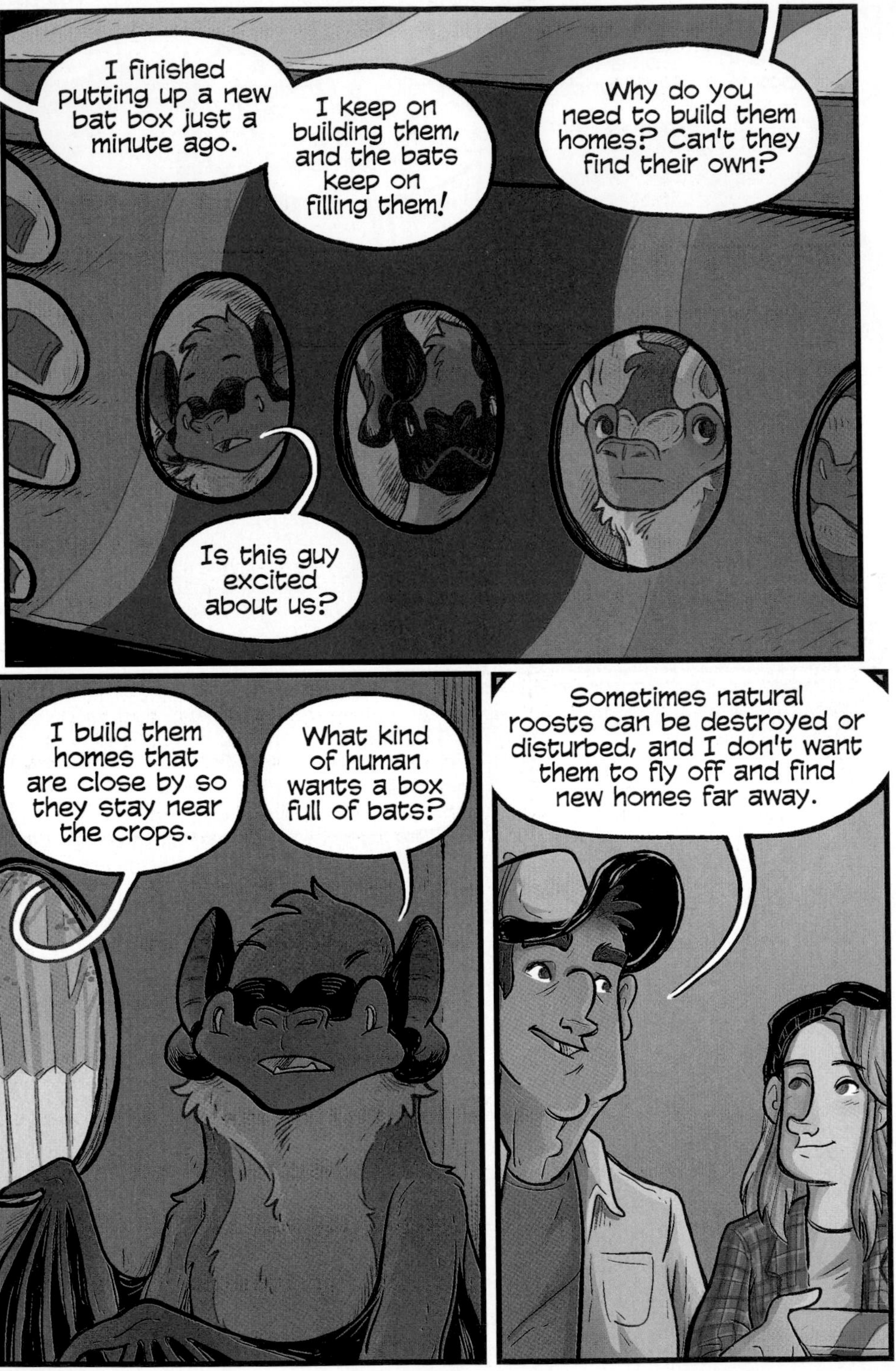
I finished putting up a new bat box just a minute ago.
I keep on building them, and the bats keep on filling them!
Why do you need to build them homes? Can't they find their own?
Is this guy excited about us?
I build them homes that are close by so they stay near the crops.
What kind of human wants a box full of bats?
Sometimes natural roosts can be destroyed or disturbed, and I don't want them to fly off and find new homes far away.

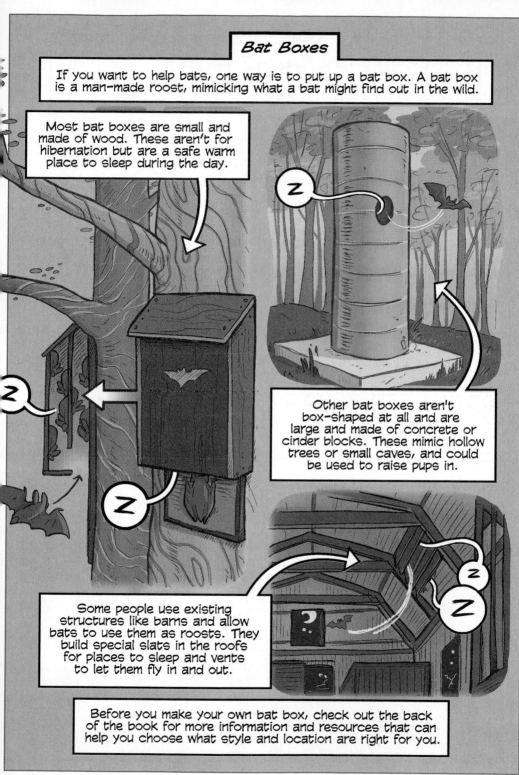

Bat Boxes

If you want to help bats, one way is to put up a bat box. A bat box is a man-made roost, mimicking what a bat might find out in the wild.

Most bat boxes are small and made of wood. These aren't for hibernation but are a safe warm place to sleep during the day.

Other bat boxes aren't box-shaped at all and are large and made of concrete or cinder blocks. These mimic hollow trees or small caves, and could be used to raise pups in.

Some people use existing structures like barns and allow bats to use them as roosts. They build special slats in the roofs for places to sleep and vents to let them fly in and out.

Before you make your own bat box, check out the back of the book for more information and resources that can help you choose what style and location are right for you.

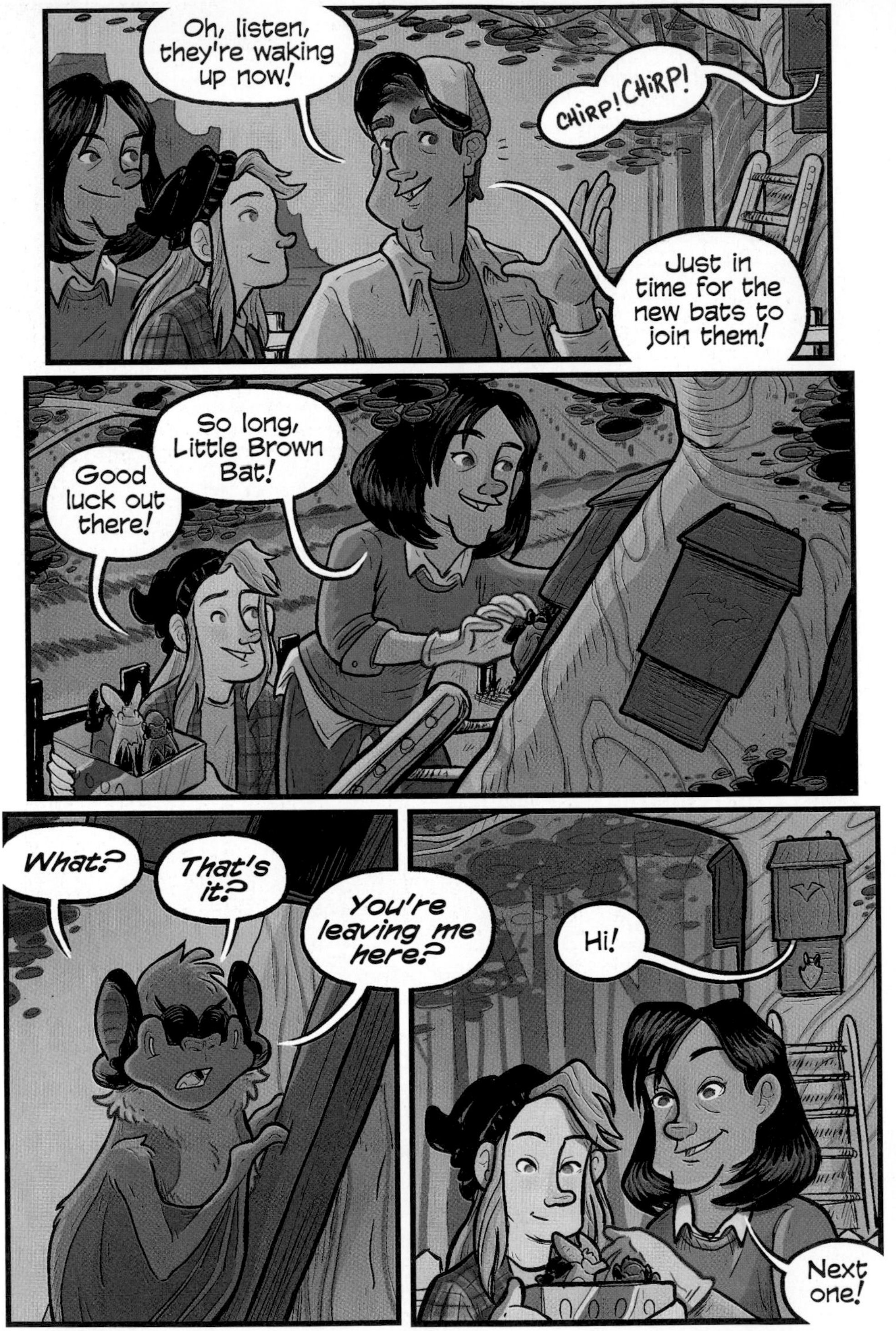

Oh, listen, they're waking up now!
CHIRP! CHIRP!
Just in time for the new bats to join them!
So long, Little Brown Bat!
Good luck out there!
What?
That's it?
You're leaving me here?
Hi!
Next one!

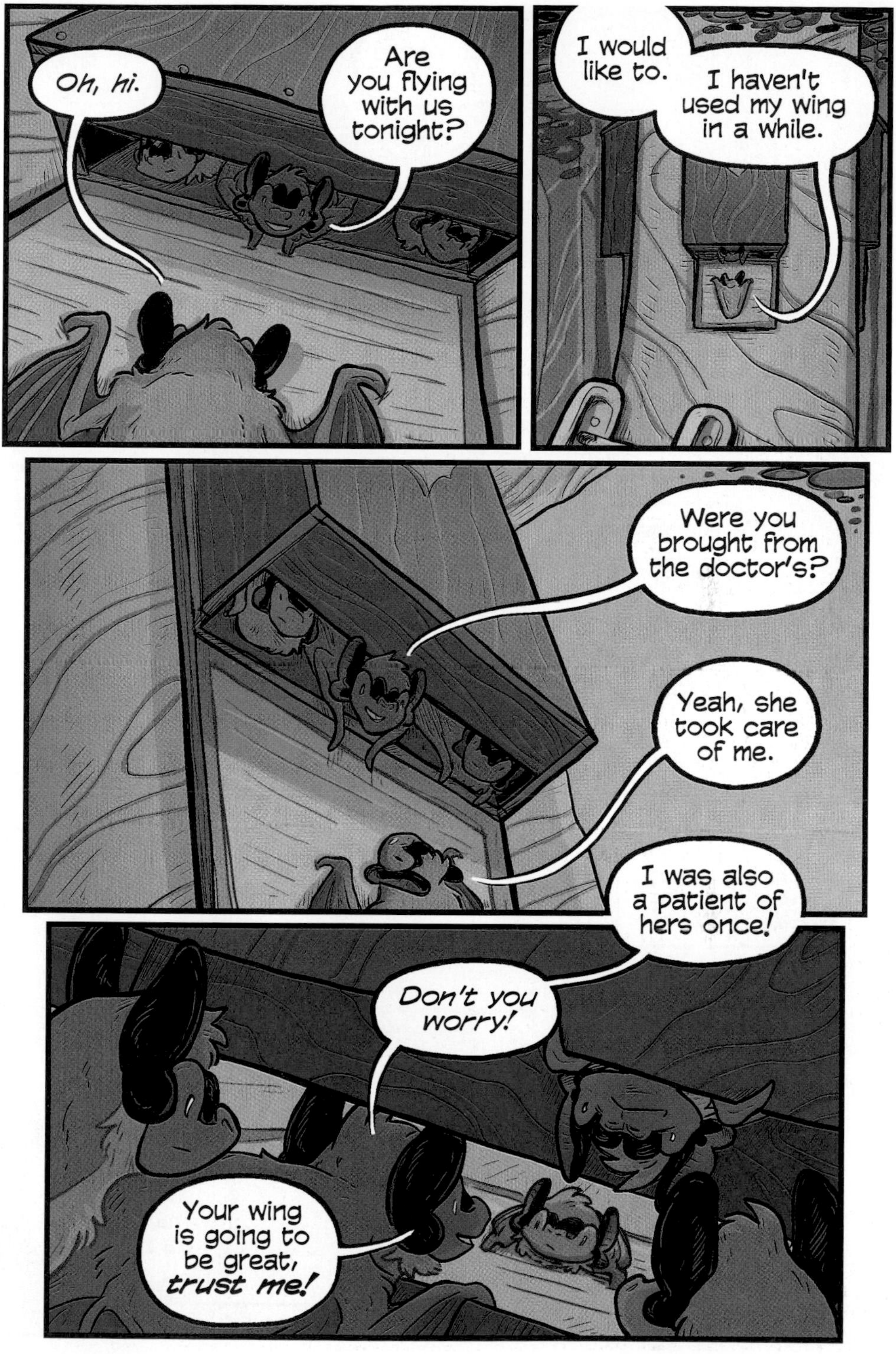
Oh, hi.
Are you flying with us tonight?
I would like to.
I haven't used my wing in a while.
Were you brought from the doctor's?
Yeah, she took care of me.
I was also a patient of hers once!
Don't you worry!
Your wing is going to be great, trust me!

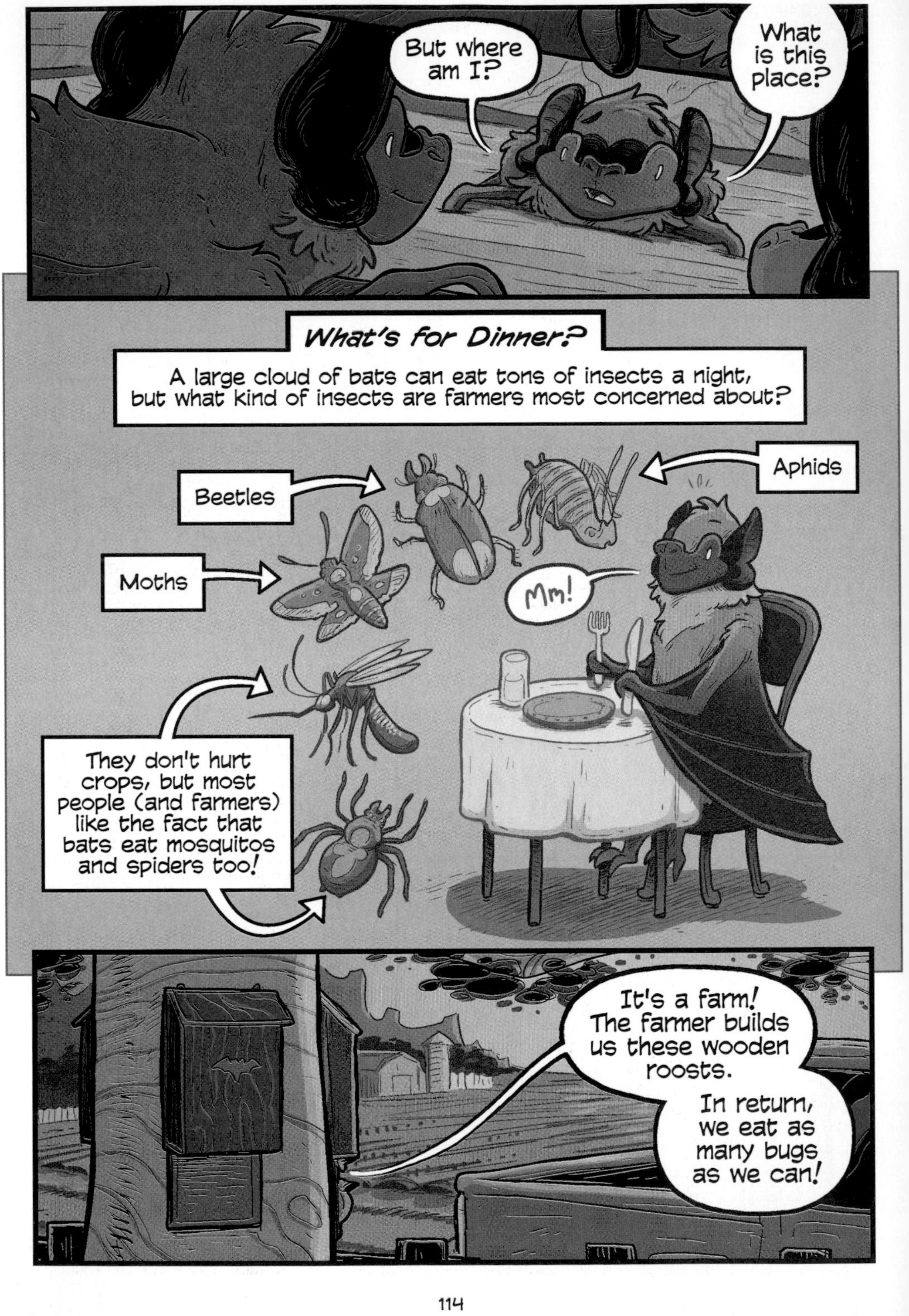

But where am I?
What is this place?
What's for Dinner?
A large cloud of bats can eat tons of insects a night, but what kind of insects are farmers most concerned about?
Aphids
Beetles
Moths
Mm!
They don't hurt crops, but most people (and farmers) like the fact that bats eat mosquitos and spiders too!
It's a farm! The farmer builds us these wooden roosts.
In return, we eat as many bugs as we can!

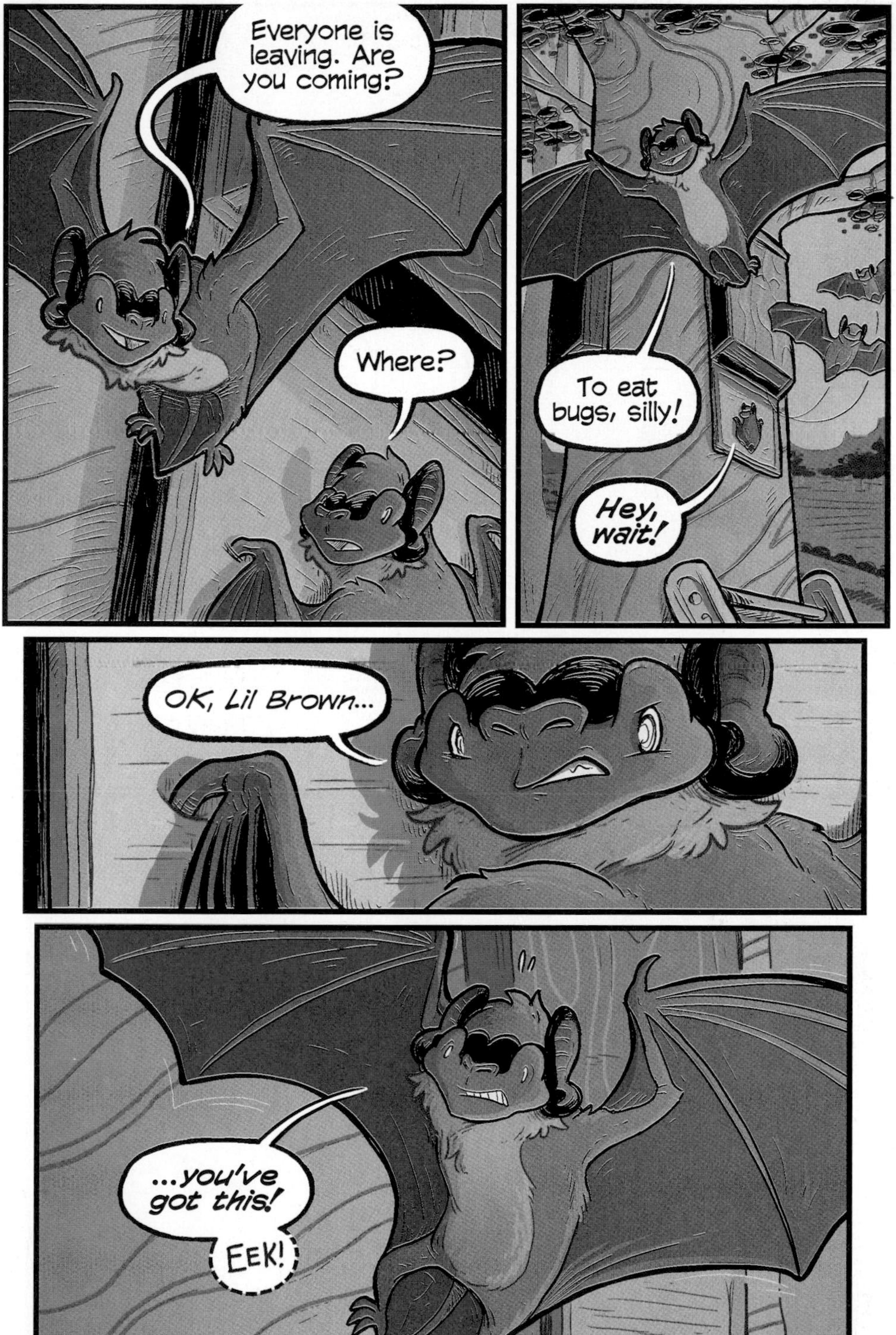
Everyone is leaving. Are you coming?
Where?
To eat bugs, silly!
Hey, wait!
OK, Lil Brown...
...you've got this!
EEK!

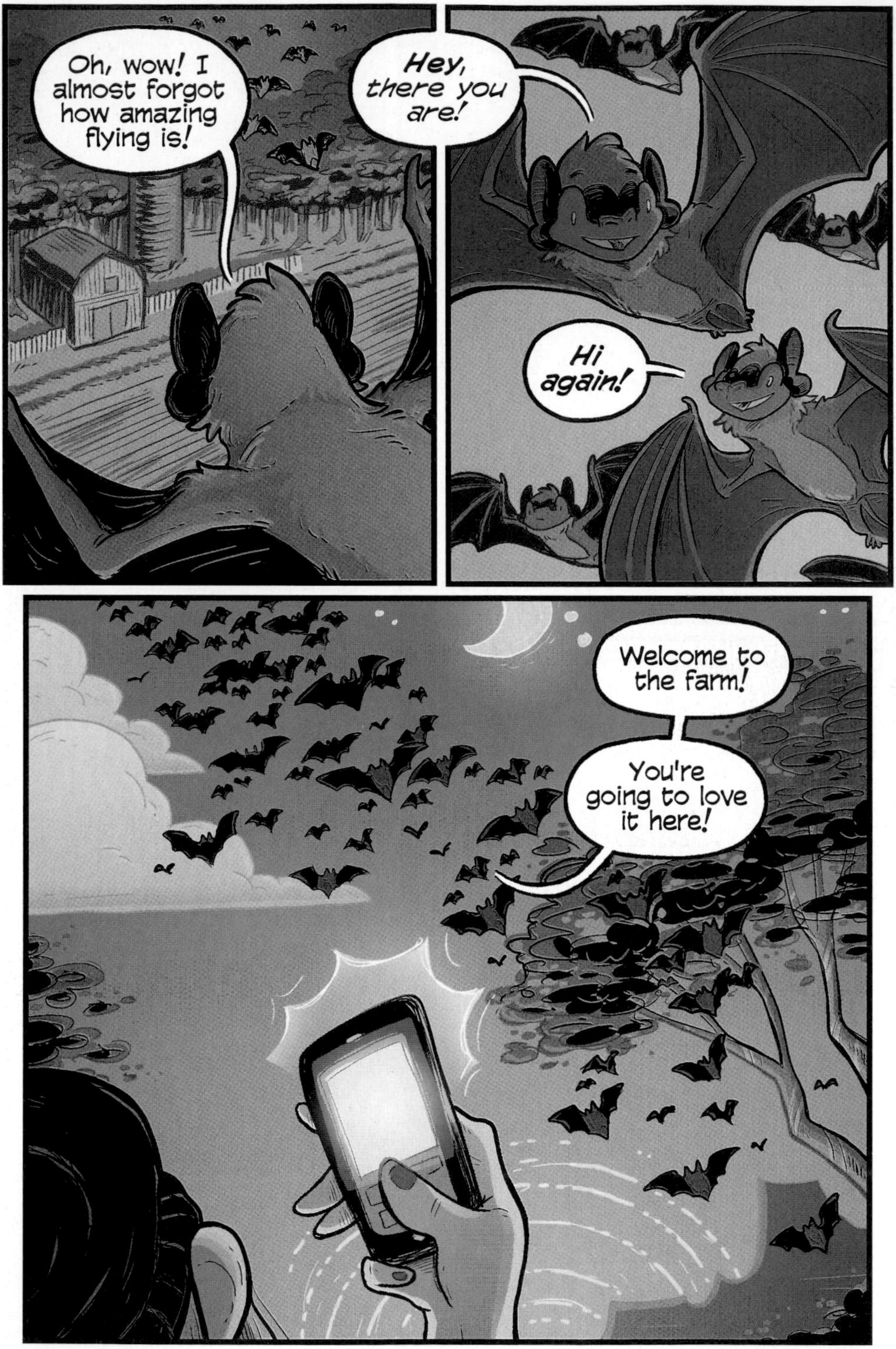
Oh, wow! I almost forgot how amazing flying is!
Hey, there you are!
Hi again!
Welcome to the farm!
You're going to love it here!

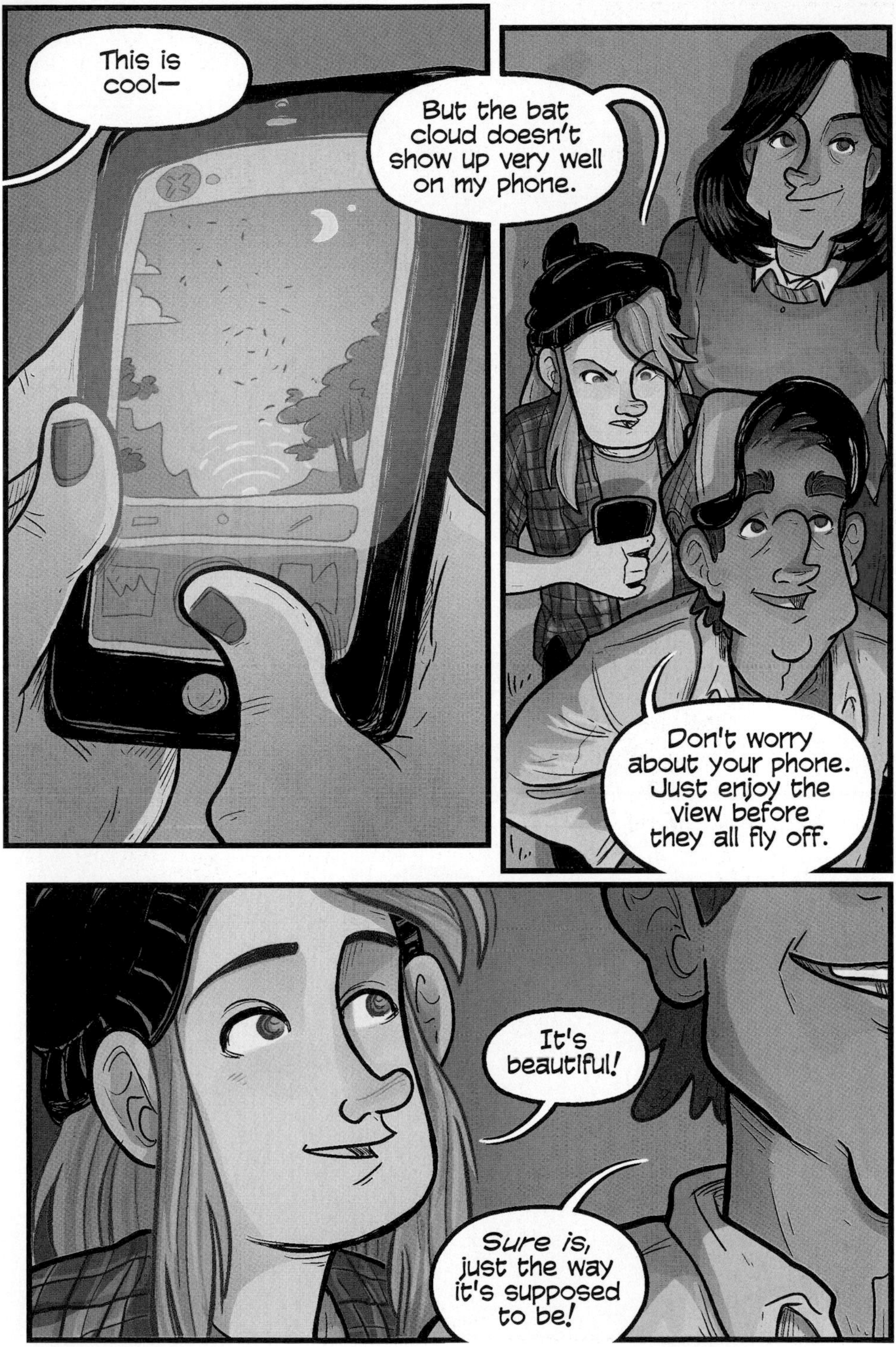

This is cool—
But the bat cloud doesn't show up very well on my phone.
Don't worry about your phone. Just enjoy the view before they all fly off.
It's beautiful!
Sure is, just the way it's supposed to be!

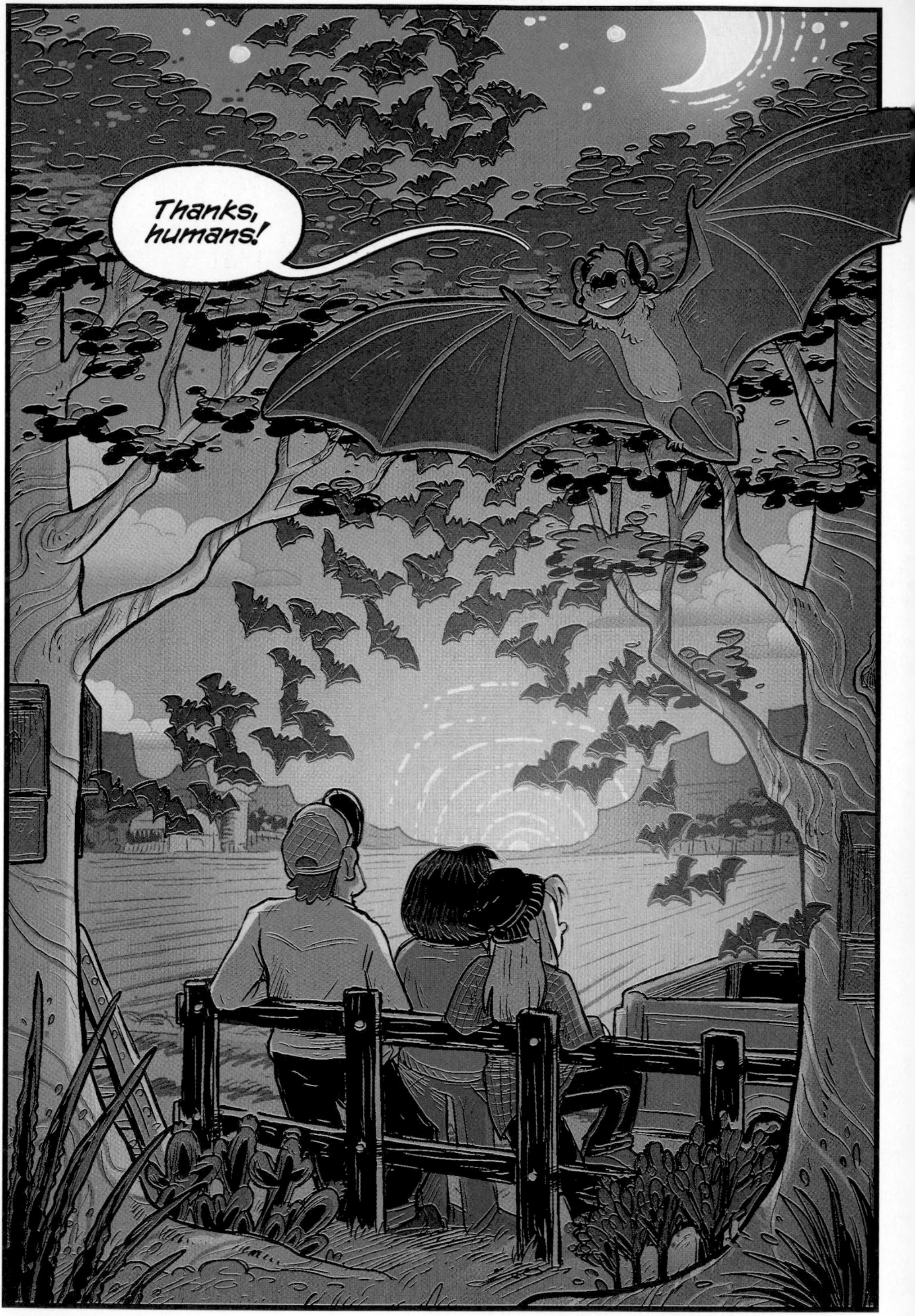
Thanks, humans!

Installing Bat Boxes at Home

Installing a bat box of your own can be a fun family project. There are a few things you'll need to consider before you get started.

Build or buy?

If you have the time, tools, and an adult to help, you could build your own bat box from scratch.

If you can't or don't want to build your own, a quick search online will show there're lots of premade boxes to choose from.

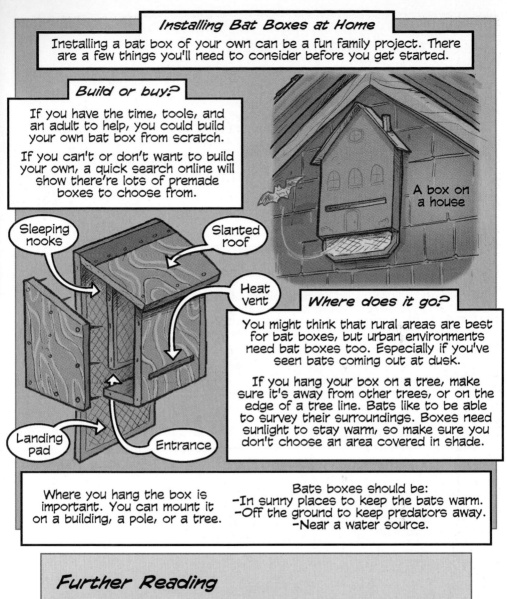

A box on a house

Sleeping nooks

Slanted roof

Heat vent

Landing pad

Entrance

Where does it go?

You might think that rural areas are best for bat boxes, but urban environments need bat boxes too. Especially if you've seen bats coming out at dusk.

If you hang your box on a tree, make sure it's away from other trees, or on the edge of a tree line. Bats like to be able to survey their surroundings. Boxes need sunlight to stay warm, so make sure you don't choose an area covered in shade.

Where you hang the box is important. You can mount it on a building, a pole, or a tree.

Bats boxes should be:
—In sunny places to keep the bats warm.
—Off the ground to keep predators away.
—Near a water source.

Further Reading

Tuttle, Merlin D., Selena Kiser, & Mark Kiser. *The Bat House Builder's Handbook*, 2nd ed. Bat Conservation International, 2013. Available for download at www.batcon.org

Gelfand, Dale Evva. *Building Bat Houses: Storey's Country Wisdom*. Storey Publishing, 1997.

Williams, Kim, Rob Mies, Donald Stokes, & Lillian Stokes. *Stokes Beginner's Guide to Bats*. Little, Brown and Company, 2002.

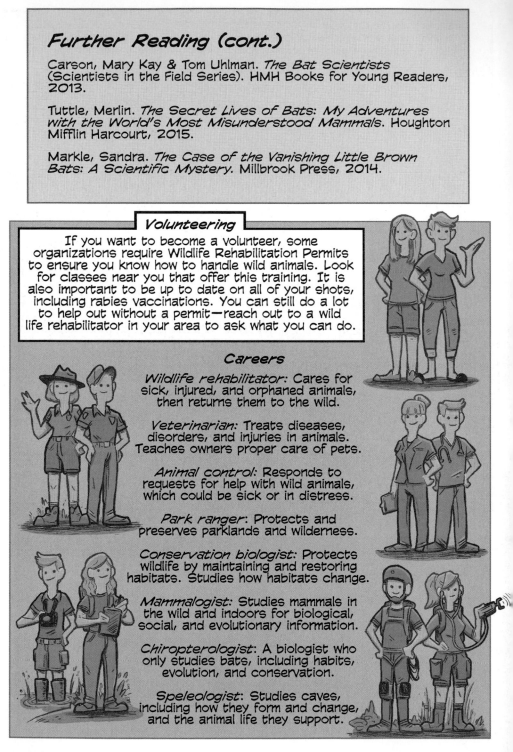

Further Reading (cont.)

Carson, Mary Kay & Tom Uhlman. *The Bat Scientists* (Scientists in the Field Series). HMH Books for Young Readers, 2013.

Tuttle, Merlin. *The Secret Lives of Bats: My Adventures with the World's Most Misunderstood Mammals*. Houghton Mifflin Harcourt, 2015.

Markle, Sandra. *The Case of the Vanishing Little Brown Bats: A Scientific Mystery*. Millbrook Press, 2014.

Volunteering

If you want to become a volunteer, some organizations require Wildlife Rehabilitation Permits to ensure you know how to handle wild animals. Look for classes near you that offer this training. It is also important to be up to date on all of your shots, including rabies vaccinations. You can still do a lot to help out without a permit—reach out to a wild life rehabilitator in your area to ask what you can do.

Careers

Wildlife rehabilitator: Cares for sick, injured, and orphaned animals, then returns them to the wild.

Veterinarian: Treats diseases, disorders, and injuries in animals. Teaches owners proper care of pets.

Animal control: Responds to requests for help with wild animals, which could be sick or in distress.

Park ranger: Protects and preserves parklands and wilderness.

Conservation biologist: Protects wildlife by maintaining and restoring habitats. Studies how habitats change.

Mammalogist: Studies mammals in the wild and indoors for biological, social, and evolutionary information.

Chiropterologist: A biologist who only studies bats, including habits, evolution, and conservation.

Speleologist: Studies caves, including how they form and change, and the animal life they support.

Bat Anatomy

Bats and humans have a lot in common, like finger bones, but bats have anatomical features that are unique to them alone.

Patagium: The skin membrane that allows for flight and makes up the wing. Each section of the bat's patagium has a name.

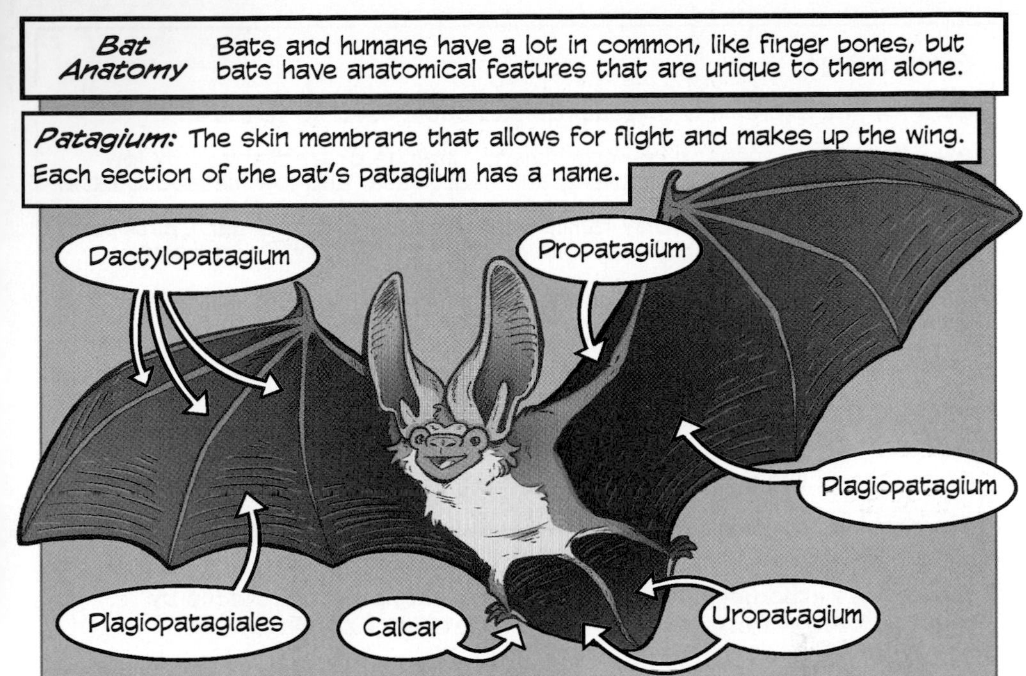

Dactylopatagium
Propatagium
Plagiopatagium
Plagiopatagiales
Calcar
Uropatagium

Cutaneous muscles do not attach to bones. In bats they are called ***plagiopatagiales*** and help give the patagium shape during flight.

Calcar: Cartilage at the ankle. Gives the uropatagium strength.

These are some common parts of a bat's face that each help with sensing echolocation.

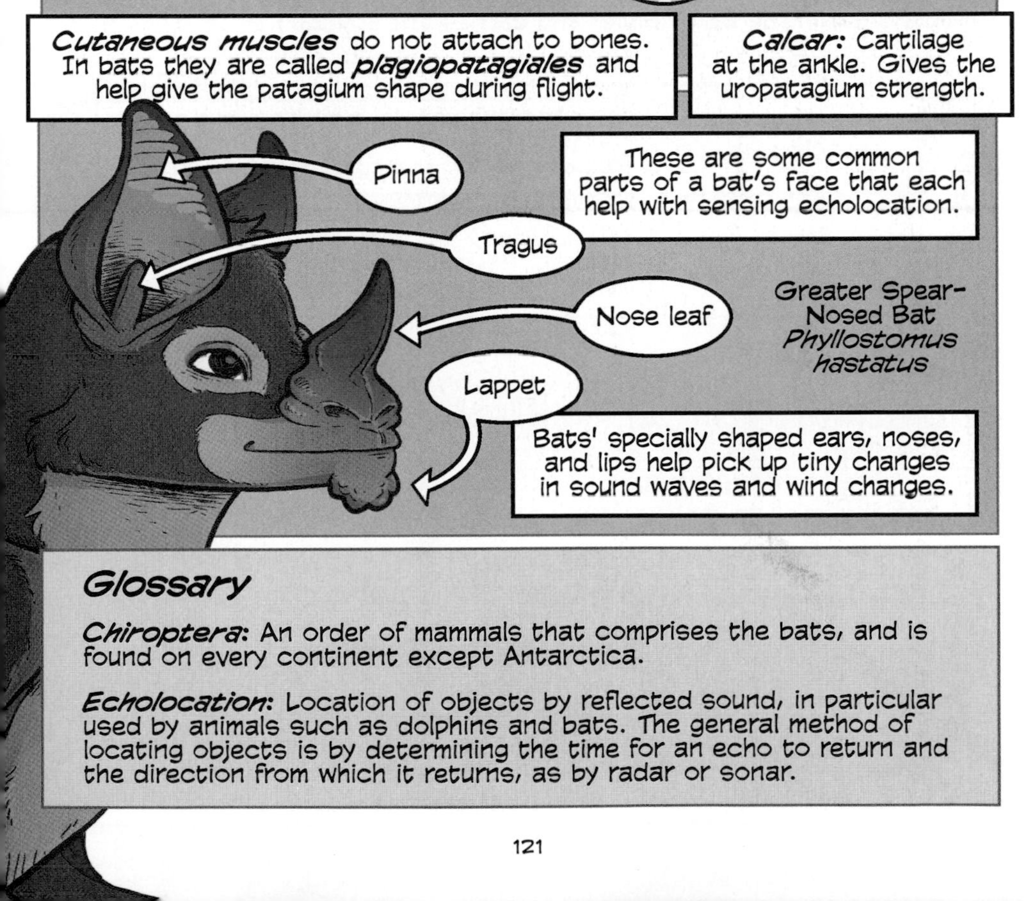

Pinna
Tragus
Nose leaf
Lappet

Greater Spear-Nosed Bat
Phyllostomus hastatus

Bats' specially shaped ears, noses, and lips help pick up tiny changes in sound waves and wind changes.

Glossary

Chiroptera: An order of mammals that comprises the bats, and is found on every continent except Antarctica.

Echolocation: Location of objects by reflected sound, in particular used by animals such as dolphins and bats. The general method of locating objects is by determining the time for an echo to return and the direction from which it returns, as by radar or sonar.

Glossary

Guano: The excrement of seabirds and bats, used as fertilizer.

Hibernation: A season of heterothermy that is characterized by low body temperature, slow breathing and heart rate, and low metabolic rate.

Megachiroptera: The only family Pteropodidae of the order Chiroptera. They are also called fruit bats, Old World fruit bats, or flying foxes.

Microchiroptera: A suborder of Chiroptera including all bats except for the fruit bats. Usually smaller sized but not always.

Nocturnal: To be active at night.

Pollination: A process in which pollen is transferred to the reproductive organs of plants, enabling fertilization and reproduction.

Pup: One of the young of various species of mammal (a seal, dog, or rat).

Roost: A place where birds regularly settle or congregate to rest at night, or where bats congregate to rest in the day.

Sonar: A method or device for detecting and locating objects by means of sound waves sent out to be reflected by the objects.

Sound wave: A wave that is formed when a sound is made and that moves through the air or water and carries the sound.

Frequency and Decibel

Bats can make very loud sounds, but we aren't able to hear them because the sound is at frequencies too high for the human ear.

Decibels (dB) measure how loud or intense a sound wave is.

Frequency measures how often something repeats. Sound frequency is how many waves hit the eardrum per second, called hertz (Hz).

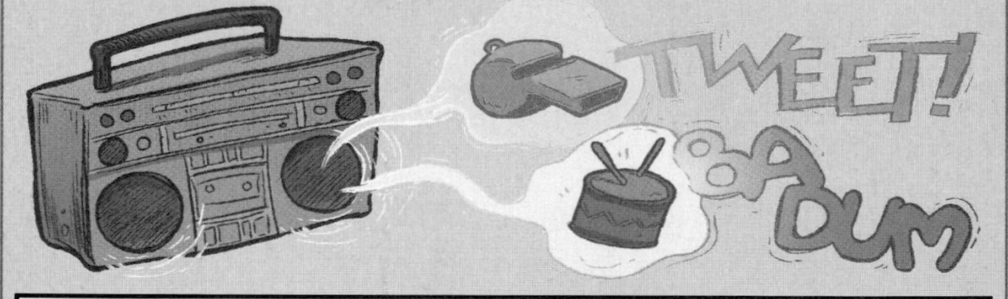
TWEET!
BA DUM

Think of it this way: A decibel is the volume on a radio; it can be loud or quiet. Frequency determines what kind of sounds you hear; they may be shrill or dull, like the sound of a whistle vs. the sound of a drum.

Sounds below 12 Hz are called ***infrasonic***. Elephants can hear these sounds, but humans can't.

Sounds above 16,000 Hz are called ***ultrasonic***. Bats can hear these sounds, but humans can't.